The Bohemian Time Traveler's Vacation Guide

By: Ian M. Gilroy

PublishAmerica
Baltimore

First printing

At the specific preference of the author, PublishAmerica allowed this work to remain exactly as the author intended, verbatim, without editorial input.

ISBN: 1-4241-0219-7
PUBLISHED BY PUBLISHAMERICA, LLLP
www.publishamerica.com
Baltimore

Printed in the United States of America

Dedication

To the memories of Nick, Barbara, Keith and John.
—I think of you often.

Acknowledgements

A special thanks to the following people who helped make this book possible.

My parents, for having me, caring and believing in me.

My daughters, Alexis and Allyson, for loving me.

My brother, Robin, and sister, Wendy, for putting up with me.

JoAnn, for all your help and love. I couldn't have done it without you.

Barb, for making it legible.

Nancy, for helping me believe in myself.

Ian, for continually pushing me.

Chris and John, for laughing out loud.

Al Gore, for inventing the internet, what a tool! Hold on, wait a minute, correction,
—the Pentagon, for making it possible to surf the net, what a ride!

"Music absolutely keys memories in your mind, memories that haven't been around for a long time. You'll hear a specific piece of music and boom, it's like time travel—you're right back there—I wonder what does that, all of a sudden you're back there—the people that were around you and what you were doing, your environment, it all comes back, like a scent returned."

Art Bell
Coast to Coast
2002

Prologue

I winnowed the chaff of the epoch.
    —Oh, I couldn't be that lazy.
I scanned beyond the ruffle.
    —Oh, I prayed I wasn't crazy.

Inspired by:

The Real Me
The Who

At about the same time Douglas Adams first contemplated writing his book *The Hitchhikers Guide to the Galaxy,* I was doing just that, hitchhiking. While my itinerary didn't include the outer fringes of the Milky way, based on probability alone, I remain certain that our paths indeed must have crossed, likely somewhere in Northern, rain-drenched France.

Beside our appetite for adventure, any common threads except perhaps the desire to write were virtually non-existent. His insatiable drive dwarfed any ability I harbored to take a dream, bring it from the matrix to the forefront simply for the purpose of succeeding. You see I am a procrastinator. What took Douglas Adams seven years to bring to fruition took me over twenty-five years just to start. No matter how hard I tried, I couldn't establish a starting point even though I AM writing this I still really don't know where to actually begin. However, upon reflection I guess in a way I HAVE started. Hey, that's a relief! Now I can explain what prompted me after a twenty-five year hiatus to pick up a pen and apply it to paper for the sole purpose of reliving my formative years.

As an entrepreneur flying solo in charge of a marginally successful cleaning company, I spent many a boring night cleaning up after others. I passed the time listening to a nuance of noise encapsulated on disc. It was while scrubbing toilets and drifting with the sounds of yesteryear that I realized I was able to unearth stunning memories. Groping, while hoping to cope with the everyday trials and tribulations that plagued my ho-hum existence, I found myself moseying through those fossilized moments in time.

I remember years ago researching Buddhism and learning of the fundamental belief of enlightenment: when a person transcends Karma and reaches a pure state. It is then that time ceases to exist and at that moment the past, the present and the future merge to become as one. In all honesty, I doubt that while listening to Black Sabbath I had reached an enlightened or pure state unless everything I had been taught over the years concerning good versus evil and the difference between right and wrong was a lie. Nevertheless, the thought of reaching Godhead by way of the dark side...hmmmm, an interesting possibility, but as I wiped the rim of a toilet bowl, perhaps not so far fetched an idea either. The notion occurred that only through the eyes of a once struggling yet proud, hippie could such interesting possibilities and ideals be justly explored.

If Einstein's theory, like the Buddhist's belief, was correct and the past, present and future can indeed coexist in the very same moment, then truly all I need do is use this walk-man to pry open my mind. Allowing music to be the vehicle to transverse the valence along the passageway through the fragile portal and into the sanctum that houses my exclusive version of the space-time continuum. Much like the course of events that accompanied Marcel Proust after he indulged himself with the pleasures of the Madeleines dipped in tea, I began my journey with a glass of Coke and a Kit Kat, akin in my mind to Proust's inspirational fare. Sadly, after blotting out all external interference and consuming the equivalent of three king-sized bars and a six pack, I must confess all I had to look forward to, based on the simple act of reverse peristalsis, was the task of re-cleaning that same damn toilet!

The author, Kurt Vonnegut Jr., succeeded in manipulating time through his thought-provoking novel, *Slaughter House five.* Even though my first impression, while still a youth in school evoked plenty of brow scratching, it wasn't until I purchased the Cliff Notes, that I ultimately brought the essence of truth to light.

> "The world is really just a collection of moments strung together in beautiful random order, if we are going to survive its up to us to concentrate on the good moments and ignore the bad."
>
> Taken from the movie *Slaughter House Five.*
> A Universal Pictures Production.

By using music as an astral time machine, I have been able to recapture and relive a moment as a memory from an observation of personal insight or as a series of moments strung together like a one act play. I have resurrected a resonating spiral of trivialized opinion, a free-flow of collection, a pastiche if you will—whoa Nelly, wait a second. I don't even know what that word means...,hmmm, how about hodge-podge? Yeah that's better, a hodge-podge of trivialized opinion. These sentiments ravage the likes of politics and religion, life and death, the natural and supernatural, and the physical and metaphysical.

"The Bohemian Time Traveler's Vacation Guide" is an ethereal ride through the humble beginnings of the hippie generation, weaving in and out of a decade that gave birth to this counter culture. It reached adolescence when I grew into mine. A mystical ethos where the vicissitudes of existence did little to change it for better or worse. The experience became a collective experience for myself and others who were drawn together during this time, all of us searching and hoping to find answers to the same questions.

However, for every silver lining there exists a tarnished underbelly. For every underbelly, there undulates a venomous snake ready to strike. So to successfully exploit the experience by quoting the lyrics, thus transferring the calling that inspired the memory, has proven by this poison to be futile.

Permission to use, tainted by greed, or the simple inability to allow for fear that the need may be questionable, forcing by association a negative interpretation.

Shit! Talk about censorship and narrowing the boundaries that dictate free speech. So, to quote or not to quote, that is the question. This pinched the nerve, forcing my hand, not to cover my mouth, but to point the finger.

> Though the experience, beholden to the memories, sculptured the imagination.
> Forces that lurked apart, allowed not; words or verses to describe them.
> Censorship copied the past, darkened the desire to use the lyrics.
> Those who control, proclaimed, freedom as the corner-stone.
> Now rolled over, to trample underfoot.
> So many died, I hoped not in vain, as row gave way, to row.
> Impervious not, the marble and stone.
> A battalion at ease, eternal the peace, the price, the names, echoed death,...to be free.
> Fascism, communism, to blanket the cold, never a chance to stand on a box.
> To soap the masses, washing away tyranny,...so to be free.

Heller was right, a "catch 22," or to catch anyone, who would dare question the legalities or sanity through this blatant act to stifle my quest, to show in verse from songs; that allowed me to rekindle.

Oh what shame! Oh, what a sham. But, alas, I'll make do. For I soon discovered that when fate closes a door, God soon opens a window.

I just hope this opening isn't a view from a 13th floor penthouse or resembles a porthole where I'm wedged passing through.

So beware, listen to your heartstrings and let the music resonate your head. To heed the lyrics may resurrect the "dream police," to arrest the mood, leaving a stench, killing any freedom to wallow in reverie.

Come all, follow me, hence,
    This place hither.
To relive, oh that which,
    Yesteryear will deliver,

Inspired by:

Wondrous Stories
Yes

CHAPTER ONE

OF MAD DOGS, ENGLISHMEN, AND ONE

AMERICAN

What we hoped was that we,
could stop the coming.
end of the world

Ken Kesey

Setting the Stage:

Peace love and the birth of a dove

Memories all, rapid the call.
    Reminding me.
        How we ignored.

Turning history's pages,
    Repenting not,
        To repeat again,
            The sins of the ages.

Inspired by:

Lessons
Rush

Noel Webster defined hippies as "long-haired, draft dodging, parasitic scroungers leeching an existence by swindling the government, avoiding taxes, and side-stepping the responsibilities adherent to adult life." Hmm, a little cruel; I probably shouldn't have asked my ultra, right-winged, republican next-door neighbor. The dictionary explanation however, is much kinder albeit less candid stating, "slang, a person who in a state of alienation from conventional society turned variously to mysticism, psychedelic drugs and communal living." Maybe the word variously should be substituted by vicariously and/or voraciously since I believe some practiced to a varying degree by opting for one category over another with most falling somewhere in between; a medley of transient dreamers in quest of happiness through hedonistic endeavor.

So where did the word come from and when was it first used? Choosing the path of least resistance, that being an anecdotal overview, it appears Michael Fallon first used the word in a 1965 newspaper article to describe the younger "beat-bohemian." He borrowed the term from an autobiography of Malcolm X, where the word was apparently used for the first time around 1939.

"A few of the white men around Harlem, younger ones who we call hippies acted more Negro than the Negroes."

I knew sooner or later I'd get caught up in this. Well now, I have to explain who these "Harlemites" were: "The Beats" (a term coined by Jack Kerouac because they had the beat or quite simply, they were in tune to what was going on) viewed the young "hippies" as beat generation wanna-bes or junior grade hipsters. This borrowed from the term that described their predecessors "the Harlem-based Hipsters" –these were black jazz musicians who traveled around the country from gig to gig turning on people to their lifestyle, lingo and drugs, especially marijuana. It's interesting to note that many early hippies especially the early San Francisco "diggers" objected to the connotation and preferred to be called "heads" or "freaks." Okay, this is as far as I go; you may ask where does the word "hipster" come from? That's a little more difficult. Likely from the opium dens where many of these musicians "reclined, resting, ever so stoned, precariously on the hip," as they enjoyed the fruits of their endeavors. This unfortunately resulted in many sliding off the hip and landing headfirst on the floor. This brought on many a concussion especially if the floor were made of concrete or stone. Upon reflection, perhaps that is where the terms "head" and "stoned" came from, from the hip to head and from the head to the floor. You know what? Sounds pretty convincing to me.

Every book has a beginning and end except maybe *War and Peace* which seems to ramble on to near infinity. I must admit I found it a lot easier to write the ending first and then gradually work my way back. I think this was partly due to those particular memories being clustered closer to the area of my brain responsible for their retrieval. The beginning of what I consider MY story was also much easier to deal with than delving back through the historical roots that led up to what is referred to as a hippie counter culture. This is due in part to the fact that I wasn't yet born and therefore, unable to experience first-hand that period when the seeds were first sown. As a young lad, the '50's for the most part, were spent sucking my thumb while wearing short pants huddled close to my mother's apron. So, I'll do my best to be both brief and relevant when discussing the pre-cursers that allowed the roots to take hold. In lieu of a history lesson or more appropriately, a spontaneous soporific intervention, I have decided to consolidate the events leading up to the hippie movement including the decade of the 1960's. Besides the idea of spending countless hours in libraries burying my intellect in mounds of research also possesses not only the ability to strain my eyes, but any discipline I embrace to undertake such a task. So lets get down to the matter at hand, utilizing my personal perspectives and historical spin, no doubt a short lesson but nevertheless an invaluable one.

The beat goes on! (What a great segue)

Warning: Read at your own risk! Contents may prove to be far too serious causing all bodily functions to fail so read this while residing on the crapper in place of the morning paper.

Free to be,
set sail with me,
Harbor not,
resentment.
For all will have a chance
to see.

Inspired by:

Wooden Ships
Crosby, Stills and Nash

Center Stage, Columbia University circa the mid 1940's, Jack Kerouac, an aspiring yet inspiring author gathered with the likes of Allen Ginsberg and William S. Burroughs. They planed the surface, threw away the gavel, so as to speak their minds. The intellects as fancy-free thinkers jettisoned the rules to explore each other sharing thoughts about existence and reason for being. They created a scale model emphasizing our significance in cosmic proportions as really being insignificant. The nuclear age threatened all including those that possessed a proclivity to procrastinate, and reclusive, recalcitrant free-spirited, disenfranchised writers and poets who were intent on preserving tomorrow rather than burying it. Life was crisscrossed by film noir and existentialism a proving ground that stenciled a pattern, expunging the contemporary parameters thus widening the literary throughway creating by expropriating a broader, deeper well from which to tap expression. With no boundaries, these free thinkers were able to brandish the spirit with a bravuran mix of spontaneity and non-linear randomness (sort of what I've been writing or should I say, putting on paper since, oh, about "center stage" on). It was a carefree style often highlighted by a stream of consciousness some of which unfortunately had a habit of running upstream, totally in opposition to not only the laws of physics but everything conventional as well. It was really quite passive non-confrontational expressionism, which bombarded society with a series of dogmatic surrealism. It's decree coated by layers of influence, daubed by the likes of Blake, Whitman, Emerson, Hemingway and Fitzgerald. It was really a state of mind or more aptly put, a mind in a state of change slowly awaking to refocus, to reprioritize, to repatriate.

> "The so-called beat generation was a whole bunch of people of all different nationalities who came to the conclusion that society sucked."
>
> Amiri Baraka

The beats or beat generation later became space-age freaks or beatniks; the name was a simple amalgamation of beat with sputnik. Geeze, that stimulates memories from boarding school. Here we use the word beat combining it was meat. You see, being a young adolescent male, both subjected and isolated and therefore exposed to the temptations enlisted through the visual erotica espoused by Playboy's centerfold; it was easy to explode when fantasizing after "lights out!"

Okay, back to the infirmary where I, as a spin-doctor, will continue to inform. The beat movement gained momentum, using San Francisco as a breeding ground where the image was honed and more recognizable. The Six Gallery the template for its validation.

The man, that crazy dude.
Oh daddy oh decked out in black and blue.
A beret and beard, shades and sandals.
Bongos next to the aromatic silhouette of Mary Jane.
The smoke filled back room where hot java was sipped and snappy words met snapping fingers.
Twitching, moving and levitating.
The crowd yet vibrating to the energy.
As the cool cats and chics roughed the groovy scene.
To speak, to scream.
To sigh, to cry.
The unadorned truth,
Is bittersweet.

"Coffee House Blues"
(Yes, it's mine)
(circa: can't really remember—probably English class late 1970)
(This was my second real attempt at poetry)

Kerouac was indeed the father and prophet, Ginsberg the disciple who carried the spirit epitomized by Neil Cassady, the quintessential "Bohemian." Cassady represented the rhythm or beat, the pounding base line, whatever happened, happened around him. His energy drove everything (including Kerouac's car which was the vehicle supplying the experience for the novel *On the Road* and later Ken Kesey's bus). Ginsberg was able to mesh the beat philosophy with the spiritual and metaphysical breaching the gap with mind expansion. He brought with him the likes of Bob Dylan and the Beatles, establishing a bridgehead between the "beatniks" and what was hippie infancy.

All the World's a Stage

Restrained by thought alone.
The sanitized walls,
Chained me not.

My hopes and desires
captured for a moment.
—Free,
To take hold.

Inspired by:

White Room
Cream

I was still removing the last remnants of rose pedals from my hair and the thorns from my ass when I realized the only thing missing was a straitjacket. But then again, if I was forced to accept this reversal of fortune, my blue blazer adorning the back of the chair would remain a permanent prop, masquerading as a scarecrow to the academic feign of heart.

The back room adjoining the library contained neatly partitioned cubicles. Each paid homage to the virgin tone, awash in a blizzard that spilled over between the black curtains, assaulting Mother Nature and her decision to trap me indoors. Any freedom, at least for now, and probably the foreseeable future, had disappeared, draped in dunes of snow. This suffered containment, a bilious benchmark, measured in weeks, bivouacked as a claustrophobic encounter, drained the spirit. As I strained to see white on white, snow blindness and a blank canvas minus a brush, I struggled to start. Without a beginning there could be no end. My head, separated, cupped in palms, braced by elbows, allowed my attention to grapple with the wooden sill. A lone magazine peered the pane, protected for the moment from the inquisitiveness of the narrow snow ridge that pressed in defiance against the frame.

I was drawn like a murder of crows, killing time, putting off the evitable, an overdue term paper. My fingers levitated the space, drawing my hand, which palmed the surface revealing *Time magazine*. Ah, the hippies and within a playground to prompt a quick retrieval.

I pushed the loose leaf, a pile of loose ends, a copy of *Siddhartha* and a borrowed sleeve with vinyl, of *Beggar's Banquet* and friends. All piled to the end, thus opening a world that staged so lavish an entrance. A red carpet presence highlighted so gaudy, yet gauche, inviting me to follow as I fingered the contents.

'The hippies have emerged on the US scene in about eighteen months as a wholly new sub culture, a bizarre permutation of the middle class ethos from which it evolved. Hippies preach mysticism, altruism, honesty, happiness and peace.'

I couldn't help but shake my head which channeled images of Ginsburg chanting "OM" as the meeting of the tribes, heralded forth, the path for the hippies, and their summer mix, a tonic of love and peace. Its aftermath, a "winter of discontent," where college campuses graduated with honors, incendiary personas, ablaze in a ring of fire, torching the scene as Weathermen and students for a Democratic society, fanned the flames. If this was to be my college experience, then maybe dropping out and challenging life head-on from the collision, a solution or at least answers to the questions entertaining the meaning to life, and my purpose from which to find the truth, to win the conflict that waged between mind, body and spirit.

I turned the page, further engrossed as a means to forget the inevitable, the overdue by a day, assignment. I shifted my blank stare to the emptiness I felt, the impetus to write, a white piece of paper, better to patch the wall, which sanitized my perception. Reality was a strange entrancement to continue to read.

'They find an almost childlike fascination in blossoms, beads and bells, blinding strobe lights and deafening music, exotic clothing and erotic slogans. Their professed desire is nothing less than the subversion of Western society by 'flower power' and force of example.'

Christ! I remembered I had been given only the afternoon to listen to the Stones. Jagger seemed to epitomize the mood, at least his background and now his dress, symbols of the desire to court and transform an educated middle class. His music only closed the ranks, forcing the march, where change kept tempo to the beating drum.

I continued to read as my hand, though tempted, only probed the album and book, pushing with it the paper, which crumpled against the backdrop of the cubicle.

'Although that sounds like a pipe dream, if conveys the unreality that permeates hippiedom, a cult whose mystique derives heavily from the ingestion of hallucinogenic drugs.'

Mind expansion, a visionary retreat, a sobering realization that sooner or later I might succumb to this avenue of choice.

The radiator creaked to moan, rattling as it convulsed, shaking the sill, making me think. I certainly had a lot to live for, but in truth, the wake-up call, a slight whistle, and a paper to start. Maybe through Siddharta, I could find solace and comfort without devoting a portion of next summer to begin my search.

Ken Kesey took his government drug experience from the confines of Menlo Park Veterans Hospital and wrote his most celebrated novel *One Flew Over the Cuckoo's Nest*. Being both supine and paralytic he probably at some point visualized rather than actually perceived what strayed over the nest. This no doubt, prompted him to crack the egg that represented conformity and smear the yolk on the face of America, replacing that hovering eagle with a white dove. He managed to fling together a fledging group of peers, the merry pranksters, who rode a refurbished psychedelic bus on a magical mystery tour, all their own.

Much of the hippie aesthetic that would infiltrate the San Francisco scene of the late '60's can be traced back to the pranksters who openly used psychedelic drugs, promoted acid tests, or wild parties, wore outrageous attire and performed avant-garde, bizarre almost dadaistic street theatre that combined the energy of Julian Beck with the concepts flaunted by theatre of the absurd. This avalanche of discontent snowed the laws of conformity and mores of conventionality ushering forth an era that blanketed the Bay area, burying in particular, Haight-Ashbury.

Space, I'm spaced,
    but still feel,
the moon wink,
through the black ink.
Heralding, the world's
    menacing toll.

Inspired by:

Space Age Sacrifice
Montrose

The Beats were the first organized group to tackle issues such as the environment. They were the first to encourage and support other movements of the 1960's. Their stepchildren, the hippies developed a cynical, often caustic view, of the traditional value system especially anything that smelled of authority or bastardized their senses. Old school, non-pragmatic, ritualistic, ostentatious displays of both pomp and grandeur, especially the tediously bound morphology of scripture, were more often than not, viewed as both moribund and morally ambiguous. Many used these building blocks of discord to become staunch advocates and activists, lending not only their ears, but also other body parts as well to support these new special interest groups. Gay and Lesbian organizations, the Feminist Movement and finally the splintered, political fringe groups, many of which evolved from the basic hippie principles emphasizing equality, civil rights, liberalism, and an united front against the war in Vietnam. The age of passive expressionism now became an age where active expression exercised less restraint by vaulting, uplifting and uprooting. From the simple sit-in to the antagonistic display; the raised fist of protest lead to the rampaging hysteria of open violence.

Frustration.
    The images of protest
    test the will.
        But still,
The winds of changes,
    Chime the cord,
    —churning the thrill.

Inspired by:

Street Fighting Man
The Rolling Stones

The hippies had mixed a love potion though many had overdosed. There is a fine line between love and hate and after the summer of love, 1967, everything changed. Over commercialization, rampant drug use, fanaticism and police intervention forced the hippies to disperse from the San Francisco scene. Many headed literally for the hills to live an obscure, rural pleasure, growing to eat the communal market garden. Each group, each individual fabricated a slightly different spin on what the hippie experience really meant; nothing would ever be the same again.

Political assassination, whether conspiratorial or not, the war, the ghetto echo of "burn baby burn" as our cities ignited in a frenzy was depicted in color rather than black and white. My Lai, mothers holding their offspring, shedding tears as frozen babies reached to touch, but no one reached back; for it was really our lie. The Democratic National Convention, the Lincoln Park protests, arrests and the trial of the seven, who were magnificent to some, and so sinister to others! Charles Manson and the helter skelter caused by his attempt by murder to incite hatred and rage. Woodstock, and amidst all the mud slinging, three days of love and peace. Altamont, and as Jagger sang Satan's name, angels from hell painted the curtain black as Jumping Jack Flash lay dying at his feet. If the name Woodstock denoted the power contained within the flower, then Altamont came to cut and trample underfoot, all the pedals, ushering forth "The End of the Age of Innocence."

The hippie movement would never be looked at in the same dim light. No more flower children and free love but a new age, an age of self examination and self discovery where crystals instead of sunflowers would act as dimensional walkie-talkies, probing the ether for mystical awareness.

By 1970 I pretty well knew where I belonged. Subsequent events such as American militaristic misadventure in Cambodia, the shootings at Kent State and Nixon's shame and the Watergate blame, only reinforced the obvious. I would soon leave to cast upon the waters a new life. The catalyst was my personal battle, the haunting realization, the fear of walking point at Hell's gate.

Revolution, a shrill,
    the minds' head,
    the bitter pill.
To change the mindset,
    will only spill,
    so lavish an outpouring.
To soak the inner fabric,
    wringing societies rill.

Inspired by:

Revolution
The Beatles

Setting the Stage:

The Transformation

If life is hell,
then death be,
Freedom to soul.
To search, to find,
A chance to exist,
in peace.

Inspired by:

Your Saving Grace
Steve Miller Band

Vietnam was a war where the rules of engagement changed. There was an illusion created by doctrine, outlining a battle plan, where strategy employed a battle cry against communism. But the reality was an enemy, elusive, fighting a shadow war, where the face, though recognizable, remained hidden from view. There existed no defined front, except a sculptured landscape where rice paddies, hutches, foxholes and Cu Chi tunnels burrowed a vista, carved from jungle, dictated the emotion, wrapped by gauze and tape, holding limbs, tethered by the smell of death. This was Vietnam, where distrust spread from our shores, fragging the fray, to frazzle the fragile, a mutiny of deception, a fresh start, parched with racism and the white powder, dusting the long march home.

While on Spring furlough, a temporary reprieve from both text and protocol, April 1971 fostered, in addition to a nerve racking and nail biting preoccupation with my draft lottery number, a chance meeting with John Kerry, and his sideshow, the Vietnam Veterans against the war, troupe. This was not a physical encounter of the handshake type or even the rubbing of shoulders variety, but an eye to eye vicarious interaction, separated by only the flimsiest of TV screens. I watched intently as he garnered, by garnishing his position against the war, sympathy, at the same time wooing the Senate foreign relations committee. I thought, Christ, here's a man who still had the balls, since many an unfortunate Vet returned home minus one or both. He even had the medals to prove it, until he tossed them in defiance over a Washington Barricade, symbolically separating the war mongers from his peaceniks.

He had seen combat, and purportedly witnessed first hand, alleged atrocities involving U.S. forces. Now I understood the term "Vietnamization." Yeah, before America left, the U.S. military would train the South Vietnamese army to do the same thing; to kill indiscriminately!

I confess, I learned one invaluable lesson while away at school. Well there were other lessons I learned, but to write this book in Latin would only inflame the soul of Nero. School taught me to always be objective, and try and look at the "big picture." Since my parents TV, or I should say, the one they excommunicated to my room was a measly 13 inch black and white one, on the fritz, I took the liberty of watching the rest of the "John Kerry show" on the brand new 27 inch color console in the family room, minus of course, the rest of the family.

I concluded that Henry Kissinger summed up the whole "bleedin' hearts" affair quite nicely, when he described Kerry's entourage as " Hippies in Uniform." The more I looked at this collection of a rag tag, long haired, misplaced turned on menagerie of ex-military cohorts, the more I realized that there were no real long haired, bead wearing, barefoot, guitar strumming, turned on hippies. Besides the anti-war stance, the two groups had only the stereo-typical turned on label, and nothing more in common. The real hippies kept their distance, letting Kerry and company do their own thing, which I'm convinced did nothing more than establish Kerry as a political entity, by giving him a political platform. He was, in truth, just another 'enabler' looking for an opening to crawl through. A typical political opportunist, using the war, as a rallying point to further his own agenda.

This polarity of personality, a flip flopping of convenience came to represent a nation divided. He took a position central to the issues, by fence sitting relative to the middle, enabling him to jettison in either direction, depending on the stakes. It was this grating experience coupled with the ideals of escapism that pulled the wool away from my eyes, but put the pillow ever closer to my face.

As a young hippie neophyte, the polarization created by the Vietnam War spilled forth in droves whether slurred and strained with prejudices and bias or accentuated by college campuses exploding in protest and violence, it eluded my senses and bombarded my life daily. I couldn't help but develop a disdain and blatant distrust for my government. The agonizing realization that the military industrial complex held firmly the reigns of power caused my brain to swell. This encephalitic muse all but implicated those in charge of perpetuating a criminal ruse, the pièce de résistance being eventual disclosure, thanks to the Pentagon papers outlining US involvement in Vietnam since the early 50's.

I had experienced during my formative years a visual representation of death and its despair, watching the lives of the Kennedy's and Martin Luther King Jr. bleeding society's tears as they lay dying near their assassin's lairs.

Being a hippie was fundamentally an existence with me. The casual observer looking across at myself, sitting on a seesaw, teetering on the brink, a dichotomy where the daily routine harbored both the manic and depressive qualities, possessed by the individual or set of circumstances that governed the times.

On the one hand, life imitated tarot or a simple deck of cards where it's easy to end up with a chump card. Everyday life was a struggle to survive.

It was due to this test of endurance, becoming almost effortless in scope that forced a cynical look at one's surroundings. This emollient, sometimes bordered on the absurd, reaching a bizarre crescendo of both sight and sound. The catalyst responsible for this jocular reaction was none other than nature's own mirthful aphrodisiac.

If combined with another anodyne, the resulting display became a sketch where comedic relief, like a narcotic numbed the pain of the psyche. It was not just the relief supplied weekly by the antics of *Monty Python's Flying Circus,* but the implacable impetus replayed incessantly, reinforcing the tomfoolery that was Cheech and Chong. I used both of these combinations when dealing with the harsh realities of life, such as the Vietnam War.

It's easy to manipulate and change history by simply altering events based on the supposition of "what if." So, by turning back the pages and tweaking the episode in question, —well not literally turning back the pages, since to engage in this act the reader would in effect read a variation of the same material again thus experiencing a form of "déjà vu." I'm certain all this would do espouse the identical overall affect, forcing the reader to seriously consider abandoning the book altogether. "déjà vu" being a French term, no doubt came into the popular vernacular beginning with the French military when dealing with the pesky English, since the identical theme had the uncanny ability to replicate itself, forcing the same outcome, where it became common place to see the French raising a "white flag." So, to avoid both literal ambiguity and the consequences of "déjà vu," or being a wacky way-out wayward victim of circumstance, one should figuratively flip back the pages and use a radicalized alternative when dealing with the issue or period in question. Plainly put, I wonder what would have happened if the American military brass, tarnished by years of exposure, had decided to use a variation of Monty Python's "funniest joke" concept, before flagrantly committing thousands of "boy soldiers' to Southeast Asia. By borrowing the talents of Bob Hope, between USO shows to fling a zinger, things might have been quite different. Everyone knew General Westmoreland had no sense of humor, but what about the Joint Chiefs of Staff? Surely at least one of these higher-ups could have seen this new and improved joke as the logical follow-up for Agent Orange. Obviously with no jungle to speak of, all those air-dropped leaflets would have easily been found and read.

NVA Officer—Did you hear about Diem in church?
VC—No.
NVA Officer—(Laughing slightly) Yeah, he passed* wind.
*(Not to be confused with the Japanese version, or 'divine wind').
VC—(Giggling) Really!
NVA Officer—It was bad!
VC—How bad was it ?
NVA Officer—It was so bad he ended up sitting in own pew!

In a predominately Buddhist south, President Diem, a devote Roman Catholic would have been vilified and embarrassed leading to his eventual abdication. This in itself would have not only saved thousands of lives, including perhaps President Kennedy himself, but also the US taxpayers billions of dollars. But more importantly, the US government, particularly the CIA would have been free of any humiliation by association to the assassination and following cover-up and coup. All this at the expense of the NVA and VC laughing themselves back to the Stone Age.

The stark realities of war forced me to recognize the opposing team and each of the key players. I had also accepted because of my lottery status, the possibility of being drafted. If and when, I decided against deferment, I concluded that the best passive approach would be to use my father's influence and become a medic. At least I would be preserving life, rather than indiscriminately taking it. I did however, make one promise to myself; the large satchel, emblazoned with the Red Cross would contain a personal survival kit. Next to the four by four gauze and morphine would be a three fifty-seven magnum, a large array of grenades and claymores, an ozi, a sawed-off shot gun, a Bowie blade and just in case I misplaced my mess kit, a Swiss Army knife.

I remember distinctly the first time I used cynicism to satirize an event. President Johnson's unflinching commitment to Operation Rolling Thunder shackled any capacity I possessed to understand the rationale behind any civilized rules of war. The continued pummeling of the north, including civilian targets simply galvanized the will of the people. The pictures reflecting the horrors of this unprecedented act of carnage brought back images of the great thousand plane raids against Dresden and Hamburg, a generation before.

In war, some things never change. We just keep on inventing better and more efficient ways to kill and maim. Unfortunately, as we expand this techno-madness, we include the possibility of liquidating those innocents caught in the middle.

I firmly believe if we had concentrated on the floundering Paris peace talks, instead to what I have dubbed, "Operation Smoldering Blunder," peace with honor would have been achievable years earlier.

I would have added however, just a little twist to the peace process. Operation, rolling the biggest fuckin' joint ever assembled by civilized man. I remember fantasizing about it to the point it became an obsession, especially when stoned and listening to Cheech and Chong. It always seemed to feature facsimiles of the same five characters following a very similar and predictable script centered around the Paris conference-center. There was, without exception, this enormous mirrored ballroom that contained one large, and I mean LARGE table. In addition, two chairs, one at either end, a small step stool, were strategically placed relative to the middle. The table provided an ample workstation, not for the distractions presented by an entourage of meddling dignitaries, but a construction site. This area facilitated the assembly for the grass laden torpedo-shaped monstrosity that was soon to follow, the contents, a bonafide windfall for the South American junta chosen to supply it. The de-seeder, the world's largest album cover, a montage of current favorites centered around *Who's Next*.

The possession included none other than Henry Kissinger, Lu Doc Tho, escorted by Hanoi Jane in a breathtaking evening gown arranged around a pair of combat boots and a large valise. Lastly, the Swiss referees who always bore the same uncanny resemblance to Cheech Marin and Tommy Chong.

Mr. Marin, in keeping with the script, ended up standing on the stool, flanked by Hanoi Jane and Mr. Chong. Mr. Kissenger stood to their immediate right with the "Duck" opposing him at the extreme left. (Not surprising based on their political affiliations).

Ms. Fonda always managed to produce from the briefcase in her care; a blowtorch, welder's mask and a chain saw. You see, it was a strapping specimen of a case, somewhat larger than a briefcase and a little smaller than a suitcase. It was almost a new category of case altogether, not a briefcase really and not a suitcase either, yet something too large to be taken on an aircraft as hand luggage, but also something too small to put with the other luggage. It didn't resemble a duffel bag or a gym bag, or for that matter, an overnight bag. Just what the fuck was it? I'm not really sure, but boy was it unique. Knowing Jane Fonda, it was probably an imitation Gucci, made from the last known Kenyan white rhino, trimmed in Siberian ermine and comprising as the storage compartment, the spleen from a Tasmanian Great White...no, not the shark, but Melville's Captain Ahab chowder chomping, I don't want to be the world's largest pin cushion, whale. Since there is no bag on the market, or for that matter on record, it remained not only a complete mystery, but fell into the same category as other similarly riddled bags, such as the one belonging to Felix the Cat.

Cheech, totally ignoring the bag, brandishing the saw and initiating a blind Mohel at the circumcision of a white whale, ops! That's just too much punishment for Moby's dick. Hmm...yeah, how about a Sperm whale? Now, in retrospect, maybe that's what Hanoi Jane should have used to make a matching trunk. I'm sure there would have been enough foreskin, sorry, a four score and many more skins left over to also manufacture a complete set of luggage for both Cheech and Chong.

Cheech, slicing and dicing, always managed to surgically separate not only Barbarella's head, but before it hit the floor, succeeded in splitting the prodigious phallus of peace. This not only left two identical papier-mâché like cadavers, but a twitching torso as well. Chong in stride, akin to a pyromaniac running amuck in a paper mill, would always light without a hitch, the now separated rolled tarp-like projectiles.

Upon viewing this spectacle, time and time again, I couldn't rid my mind of the serious application of the cirrus layers of smoke that congested the ingester. This invariably brought about the predictable bouts of coughing and wheezing.

Like a knife, this gashed the war clouds leaving a peaceful fog, soon muttering with the attempt from those it blanketed to utter and hence, communicate.

I've never seen two stoned people become confrontational (I'm sure this is one reason why America lost the war.). The resulting verbal engagement always contained earth-shattering dialogue punctuated by the slow repeated use of high octane hippie jargon.

"Wow man! Can you please stop playing with that head." The biting inflection hinted strongly of a Prussian swagger.

"Sorry, dude!" The voice offered with an Oriental dialect, a conciliatory position. "Watch this," the same silhouette, drop kicking the head, looking like a hazy wax figure of Pele, as the motion of the follow-though arched the ball, I mean head, through the open door. "I guess we better come up with some sort of agreement, or heads will roll!"

With his almost Confucian like wit, the fist signs of extemporaneous laughter. The laughter is soon separated by a slow, almost tedious Jewish twang.

"You know something, man? My eyes look like yours. Tiny little slits. Now I know why you guys can't drive."

After more bouts of insane laughter, a more pronounced resonating voice that teased the listener with an Oriental slur.

"Yeah, dude. I can dig that but I can still see, even with these tiny grooves that you like me, could use something to munch on. I tell you what, let's sign this bloody treaty and I'll treat you. How's Chinese sound?"

More laughter. "Only if I can have your fortune cookie. I don't trust those Chinese."

"You know something, man? I don't trust those cats either. Talking about cats, whatever you do, don't order the chop suey."

DaDa, Dadat, Dadat, Da, cymbals (curtain!)

What can I say, you spend eight years away at boarding school and see if your mind doesn't suffer some sort of brain damage. It's just unfortunate that the harsh realities of conflict always produced a stubborn arrogance that superceded any tangible reference introduced by common sense. The agonizing standoff produced by war, followed me throughout my tenure while away at school.

Please stop the world
I must get off.
I do protest,
Refusing drink,
Lining the trough.

From the insight of human disgrace
And its rubble,
So to,
I leave to hide from all its trouble.

My 1st real attempt at poetry.
Stoned, behind the ice rink
Circa, early 1970

The obvious lessons, not from the poem, forget the damn poem! But, concerning the quagmire that was Vietnam was that for every action there is an obvious consequence and the lingering question, why didn't the United States military simple leave? The answer? Honor! Come on! It wasn't an eighteenth century duel. Just how differently would the hippies have handled it? Put it this way, being the love generation, we would have never been there in the first place. Okay, let's say for convenience sake we were chosen to broker a peace. You know, the shortest straw wins or in this case, loses. Since the most radical faction of the long hairs, that being the Democratic seven were busy doing their own version of a sit in, sadly behind bars, it would have, no doubt, been a more passive display. If a love in, or a three day festival failed, we would have collectively shrugged our shoulders, given the universal peace sign being very careful to display the palms in the direction of the receiver, turned with precision toward the setting sun and ran like hell along the road to the dawning of a new day.

Wait a minute! Sunset, sunrise, right! That would have meant splitting into two groups each walking or I should say, running in different directions. Confusing, yet effective, especially if both groups, lets say a hundred thousand strong, whistled the theme from the *Bridge on the River Kwai.*

The important issue here is that the American government neither possessed the will or for that matter, the cahonies. So, Uncle Sam as castrated as he was, couldn't walk away disguised as a paper tiger with tail firmly tucked between his legs since it had the awful habit of wagging the dog.

All they needed was an exit strategy, which I believe is essential, just in case. If in place, they could have retreated, (ops! Wrong word), escaped, (can't use that one either), withdrew, (un huh!). Let me think for a second. How about bid adieu, (no that one's already taken, used by the French about twenty years before, right after Dien Bien Phu). Hold on, I've got it. Vamoose. The military vamoosed, simply declaring that the United States government had met all its strategic initiatives. This was technically feasible by using the already drastically inflated end of the week body count, ready for prime time propaganda reports and the bombing campaign. Now the quick changing of the guard by way of the simple, but never understated communiqué, (In triplicate of course with the CIA receiving the customary pink copy).

"We're out—a—here, (stop)
Good luck, adios, and
good riddance (stop)
We have a drug war to fight!"

It's really not difficult to save face by simply covering it up by using a mask, or better yet, by masking the truth. Since with or without our help, the South was doomed.

Dead Babies

As men died,
    screams echoed
    bleeding their fate.
As children played,
    a nation paused,
    a breath to take.

Inspired by:

The Ballad of the Unknown Soldier
The Doors

The flame from the candle danced as the smoke rose in a funnel shaped column toward the hole in the ceiling. I made a feeble attempt to form with my hand the silhouette of a dog against the backdrop provided by the wooded slats. As many times I have stood, balanced precariously close to the edge of the chair, I had never paid attention to the graffiti of names carved or notched into the knotty pine. Surprising, many were in German; names like Von Rickthofen, Brandenburg, and Schultz.

Amassed, a hall of records containing an archive of memories mirroring generations of Tom Browns, a time capsule of closet relics bearing the crumpled and faded names of De Maurier and Rothman.

I looked over at Al, his face almost Halloween like, a contrast in texture, highlighted by marionette lines that gave him an eerie reaper like appearance. He exhaled, the smoke merging as if programmed with the wisps of candle vapor that seemed to flirt in anticipation.

He passed me the pipe that still glowed hot, a single ember, a small red dwarf waiting to be extinguished. I placed it between my lips and drew its last breath

I had certainly come a long way since first being introduced the previous summer to the euphoria contained within the THC molecule. I exhaled, coughed slightly and as I handed back the pipe, remembered the carved names.

"Al, I feel a little claustrophobic, you know, like Charles Bronson, in the *Great Escape'!*

"Yeah, it's a little confining, isn't it," handing me back a now reloaded pipe.

"Listen, dude. I'm blasted," my hands obviously out of sync with my brain since the pipe was already well on its way toward my mouth.

I paused momentarily as the faint sound of Alice Cooper permeated the narrow box shaped area that held our heads.

I blew a short spurt of air toward the candle, causing the ripples of smoke to gyrate out of control before reforming its disciplined spiral toward the hole.

"Okay, one last hit," my voice sounding raspy yet willing.

I closed my eyes as he re-ignited the bowl, drawing in the harshness of both the new hash mixed with the residue of past pleasures. I coughed again and placing my hand over my mouth displaced the exhalant into my eyes.

I felt trapped and thought about the North Vietnamese sappers living and fighting from areas not much bigger that this. It sent a shiver up my spine culminating with a tingling sensation that exacerbated the ringing in my ears. The war was all but over, but I couldn't help but dwell on the possibility that I might end up being a late inning replacement. With my luck, I'd find myself with only a first aid kit, walking point down some defoliated jungle path. A survivor, only to return to be jeered as a "baby killer."

"Al, I'm fucking ripped. I've got to lie down. I'll see you at dinner."

When I awoke, there was the distant din of voices competing with the sound of cutlery meeting china. Christ. I had missed dinner! As I sat up in bed, my hands frisked both pockets searching for any evidence suggesting the presence of loose change. The hunger pangs gave me only one choice. Pizza! I walked cautiously down the hall toward the payphone, bouncing the dime from my left hand to the right and back again.

I heard the faint sound of a man's voice coming form the television room. I stopped just short of the door, angled my head around the barrier, catching the image of Walter Cronkite being bathed in effigy by the setting sun as it channeled through the window next to the TV set. It was the "living room war," beaming in Technicolor, concentrated hues of red.

"To recap tonight's top story. The US resumes bombing of the North."

The Gang:

A Melting Pot of Psychobabble

I'm a child, albeit a man.
Drink I must not,
    the chalice of an age.
To fornicate, the lust.
    sacrifice the bust.
The boy, the man,
    dead before he wakes.

Inspired by:

I'm Eighteen
Alice Cooper

We came from different backgrounds. Some were upper class, some were working class and still others straddled the middle. Our parents were professionals, entrepreneurs and skilled laborers. It was a wide cross-sectional representation of the traditional British stratified class system, a true socioeconomic melting pot.

Our parents had given us life and for that we were eternally grateful. Through this simple act of procreation, we were given a chance, a chance to live, a chance to grow, a chance to learn. We would go to school, enter a structured world, find work, marry, have children, pay taxes and hopefully, live long enough to watch the process repeat itself. A cycle within a cycle, a wheel within a wheel, and as long as both turned, independent, yet dependent on one another, the world turned.

However, we saw it differently. The extreme factors that

subjugated our existence also stymied our desire to establish a symbiotic relationship with society. There are many factors, many of which mimic those that initiated the hippie movement in the US. Even though Britain shared this theme, she never really established an identity on the world's stage after the Second World War. She had won the war, but had lost an empire.

Where exactly did she fit in? Where, as a people, did they belong? Many as a result, left during the brain drain of the fifties. One was my father. I however, upon leaving school chose to return. This move circumvented the conventional, or should say the unconventional wisdom of the period, since many "Yankee" wannabe hippies gravitated to the American Southwest, and the sun to help bleach free a mindset tattooed and consumed by the "American dream." I chose the Southwest of England and the rain to help wash away disillusionment levied against the establishment and status quo. Even though I managed to land feet first rather than on my back, my instinct as a hawk, rather than a hawker, marked my new territory. Plymouth was now my home, but to headquarter an existence, a roof over my head, I struggled to find, until I walked through the doors that would forever change my life.

A Stairway to Heaven

A new day will come,
    the path will take,
    the vale will break.
Follow the dreams,
    I hope to make.

Inspired by:

Stairway to Heaven
Led Zeppelin

The palm trees swayed in unison as though dancing with the wind, which tickled the bottom of my feet. The sun burned the sky and caressed my hand, as the sand blushed, dispatching as a stream, through the cracks between my fingers. As I raised the Pina Colada toward my reckoning lips, my moustache ran interference, spilling the contents. The outpouring avalanched down the gully that lay between my hairy pecks, carrying the crushed ice with it. Without intervention, it disappeared leaving only a slight trail toward the repository that formed just inside my bathing suit. As a marker, the small pink parasol stood triumphantly upright, parked firmly in my belly button.

"Bloody hell!" I bolted erect, shivering from the shock. Hold on, it was only a dream. I must have inadvertently dozed off on the settee in front of the fireplace. Luckily no one in the pub had noticed. I quickly wiped the drool from the corner of my mouth, licked my lips, yawned and reached by instinct, above my head in anticipation of a pint. Sadly, none followed.

"Ah, soon enough," I thought. It was just good to be inside. I

heard the wind chastise the door, which cheekily responded as it thwarted any attempt, except for a slight draft, to enter. A smattering of cold nibbled at my feet and as I looked down, to my amazement, they were bare.

"Christ!" I must have walked over in the snow without my socks and boots.

"Late again." The voice was without form, since only the words were present. I looked around and to my astonishment the pub was now empty. There was a chilling laugh and the door opened. The cold nip was quick to inflict a frenzy that startled the hair on my legs to rise.

"For God's sake, shut the bloody door, please shut the door!" I shouted.

"It's ta, ta time to mo, mo, move."

Now my sixth sense told me I wasn't in a pub, but propped in the corner like a frozen yogi with only a not-so-great coat. My eyes opened and stared in abandonment at the Yukon, which during the summer was actually the foyer acting as a buffer between flats that comprised the residence. Reality had provided a cover, which had given me the temporary protection provided by a dream, lingering within a dream. Now the real nightmare was about to begin again, fashioning a test of endurance, pitting myself against my own stupidity.

Why the fuck did I ignore the clock when I knew deep down inside, hugging my frozen kidneys that I wouldn't get laid.

Now if only my dependence on testosterone and its relationship to my masculinity could duplicate the affinity that existed between antifreeze and the taxi that dropped me, maybe, just maybe, I might survive the night. But again this self imposed exile to the local Siberian Hilton was indeed my own personal gulag, truly a sweat shop, equipped not for my survival, I was in essence, fucked!

As I shivered with contempt at my own hormonal driven dementia, I remembered from my grammar school

Shakespearean experience, an interpretation of the verse, which summed up best my predicament.

"When my love swears that she is made of truth,
I do believe her, though I know she fucking lies!"

Shit! What did that prissy dressed poofter know anyway?

"OH what a tangled web." Crykee! I must be suffering from the first sign of hypothermia. I proceeded to adjust my recently bartered Oxfam army great coat, hoping to cover my numbing feet without revealing my already anesthetized ears.

The need-jerk reaction, that was my head responding to a sign, proved all was not lost. It was the muted sound made by wood, creaking as it recoiled from the weight as though someone or something was trekking down the stairs.

I was secluded in the dark corner, a voyeur to a world, the flicker of which was rapidly fading. As the door opened, I peered with one eye, catching a glimpse of a hobbit like silhouette, bidding farewell to a mysterious sojourner. God, I was really in dire straits now. Maybe this was a near death experience and he was here to appropriate my soul, shuffling it off to hell.

He pulled the door, inching it open. It remained rigid as it stood guard, protecting the sanctuary that was his home. Statuesque, he still appeared as a necromancer, fabled by a trick of light that trickled through. I managed to filter his nefarious quality and as more light freed the room, it was though the "house lights" illuminated him, an emcee at a benefit concert where I hoped to be introduced momentarily as the man of the hour, the guest of honor.

"Hard luck mate, missed 'lights out' did ya?" I sensed sarcastic pleasure, as he pointed to the entrance.

As I nodded, I felt my heart rescinding from the rush, returning quietly to my chest.

"Yeah, I'm so fuckin' cold, even the voices in my head are a stutterin' and a stamerin'."

He giggled as my segue, like an ice pick chipped the freeze, defrosting the mood.

"Well, look at it this way. It could be a lot colder." He hesitated, rubbed his hands together and with the acid that dripped from the corner of his mouth, dipped his tongue and continued, "Just think, those damn commies could launch a sneak attack tomorrow and by the weekend, all of us, at least those who survived, would be sharing body heat, during the fall out of Nuclear winter."

He turned, completed the process, forcing the door to relinquish its hold. The light spilled into the room like a torrent, attacking everything between his space and mine. Like Bella Legosi at sunrise, I reached to block my eyes, pulling myself up, using the wall as a crutch.

This time I could see a beard, which lay siege to his face, giving way just below the eyes, which now targeted mine.

"Well, just don't stand there, come on. It's a lot warmer where I'm going."

"Thanks," I said and before I could follow with my name, he introduced himself, continuing the passive interrogation without a breath.

"I'm Fluff, and you must be the 'Yank' and from the sight of things, you didn't quite make Shaggers' curfew did you?" Mocking me playfully with his finger.

"Yeah, I am he and nope, missed it by that much," forming a slight gap between my forefinger and thumb.

He smiled, laughed again and pointed toward a seemingly endless batch of stairs. I followed without hesitation, saying nothing as he marched toward the source of the bright light that dominated from atop. At first glance, it appeared somewhat eerie, but as I drew closer, it seemed to offer not only sanctuary, but also warmth. I felt I was almost floating toward it as the numbness in my legs still hampered my ability to walk. At the top, Fluff, with almost regal flair announced, "Visitor everyone."

Upon making my grand entrance, I noticed a large round table that hinted of Camelot. A sea of denim surrounded me, almost acting as a ring. As I strained to see through the maze of hair and smoke, the collective turned in harmony. It was like a swarm of starlings, avoiding with radar like precision, impending disaster. Remembering the revolutionary battle cry, I looked pressingly for the white of their eyes. This proved somewhat futile since to a man, each bore shades.

I hesitated to speak, swallowing to gain composure. It was then I heard through the haze, "Hello, my name's John. My friends call me 'Blade'." There was a short pause. "But you," his voice becoming rather sullen as it dropped ten octaves, "can call me John."

There was some snickering but mostly whispering and the distinct sound of china meeting wood.

"Just kidding!" And for the first time I saw his face, dominated by a thick black beard as he presented with a wide cavernous grin. As he stood up, he reached for my hand, initiating the all to familiar clasp. He then spoke again, "Welcome to heaven, friend."

As a group, we were reborn. We were blind to the establishment and not trusting anyone over the age of thirty, further entrenched our position by first ridiculing and then abhorring the age-old theme of having to either live or die for the dreams of our fathers.

Our parents had known suffering and deprivation, first living through the depression and then finally surviving the Second World War. From the ashes of victory, they scrounged an existence, reaping the benefits of working hard so we, as they often preached, wouldn't have to. Funny isn't it? We took it to mean that we wouldn't have to work at all.

However, we did feel a kinship for the heartfelt period being the war, even if only on a very basic level. They had experienced rationing and in a sense, their monthly ration book was very similar to our monthly gyro. If they could survive, so could we. While they were being bombed each and every night by hoards of marauding Dorniers and Junkers, we were busy absorbing hits of our own; getting bombed nightly. While they suffered through Hitler's unrelenting blitz, we were busy rolling joints in anticipation of getting blitzed!

So you see, the world can be a very cold, insensitive and inconsistent place. It's all relative and simply a matter of perception. We tried in our own warped way to change the world and in the end; we only succeeded in changing ourselves. We were disillusioned and disenfranchised, quickly becoming a lunatic fringe teetering on the edge. From this precipice we were not only alienated but also marred and in many cases, barred. The longhaired freaks became a sideshow of psychedelic psychobabble. We were more than just "far out and cosmic." We were a light show of lasers and strobes, both crazy and manic where lunacy was the norm.

THE PLAYERS

(The 'New Age' Pranksters)

Swirling with the wind,
    the tempest to bring,
    shadows and faces,
    where friends greet.
The memories,
    are forever sweet.

Inspired by:

Travelers in Time
Ur1ah Heep

The names and faces gave been changed to protect the innocent. To all those poor sods, we hustled, hassled, humiliated, harangued, bamboozled or hogtied—Get a Life!

THE COUNTER CULTURE AND COUNTER REVOLUTIONARIES

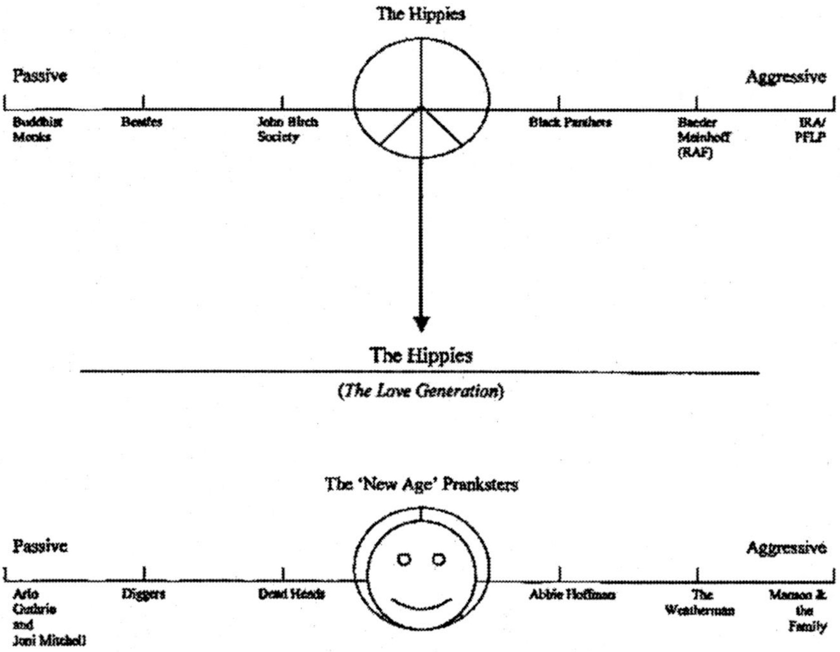

NAME: Ian G
Nickname:The Yank, Mr. Manic
AKA: The Seeker

MO: To settle down with a nice chic. A bilingual mute, only able to sign in French or Italian. My ultimate goal, to be a roadie for Marcel Marceau.

I wonder, if life will tell,
or will I sift the sands.
Each grain,
  one less, the hourglass,
  the lifeblood,
  my life, draining unfettered.

Inspired by:

The Seeker
The Who

My parents were quite well to do. Having passed through the shadow of Ellis Island, they carried much of the traditional British caste system with them. By age ten, I found myself watching Dudley Doright reruns on location at a rather isolated Canadian boarding school. My future, and career aspirations were indeed being designed and mapped for me.

By being insulated for the most part, from the frigid weather and the rest of the world, life became a series of 6:00 a.m. to 9:00 p.m. bells, which included chapel, classes and a chance to compete in the sporting arena. The Vietnam War, the cold war and political unrest seemed almost surreal, appearing more often than not on page two of the newspaper. Woodstock was simply a picture on an album cover. I was taught the hippie movement epitomized the counter culture, which in turn fostered rebellion and anarchy.

This stirred my curiosity just enough to spark an interest. I decided to remove my rose colored monocle, and look at the world in a different light. The hypocrisy, especially concerning the Vietnam War gradually stripped away at my protective shield. The hippies became a symbol of change. It embodied a set of ideals that promoted an alternative life style, set apart from the norm. It was not just anti-establishment; it was in fact, anti-everything! It offered a different approach, a different path; all I needed was a compass.

I remember reading about the Leakeys. I visualized my alter ego awash in emotion and anxiety, examining fossilized bones, and while clutching them to my heart, I closed my eyes and felt my history. However, studying Homo Erectus didn't come without the obvious ambiguities. I confess, it did imply on a very primitive level "gay pride." I mean, think about it. Homo Erectus. Doesn't it conjure images of a queer standing tall, with a massive hard-on? Somehow I could connect to the vibrations of the past and feel the energy that existed in the souls of primitive man. I found myself merging with the past and relating it to the present, hoping to capture a vision of the future. But alas, to wallow in sentiment diluted by tears from years of resentment did nothing but exacerbate the anger that already hounded me. Consequently after returning to England to further my education I cast asunder all that was mine. The astringent basis for truth, allocated the desire to collar a chance for redemption. The simple lessons of life could not be taught in the classroom.

I was headstrong, quixotic, cynical and detested criticism, especially from a wanna be pundit or authoritarian figure. I was now lost, yet free to rollick and romp in my own personal anomie. But it was my love of adventure and my desire to push the envelop to the edge that defined my character. I found it easy to encourage and even manipulate a situation with the sole premise of creating pandemonium and revelry. If given the opportunity, I could find humor in anything. However, at school, if you were caught having too much fun, you were tied behind the Headmaster's Rolls and dragged repeatedly through the "Rose Garden."

But in time, the more I was exposed to the insanity of the real world; the more I chose to withdraw. I was again insulating myself from the rigors of life. This was easy, and the artificial cocoon I found myself sheltered in was woven from the panacea shaped like a joint or a pill. I was soon convinced I could live like this forever. Never a worry, and never a hassle. There was only my world. I was suffering from the Peter Pan complex. I would buy ten acres somewhere in Cornwall, further insulate myself. But deep down inside I knew and understood the stark reality. In truth, it was difficult living with myself, and surely one of us had to go. But which one? The manic deviant or the soul survivor, clinging to the depressing realization that never, "Neverland" would never, never be.

NAME: Ian D
Nickname:Fluff, The Gnome
AKA: The Pacifist

MO: To get into the *Guinness Book of Records* by breaking John Lennon's and Yoko Ono's record for staying in bed. His companion; a twelve-string acoustic guitar.

I'm not sleeping,
I dream with one eye open.
My life as stories,
so destined to change,
my life within reach,
to drift, out of range.

Inspired by:

Spill the Wine
Eric Burdon Declares War

He reminded people of a garden gnome, or a fluffy cuddly bearded troll. However, if I closed my eyes, he captured the spirit of Frodo from Tolkien's, Lord of the Rings. A typical Hobbit, living a laid back, fancy-free existence, without a care in the world. It was easy to visualize him, frolicking innocently amongst the daisies, or catching a few Z's, napping in a haystack.

Fluff never let things bother him, or if they did, he never switched on the neon sign advertising the fact. He was cool as a cucumber, probably the most even keeled of the group. The antithesis for the character more often than not depicted by Pete. His approach to life, and all its challenges could be summed up effectively by reading between the lines from some of his more profound sayings.

"Being young and full of vim and vinegar, there is absolutely no excuse in ever being tardy—so when its your turn, get your fucking ass out of bed and, for Christ's sake, make it to the damn dole office on time!"

He was a loyal party man, and showed his steadfast support, to her majesty's government.

"Remember, be happy, smile, and count your blessings. It's simply wonderful to have elected officials in power that care enough to pay you not to work."

You know something, he was right. Life doesn't have to be so damn laborious or complex. Just take the time to simplify it and make it work for you. Pretty simple really!

He possessed this uncanny ability to sense when aggressive male posturing had the potential to escalate into all out conflict. He used this gift on more than one occasion to stifle tension within the group, before fists had a chance to fly.

NAME: John B
Nickname: The Blade
AKA: The Lone Wolf

MO: To be hired as Princess Margaret's bodyguard with the sole purpose of shagging her and then leaving her high and dry in Monaco.

I'm a loner,
I'm a stoner,
but through the ugly stories,
I'm a man.
Where my bond is true,
and my hand,
like a Celtic cairn
is unyielding

Inspired by:

Desperado
Alice Copper

John had encountered more by the time he was 21, than most people elicit during an entire lifetime. He had been stationed with the British army in Northern Ireland, and as a biker had crossed paths with the Hell's Angels. His life harbored a grail like quest in search of purpose through enlightenment.

He was a modern day Knight's Templar or Arthurian throwback. Not in the image of Mallory, but like a figure rising from the mists of *Historicus Britannicus,* standing firm atop Glastonbury, holding on high a sword reflecting the mid-day sun. There was a certain aura attached to his Viking veneer which like a thin coat of Armour, surrounded and protected all those that chose to stand with him.

The Blade had a code of justice and felt he had to stand up for the hippies, because for the most part, they couldn't physically stand up for themselves.

He became our protector. In this respect, he was a combination of Brando's "macho" toughness, brought to life in the *Wild One*, and Peter Fonda's "cool" confidence, which marked *Easy Rider*.

However, there existed another side to John. Deep within there lurked a desperate force that gnawed at his fragile persona. Instead of the enigmatic rugged individualist, chain-smoking Marlboros, a warm and sensitive side presented, changing by definition, the man.

He had learned to balance the two halves, stabilizing each, but allowing just enough of a mystique to keep all those outside the circle at a safe distance.

NAME: Nick
Nickname:Sputnik
AKA: The Explorer

MO: To purchase HMS Eagle as scrap and refit her as a floating retreat for wayward hippies, using the flight deck for free festivals and the occasional sit in.

I'm a mover, I'm a shaker,
I've traveled, and I've seen.
I'm not shackled, tethered, but bound,
to new places I've never been.

Inspired by:

Goin' Mobile
The Who

He would say, the world, the universe is yours. It's where anything and everything is possible. He was a cross between Ptolomy and Phineaus Phogg. As a first impression he seemed to place himself at the center of the universe, but when you got to know him, you realized, all he really wanted to do was travel across it.

Strength, fortitude, drive, confidence and a belief in one's dreams can take the believer anywhere. He often told me, grab the gusto while you can, and don't savor the moment too long before moving on. He pictured life as a platter of cold cuts, where his appetite for living had him reaching for the roast beef instead of the bologna. When he set his sights on the seemingly impossible, he was able to re-define the rules and change the outcome. He never quit, and if you shared his space long enough, his lifeblood inevitably spilled forth and saturated you. Consequently, he was able to scale the highest mountain, to drink from life's fountain. To him it was a little more than a hill, and the climb simply an enjoyable afternoon stroll.

He loved adventure and by believing in himself, could and did on more than one occasion; leave England with only a small backpack. His search for Shangri-La involved sacrifice of the material. Well not all of life's luxuries, but just enough to achieve spiritual enlightenment and cleansing of the soul. This alone inspired me to do the same.

NAME: Rob
Nickname:Robbin
AKA: Robin Hood

MO: To win a seat in parliament for the wild party and then move the Royal Navy from Plymouth across the Tamar River, to Torpoint.

I have given, and I've taken.
I have borrowed, and I've forsaken.
I'm a toker, and a broker,
a rabbit on the run.

Inspired by:

The Battle of Epping Forest
Genesis

I met Rob through Nick. They had grown up as best friends. To the casual observer, Rob appeared in all his glory, the prototypical hippie. He looked the part and dressed the role, skimpily clad; a symbol of defiance.

There was the flim-flam man and then there was Rob, the flip-flop man. His lack of proper footwear became his trademark. He wore flimsy thongs yearly, barefoot in the summer and with socks in the winter. He was a simple man with simple tastes.

He was a stanch advocate of hippie doctrine with one glaring exception. He abhorred the whole idea of being a new age cohort or a by-product of its hysteria.

He epitomized a back-to-roots movement. I'm convinced if he had been offered a small plot of land, a mule, a lifetime supply of cannabis and a one room cottage, he would have been content for life.

As an outcast living outside the line, queuing conformity, he was viewed as an outlaw who more often than not out flanked and out witted his foe; a true survivor in every sense of the word. His legacy no doubt will reflect the saga where he resurrected the collective spirit to become the savior of hippies, vagabonds and thieves.

Like many hippies, Rob found himself migrating to the southern most part of Britain as the weather changed. The only draw back, no matter how far south one ventures, Britain still remains an island, frozen in the firm grip of Thule. Consequently, the winters are rather cold and blistery.

As a group, the hippies had a choice, settle on the Scilly Isles which I thought sounded quite appropriate for such a misfit group, or St. Ives.

The problem with the Scillies, the group would have to share this piece of rocky real estate with breeding Atlantic gray seals. The notion of ritualistic combat over territorial rights was at best, not very appealing.

On the other hand, St. Ives was a haven for both the "old rich" and the camera-toting tourist.

The choice was simple; now all they had to do was blend in and survive.

Rob's notoriety as a second story man became apparent early. He not only took what he needed, but was more than happy to circulate his booty among the group. This act of kindness though appreciated amongst the destitute, finally led to his downfall and capture. The newspaper proclaimed him the Robin Hood of St. Ives and the legend was born.

NAME: Clive
Nickname:Cleaver
AKA: The Teacher

MO: Liked to tinker with cars and motorcycles. Currently working on developing a two-wheeled bubble car.

I'm still searching, but when I find,
I'll reach out, and speak my mind.

Inspired by:

Teacher
Jethro Tull

Clive, like the rest of us, over-indulged in the daily rituals that comprised hippie protocol. But while we were sleeping it off, he somehow managed to crawl out of bed and make it to work. Yes work! That four-letter word we all inherently despised. Cleaver was an apprentice at Her Majesty's dockyard. An enviable position, no doubt, if only to learn the finer points of preparing the tea four times a day for the rest of the crew. Needless to say, Clive refused the identical duties at the flat, instead bestowing the same on the low man on the totem pool. Pete. When he wasn't in the kitchen instilling the esoteric principals of boiling water, he read.

He possessed a mind, saturated with a plethora of arcane truths and knowledge.

To engage him in debate was like challenging white water rapids without the luxury of a paddle or, for that matter, a raft. He was the human variation of a main frame. Anything to do with science or the paranormal was fair game, programming a lengthy response; a recital awash in a torrent of data, drenching his adversaries with fact and theory, drowning all those present. What a way to garner gobbledygook without the inconvenience of having to scan either text or dictionary.

Yet, this was truly hard to fathom, when watching him burn the midnight oil, up to his elbows in grease, tinkering with his BSA motorcycle and a massive array of spare parts.

NAME: Steve
Nickname:Cornish
AKA: The Conniver

MO: A known Cornish Separatist and leader of the C.F.A.L.C.P.H (Cornish Farmers Association for the Liberation of Cornwall and the Preservation of Hedgerows). His goal in life, to retire to a remote tropical island and become a millionaire by growing just enough "skunkweed" to sell to himself.

Till the land, lend a hand.
Bend the rules, forget the tools.

Inspired by:

Tend My Garden
James Gang

He came across as a typical country bumpkin, the stereotypical Cornish Farmer, if you will. If you talked to him while he was intoxicated or stoned, it prompted the listener to automatically deduct a hundred points from his IQ. It was like listening to a turnip farmer, who had just fallen off the back of his tractor, suffered a closed head injury, only to be run over by a large transit van.

The interesting thing about Steve was, while assimilating the role of the village idiot,, he was busy behind the scenes. In addition to his primary use of the Medulla Oblongata, he was in effect, using parts of the brain, long thought by scientists to be dormant. He could in plane truth, analyze a situation and adapt to a role depending on that situation.

I truly believe if permission were granted by the Vatican, and Steve was allowed fifteen minutes with the Pope, he would actually have his holiness believing that Jesus Christ was not just a super star, but a space alien; a true conniver in every sense of the word.

NAME: John F
Nickname:Big John, J. F.
AKA: The Cat

MO: To take part in a rugby scrum against the entire Devon Cornwall Constabulary.

The shadows play, the cat on the roof.
Thinking with his eyes, hypnotic and aloof.

Inspired by:

Moon Shadow
Cat Stevens

John was a hulking figure of a man. He stood almost six foot, three and weighed in at an impressive sixteen stone. He was an ex-rugby player, and was the first bloke I ever saw use a head butt. It was part of an impromptu ritual with John. You see if he hadn't seen you for some time, instead of a handshake, well you get the picture. The meeting of skull with skull was reminiscent of a trip to the planetarium whereupon, the impact of star cluster left the observer somewhat shell shocked; very invigorating to say the least. Yet, the resulting headache could be devastating to the recipient if he was already suffering from a hangover.

John was a man of few words, a gentile giant until he drank. If inebriated his demeanor could change at the drop of a hat. Upon which it was not uncommon to see him swagger about, being rather loud and obnoxious.

However, the biggest irritant during this gregarious display of pent up aggression was his lobotomized rendition of Cat

Steven's "Moon Shadow." He would pick up Fluff's twelve string acoustic guitar and belch out the words incessantly, repeating the lyrics over the course of the entire evening.

I must say, it brought the group to thoughts of mass suicide on more than one occasion.

NAME: Pete
Nickname:Cochise, Sordid
AKA: The Recluse

MO: To become a member of the fabulous Furry Freak brothers with the sole stipulation that Fat Freddie's Feline be replaced by Fritz the cat.

I sit in black, and crave life's madness.
I smile in tune to each, their sadness..

Inspired by:

Aqualung
Jethro Tull

He looked like a cross between the Apache warrior, Cochise, and Oliver Twist's Fagan. He was dark, almost seafarer worn, and his jet-black hair loosely strung, weaved just past his waist.

He was coy, yet opinionated, operating from within a contrived ingenuous platform. He spoke his mind, but tended to reap the harvest, by allying himself with the harsher side of reality. He represented the external pessimist, balancing the scale by infusing just enough dark matter to keep us in the loop.

Pete was passion wrapped in pathos. He was the straw that both stirred the drink and yet broke the camel's back. He was the bloke you wanted standing next to you if trouble reared its ugly head. Sort of liked the tough loner depicted more often than not in most Hollywood war flicks. You know, the soldier in the foxhole, who unselfishly throws himself on the live grenade to save his comrades. Ops! Upon reflection, I'm probably the idiot who accidentally dropped it, after inquisitively removing the pin. Oh well, just a little more guilt to deal with, while the others debate whether in all likelihood, Pete was actually pushed, rather than heroically pouncing on the shrapnel bound pineapple.

NAME: Jim
Nickname:Jimbo
AKA: Mr. Excess

MO: Fast times, fast cars, fast women; and fasting when the money ran out.

No time to sleep, his eyes fight to lift.
As dourness swings the eve, to cleave the daze

Inspired by:

Life In the Fast Lane
The Eagles

Jim's sole ambition in life was to own and operate a chain of Chemists. Of course he would accomplish this without passing through the doors of either a bank or an institution of higher learning.

He was tall, lean and sculptured. He bore an uncanny resemblance to Eric Clapton, without the fanfare of being a guitar aficionado. Women adored him, and seemingly paraded themselves in an attempt to capture his attention. I think it bored Jim. But for the rest of us, provided a cornucopia of poontang. It was an assembly line of promiscuity which we harnessed through the allure of the moment, seizing and perpetuating the theme; sex, drugs and rock and roll!

And All the Rest

We're all in this together.
Some chose to question, while others did not.
Most watched and just smiled.

Inspired by:

A Little Help from My Friends
The Beatles

Clairemont or '*80*', as it was affectionately; or in an isolated case or two, infectiously referred to, was an old Edwardian terraced home, converted into two flats; an upstairs/downstairs marriage of convenience, where a menagerie of debauchery co-existed with a sense of warped purpose and misguided chivalry.

The main cast of characters resided upstairs, albeit not at the same time. People came and went, many using the downstairs as a training center before actually graduating to the big time. The two permanent residents of the lower floor used their digs as an oasis or safe house to escape the twenty-four/seven party zone that existed just above them. There was Wings, the aspiring rock star who was known more for his head of hair than his wielding of the axe. When the wind blew, his hair would levitate like aircraft wings. All he needed was two Rolls Royce Pegasus engines and flight could have been achieved without hitting the communal bong.

Hagus or "Shagger," on the other hand, was an unobtrusive Scotsman, who possessed the unprecedented ability to smell out any enclave, no matter how small, containing the best in resin.

He was a minor dealer, but by securing only the best, managed to fabricate a decent living.

The two geezers that made the scene more often than not were Roy, the Thug and Denver, the proto typical "New Age Frontiersman." Roy acted as Hagus's bodyguard and chauffeur, and always seemed to have a different set of wheels. Both, he and the Scotsman dressed in black, chauvinistically gave the house a gothic feel, blending effectively with its cobweb ambiance. They became known as the two Ronnies. This had no bearing on the TV show of the same name, which our parents faithfully watched, but drew from their affiliation with the Ronnie's after hours night club. Shagger could be found displaying his wares in the dark musty corner adjacent to the Looe, while Roy guarding the front door had the reputation of tossing anyone who simply looked at him in the wrong light.

Denver on the other hand, was a Davy Crocket clone, all buckskin, hoping to bond with anything and every thing that possessed the ability to migrate. It's funny really, because the closest he ever got to "convening" with nature was putting up his pup tent in the sitting room. Here he could be seen reading one of Blade's *Soldier of Fortune* magazines while listening to cassettes featuring New Age music. This serene serenade blended cavorting fowl with cascading waterfalls, rather than Ted Nugent's Gonzo rock hysteria depicting "If we're going to live outside, we might as well shoot 'em and eat 'em before they head south," mentality.

CHAPTER TWO

THE RITE OF PASSAGE

Every man has by the law of nature a right to such a waste portion of the earth as is necessary for his sustenance.

Sir Thomas More

To Be or Not to Be (101)

If freedom is the backbone,
then why do so many struggle just to walk?

Inspired by:

Simple Man
Bad Company

What defined the parameters of "hippieness?" What drove teenagers and young people to adopt and adapt to this subculture? Biological influences many affect behavior, but the determining variables, including environmental, are many.

Even the different schools of thought, I'm sure, would conjure a myriad of reasons why behavior could influence an individual to give up the straight and narrow to accept this alternative life style.

Just look at Freud, who placed great emphasis on irrational, unconscious influences, including sex, on behavior. The centerpiece being that all human behavior is motivated. Anthropologists like Margaret Mead stressed that culture influences personality. Social psychologists including B.F. Skinner stated behavior is a function of a payoff, depending on the amount and kind of reward and punishment it fetched.

All behaviorists need to do is study in depth, the world of the hippie. It's a no-brainer! Each camp would be able to draw on something.

Hippies came from different socioeconomic backgrounds, hence environments. Each individual exhibited different capacities to learn and assimilate, depending on intelligence and other biological components. A great number are passive, complacent and indolent.

I'm sure as scientists unravel the double helix, and examine in fine detail the chromosome, they will find in the minuteness of the gene, a common thread linking all known hippies.

This breakthrough hopefully, will occur many years after my death, therefore sparing me great embarrassment; the long awaited discovery of the gene that governs inactivity, which in essence fosters laziness. Coincidently, this gene pool will probably be found in certain ethnic groups such as a branch of the Celtic family currently residing in an area located just south of Ulster.

In plain truth, most hippies except those presently incarcerated on drug charges, are not easily motivated. If this study was expanded to include other animal species, it would prove easier to convince a sloth to temporarily relinquish its upside down position, to move one tree over to again resume the same upside down position, suspended however from a slightly different branch.

The only way to motivate a hippie was to introduce a panacea creating a panache promoting both sex and escapism. Here the participants simply found a temporary release where erotica, bliss, harmony and finally love removed all scourges of the anomie or alienation brought on by the stress of the real world.

Life for the hippies therefore, became a simple variation of the Skinner box. Due to environmental constraints, freedom was compromised. It became the hippies' perpetual quest to escape, thus avoiding any of life's adverse conditions that continued to drive the troop. When the red light went off in the brain, the hippie simply looked for release. This usually manifested itself as a positive reinforcement offered through the swill and resulting thrill of the joint.

The bond between group members, like a band of brothers and sisters, created a sense of purpose. You band and bond with your own kind. The attraction of the group hopefully, motivated individuals to develop common goals and similar viewpoints. As in any typical group, as subtle changes occur, the members change or adapt within. But based on the traditional hippies' narrow frame of reference, change is often slow and tedious.

I think it's more likely there will be a woman wearing a funny hat sitting next to all those old men wearing funny hats during high mass at the Vatican before the true blue prototypical hippie indulges in any form of serious change.

The hippie movement may be a fad, or subculture destined to follow the way of the dinosaur. It however, may well spell the way back to a simpler time, a viable alternative to our current out of step existence. Time will tell, but it may behoove Margaret Mead to look no further than her back yard, rather than New Guinea when studying group behavior. I mean this literally, since I have been told that while she has been away, squatters have set up a functioning commune inside her garden shed.

The ethos of a hippie was really a frame of mind. In it's elementary form, one had to simply look and act the part. The wardrobe was basic and inexpensive. It was comprised of jeans, tie-dyed "T" shirt, sandals and/or tennis shoes. However, I once witnessed Rob wearing one of each; a social comment, I think. Oh, don't forget the customary dab of petulia oil under each arm, but be careful, repeated use of this tincture of the odious persuasion perpetuated the formation of olive green colored blotches, which unfortunately distracted from the whole idea of the tie-dye psychedelic pattern concept.

In addition to the long hair and optional headband or floppy hat with one lone eagle feather, one needed a cause, any cause. Since most of the really good causes had already been snatched up, you needed to be vigilant. It also helped if you possessed an over active imagination and pertinacity. However, with a little help from Mother Nature, you could always invent one. Ahhhh, here's a good example. Making it mandatory for everyone to wear Carmen Maranda hats (with optional pantenes instead of bananas), to all public events with the exception of Ascot and the Henley regatta, where all forms of headgear would be banned. This no doubt would have caused quite a stir across class lines.

Most hippies would agree, that the overall learning experience leaned toward spiritual maturation. This congruous alignment of overly zealous zealots produced a frenzy of new age fads, most of which emphasized a merging of souls to stimulate and then seduce the collective vibration between man and his creator. Meditation, Yoga and even in some cases, simple chanting were signs that the quest for knowledge and truth through spiritual enlightenment were in progress.

We dabbled, but the incessant mumbling of both Mantras and monotonic chanting of one syllable words like OM, were just maddening enough to drive us to drink.

Consequently, it was not uncommon to experience a slightly out of sync, mostly out of tune, desperately in need of a barbershop, quartet struggling mightily to regain a secure foothold before beginning the torpid climb upstairs after last call.

Do, da, do, da.....
I don't care if I do go blind!
Do, da, do, da, ...
I don't care if I lose my mind.
All the do da day.

Not all education was a simple process involving dropping of the shades, the lighting of incense and the mysticism provided by the faint sitar solo emanating from Ravi Shankar's greatest hits. Believe it or not, hippies were required to graduate with honors from the institution of life, or more commonly referred to as the school of hard knocks. Here knowledge was garnered by simply sitting down and rapping with an older and hence, wiser hippie scribe. These sessions included being schooled in five major areas.

1) The role of the Rastafarians and their place in existentialism.

2) The history of communal living and its impact on western civilization. (This is not to be confused with conflict, confusion and corruption; the brief history of the Kabbutz.)

3) Altered states: The psychology of dealing with the bummer.

4) All that is wrong with the world. Perceptions, conspiracy theories versus the truth.

5) The qualitative and quantitative alchemist's handbook for the aptitude and analytical differentiation of resins or simply, getting to know your stash.

Mandatory reading included "Ganja and Me;" the unauthorized biography of Bob Marley, a years subscription to both *National Lampoon* and *High Times* magazines and closing your eyes and randomly picking any one page from either volume one or volume two of Madame Blavatsky's *Secret Doctrine* and memorizing it.

After six months internship as an exchanged student, more common than not, either Amsterdam or West Berlin, the new convert had three years to make the compulsory pilgrimage to the holy city of Katmandu.

Reaching New Heights

To be oppressed, and forced to tow the line.
To be free, and allowed to break the chain.

Inspired by:

Rainy Day Women
Bob Dylan

The hippies' epithet was also the epicenter of his existence. "Everyone let's get stoned." The irony of using the term "stoned," was that in some cultures if you're caught getting high, they will actually as a form of punishment literally stone you to death! Not a pleasant thought; but somehow that particular practice was never discussed between participants, usually due to other blatant distractions such as extreme hunger panging. This sensation was quickly eradicated by the mass consumption of what we considered culinary delights. It included such staples as Rolos, Mars bars and the all-important Kit Kat.

The art of getting high was a form of initiation, or right of passage for the newly ordained hippie. This included the understanding and acceptance of both the elevated state of consciousness and the resulting constriction of both nasal passages. Now I fully understood why God gave us a mouth. It was not just to consume mass quantities of sweets when stoned, but also to stay alive by allowing one to breath.

My first tutor was none other than my long time compatriot and cousin, Nick. He had become the consummate connoisseur of cannabis while away at boarding school. This was another thing we had in common. I was sent away to the frozen Canadian steppe, a bastion bathed in an icy bleak isolation where the spirit would often succumb to the cold-hearted. No doubt many a discerning critic drew one, and only one conclusion. Homosexuality must be the opiate that lessoned both the tedious and humdrum daily routine and provided the extra BTU's during those wintry and often-hibernal nights.

It's strange. I don't remember seeing any glory holes in the locker room or finding any used gum dams on the football field. I never barged inadvertently into a clandestine meeting of the secret society for closet queens or for that matter, remember any classmates graduating Cum (Hey! What's that stuff on your face?) Laude, after majoring in "skull buggery."

I do, however, remember clearly being introduced to the local "drug" cottage industry, which coincidently sprang up on every street corner surrounding this internment camp I called home.

I initially avoided the allure of drugs, opting instead for such invigorating past times as trying to catch up on extra sleep during a slipper fight or playing cricket during a thunderstorm.

However, it all seemed so fitting, since I have been told that getting high is also a learned behavior. The user must generally learn how to smoke pot, how to connect and recognize the effects and therefore, how to feel high or stoned. Maybe this is why beginners, including myself, express feeling nothing. It wasn't until one summer vacation that Nick became the mentor and I, his enthusiastic protégé.

Holy Smoke

Let's escape together,
to begin life anew,
like the sunrise,
birthing a fresh view.

Inspired by:

Are You Experienced
Jimi Hendrix

Everything seemed so methodical, so calculated and so very precise, as he laid out the whole pattern onto the tablemat. It was absolutely massive, comprising no less than ten cigarette paper or skins. They were two abreast and five deep with a narrow corridor of tobacco running almost the entire length.

I stared transfixed as he removed a tiny clump of hash from the tinfoil he had hidden in his wallet. I watched in amazement as he held the small rock like brown piece between his thumb and forefinger. He began to heat it with his lighter, obviously singeing the tips of his fingers as he did so.

He winced a little, dropped the lighter and proceeded to rub the tiny clump between the same thumb and forefinger, showering the Turkish blend below with a Moroccan blizzard creating a cosmopolitan delight.

"Now watch closely" as he grabbed the mat at both ends. Like a magician, he rotated the mat and before I could blink, brought it up to his lips like a harmonica, sealing it quickly from left to right with his tongue.

He paused, peered over, smiled and brought the magic wand

into full view, placing a rolled number six coupon into the open end.

"Now we're ready for business," he exclaimed with a confidence of a seasoned veteran.

He placed it firmly between his lips and lit it. As he inhaled, his lungs filled like two bellows, forcing his chest cavity to expand like a yellow-bellied sapsucker in heat.

He proceeded to look at me and with his eyes rolling back into his head, attempted to speak. The whole process reminded me of a novice ventriloquist, as his lips seemed to quiver ever so slightly.

I soon determined he couldn't speak since his cheeks were also swollen looking rather like a Japanese puffer fish in defensive mode.

Without warning, he exhaled, covering me with a blanket of smoke and a little saliva for good measure.

His words were now very slow and almost synthesized. "The whole idea…like wow!…Is to keep…now" slightly smiling… "What was I saying?"

I repeated back to him eliminating the pauses, what he had attempted to say.

"Yeah, now I remember," nodding as he slurred his words.

"Like wait a minute man. I'm just going to take one more hit, cause I want to get the full effect…okay man?"

After he passed out I was able to pry the joint out of his clenched hand. To my amazement, it was almost gone, displaying a burned out carcass, as ash, making even the spirit of Humphrey Bogart proud. I had learned an invaluable lesson. Instead of using just ten skins when instructing a student, the entire effect is better achieved by using at least twelve..

The Great Pyramid of Leisure

With a future uncertain, death always near.
Live life to the fullest, drown away the fear.

Inspired by:

Roadhouse Blues
The Doors

Its interesting that both the British and Italians share a commonality, besides both residing somewhere on the continent of Europe. Each possesses a copy of one of the most slender and slight sleeves of all time, and to compliment it, one of the most prodigious and prolific publications on record. The Italians have a very lean, yet sleekly bound copy entitled "The Complete All Inclusive History of Italian Ware Heroes." This is in stark contrast to the very voluminous collection of delectable delicacies contained within the prized culinary bible, known as the "Very Secret Book of Italian Recipes." The British, on the other hand, exercise the exact opposite. The bound copy of 'British War Heroes' from Alfred the Great through Nelson is a three-edition set proudly on display at the Imperial War Museum. However, the same cannot be said for its counterpart, the British book of "Gristle, Garnish and Stuffed Entrails." This is highlighted by nine pages of mostly photographs, complete with parsley garnished entries featuring the likes of fired bread, bread pudding and toasted bread adorned with a choice of fried egg, Spam or baked beans. The success of this publication was immediate, being the best thing to hit the shelves since sliced bread. It sold an incredible twenty-two million copies the first day alone. Most were purchased using government grants by the very peekish Bed and Breakfast Association of Great Britain minus Northern Ireland. Why? Because no one ever goes there. The rest were gobbled up by all the four and five star hotels, north of the Lands End and south of the Shetlands, except for Fort William. Why? Because no one ever goes there either. It's interesting to note that the hard copy version is still eight pages longer than the double spaced book containing the decorated Italian Combat Veterans.

The British were conniving enough over time to deftly merge the contents of both books. Having a somewhat veiled recollection of past events, no doubt from a previous incarnation, I managed to thrive for a short time—I mean extremely short time on the Western Front. I can safely attest that the general staff gave its blessing, allowing the British bland, boring and half-baked but mostly fried diet, the dubious responsibility of producing in rather large quantities, enough gas to make life miserable for a mostly ill prepared German army. Though not as deadly as mustard gas, this formative foray of flatulence nevertheless proved to be a formidable deterrent. To this day, visiting Germans instinctively shy away from the traditional English greasy spoon or truck stop.

It's a little wonder why the hippie clan, particularly the English hippie bastion, became devout vegetarians. It's truly amazing just how many ways there are to prepare, disguise and even enhance the flavor of dandelion greens. Due to this, there appeared to be one constant within the hippie mystique. I don't ever remember seeing one overweight peacenik or flowerchild. Well, except maybe Momma Cass and that cat from Canned Heat. I know the "Heat" played Woodstock, so I don't know if that really qualifies or not.

Put it this way. It's pretty hard to gain weight when you're constantly famished. Food was never plentiful, but I think the whole skinny thing was more by design than an act of famine.

Our diet was bland and based on the three L's, and I'm not

referring to three little Els from the long departed Lemurian elder race. The three L's comprised the foundation of the food pyramid; the basic foodstuff being 1) Legumes, 2) Lentils and 3) Light Brown Rice. Mmmm, Mmmm good! Even now, the thought of diving into a full plate of this mish mash makes me immediately salivate and drool. God, where's a bloody napkin when you need one?

This pyramid housing the essential building blocks of our meager existence, if sketched by a dietician, bore little semblance to the great Pyramid of Giza. Our storehouse of sustenance was really an unfinished two-tiered prototypical facsimile, structured more like a plateau than Cheops' chiseled cone-shaped conundrum. The overlaying layer, resting precariously a top the edibles, was the means by which we ultimately washed the gruel down. Kegs of beer! The seminal constituent, yeast allowed a chemical reaction to occur, which conceded mass quantities of methane and other gaseous by products to ferment internally; the result, the Biafran bloat, which if you were lucky, took away the feeling of hunger for up to four hours. So if you were to discipline your palate to stomach this polyunsaturated pastel colored plate of palatable paste, you were good to go. The downside; you had to repeat the process three times each and every day.

This nutritious combination gave new meaning to the word dysentery. I can't tell you the number of times I looked skyward upon hearing the drone from a low flying turbo prop aircraft, hoping it was a C-130 with the UNICEF logo printed on each wing.

It was not unusual for anyone who survived a meal to experience, when standing, severe panging similar to the sound of an old Model T when if first engaged. However, the process was a little more earth shaking for me. After I finished, I politely wiped the corners of my mouth with the back of my right hand, looked at the chef, smiled and spewed forth the necessary complimentary phrase.

"Boy that was good!" Then I would stand, producing a gurgling sound from my stomach, which I likened to someone dropping a bowling ball down an elevator shaft. I estimated I only had thirty seconds to reach the bog before the gut grenade exploded against the inside walls of my sigmoid colon.

"Hey guys, be back in a flash, got to brush my pearly whites."

After evacuating both a ten square mile area and my bowels, I would commence to a whistling, wash my hands and reach above the hot water heater. Ah, the brown paper bag survival kit containing a real meal. Ravished and weak, I proceeded to devour a Cornish pasty, sausage roll and a bag of salt and vinegar crisps, swigging from a can of coke at ten second intervals.

The entire process from start to finish took approximately five minutes. This was just enough time before the Bombay doors opened on the next victim, expelling from the black hole, Calcutta.

In all honesty, the sober reality of the hippie cuisine prompted us all to snack. Thank God, the local chippy and Chinese Take-away were conveniently located kitty corner and within walking distance. If the mood struck, usually in the form of quick onset 'munchies,' a normal result of post-traumatic stoned syndrome, we might, if motivated, actually stroll down to the local market. Luckily it didn't cost anything to look!

On the Home Front

Shelter my life from the rain.
Insulate me from all its pain.

Inspired by:

Gimme Shelter
The Rolling Stones

I remember hearing the reference from a passage, "Every man's home is his castle," or words to that affect. What a crock! Since man has espoused to the concept of shelter, this statement couldn't be further from the truth. It rings true for only the ruling class, the elite and the very wealthy. It's better written as, "Every man's home is his hut, tent, shack, tenement, abandoned bus, cardboard box;" well you get my drift. I'm sure statistics would bear me out that probably less than Twenty percent of the world's inhabitants can truly relate to, "Every man's home is really his home." However, the abode is still likely owned by either a mortgage company, bank or some other third party concern.

I don't think Britain ever fully recovered from the devastation caused by the German Luftwaffe. The housing shortage became critical only to be aggravated by pandering, self-indulging entrepreneurs, whose primary concern was lining their already fat pockets. This greed created council house waiting lists and extravagant rents levied against the aged, infirm, student and young couples struggling to find their way. Oh yes, and then there were the poor, unemployed and undesirables, including immigrants and well, you guessed it, hippies.

From the hippies, some chose shared digs even establishing, by definition, communes. Others traveled like Gypsies, while still others struggled living where they could, usually in down trodden urban areas awaiting the giant wrecking ball.

The Commune: The 70's From 80

To toil the soil,
    its bounty be more than just,
    stones and weeds,
    that clutter the field.
Lost in the fallow,
    That touches,
    So barren the mind.

Inspired by:

Now I'm a Farmer
The Who

The group was initially very lucky. The original digs; Clairemont was a student flop house. Out of the original contingent, Fluff was the only holdover. As the student body fulfilled their academic requirements and vacated, we moved in. So one by one the college slide rules, desk top calculators, text books, cheat sheets, rag mags, keggers and the occasional box of blues, were replaced by stereo systems, guitars, incense, stash, porno mags, keggers and the occasional micro dot.

So, on paper it remained a student residence, but on the streets it came to be known as a loose haven or refuge where people gathered to escape and have fun. If you were destitute, hungry and vagrant, our doorstop became a safe zone. We weren't a "poor house" but rather a "safe house" where many a transient youth found a dry bed and a meal. In truth, I doubt we saved any lost souls. Most, if not all who strolled in, left the same way. They still carried the weight of despair along with their rucksacks firmly on their backs.

However, most were better off for having taken the brief time to share bread and a good laugh. We, in fact, imparted little knowledge. The handshake or pat on the back and the complimentary smile as each and everyone uttered similar words, "Is there anything we can do to repay you for your hospitality?" The sincerity that steeped their eyes and the occasional embrace; these were all rewards in themselves.

Was our little world, which we loosely referred to as a home, really a commune or a variation of the communal theme? In practice we shared not only the resources, but chores as well. However, what you came in with remained yours. It could be loaned or borrowed, but never claimed or stolen.

In order to satisfactorily answer exactly where we fit in, one has to understand how and why communes came into being. Contrary to popular belief, hippies didn't invent the commune, but in a sense, reinvented or redefined the universal collective wheel. By the mid 60's rents went way up in areas of California such as North Beach. The new bohemians needed new pads or digs so they found a cheap area in San Francisco east of Golden Gate Park, which became the infamous Haight-Asbury. The rest is based on simple mathematics. It's a hell of a lot cheaper for a group of people to share expenses rather than being deferred to the lone renter or a couple.

So, the communal ideal is really a cradle-to-grave welfare system where altruistic endeavor led to the pooling of resources, establishing both common ownership or sharing and a division of responsibility or labor.

Religion, especially Christianity, Judaism and many Eastern sects, delved into aspects of communal existence hundreds of years before. Both Buddhists and the society for Krishna consciousness established franchised representation in the United States and later the UK. Here the Krishnas were able to reach out passionately for converts and donations. They could be seen line dancing like the Rockettes with both a wooden flute and tambourine. The only problem this version of *A Chorus Line* only added to the confusion and maze of dampened anxiety that already spilled forth like a broken spigot, flooding the overcrowded bus terminals, train stations and airports. Talk about religious tolerance, even the hippies had an axe to grind due to territorial infringement. I admit, I was tempted on many occasions, to grab one of their out-of-tune wind instruments, smash the glass case engraved with the words, "Break in case of fire," and remove the elongated hatchet. By spitting on my hands, it lent just enough insult to proclaim an impending and fleeting demise. I would grit my teeth in defiance of conscience, raising the weapon to then whimsically wield like a Saracen's scimitar to swish and swoop my way through their orange blossom entourage. In desperation's wake, leaving mounds of sirloin burger to be distributed as soylent green to the starving masses of Bangladesh and the Indian subcontinent.

Doing my best impression of San Peckenpach, I might as well dismantle by decapitation any and all Scientologists. I'm certain, based on reputation alone, these dapper clad heuristic harlequins would be found cowering on all fours behind what was once a passive like formation of Zulus in white face.

Secular communes, especially political spin-offs or in some cases, cast-offs, gathered in intentional and identical communities. Here they advanced their political causes, promoted social reform, homesteaded and in some cases even dabbled in the fine arts.

Sanctuaries like the villages of Woodstock, Drop City and Tolstoy's Farm were thriving centers, well before Kesey and company established their free wheeling communal societies. Haight-Ashbury and the East Village were really carbon copies. In San Francisco, the Diggers, besides assisting the destitute hippies, also passed on their communal life style. After the summer of love, it was a downhill roller coaster. These urban communities sled into rapid deterioration cultivating a rabid infestation, causing a rancid love canal-like cesspool of hardened crime and hard drugs. This forced most hippies to either head for home, or for the hills.

The typical country setting whether Colorado, Arizona, northern California or the Pacific Northwest, offered open membership to anyone willing to give corporate mainstream America the preverbal bird. This loose fancy-free lifestyle provided a support mechanism. Here bonding and sharing with your own kind promoted everything from the ritualistic passing of the joint to unabashed sexual freedom. This grassroots, back to basics field trip created a patchwork, make shift existence where turning on, tuning in and dropping out became the only things that mattered. Even the very lethargic and apathetic, the quintessential of all parasitic scroungers were able to join with nature's children to reap an existence and then abdicate stealthily, weather permitting, at winter's end.

This seasonal perverse act was beyond the normal perception of most hippies who, by hibernating, were not perspicuous enough to avoid being duped. This was due in part to their senses being dulled by the constant unrelenting exposure to intoxicating aromas that permeated most campsites. When you walk around dazed and confused, barely able to focus, it becomes bothersome and thought provoking in terms of rationalizing, just what the hell is going on around you.

The rural infatuation was more difficult in Europe, especially England where land was rare and if available, prohibitively expensive. The idea of living off the land did simulate endorphins, but once we came down and realized the potential pitfalls, this yearning soon scattered. The realization that we would have to sow our own bounty, weed and feed it (using real animal waste), cultivate and then harvest the crop, not to mention preparing and actually cooking it, gave added dimensions to the meaning of the word, WORK!

The general consensus within our group, with the exception of Rob and Cornish who loved getting their hands dirty, was that any greens we needed to accentuate a plate of brown rice and lentils could usually be found at or near the top of the Farmer's Market rubbish heap.

There is a reason why rectory and rectally are located so close to one another in the dictionary. It's the same with commune and communism. This is where we differed from the traditional commune. The perpetuation of the socialist state through a so-called equal division of responsibility and labor never worked. There was always the problem of the cream rising to the top. With leadership, comes not only the role of comrade-centurion but the special perks that after all, ordained it. The old adage, with power comes corruption, can be re-engineered to include and with corruption comes exemption. This was true even in a communal or hippie world. The all too familiar power trip can and did breed dissention and resentment. So short of the comrade general being purged or being removed by proxy in the form of a passive coup d'etat, there always seemed to be the possibility of friction at the top.

So for the most part, we stayed away from this stereotypical model and opted instead to adhere in principal to the ideals brought forth from the motto: "put off today that which can be done tomorrow!"

But since we lived for today, there was no tomorrow. Since tomorrow on our plane never came, today remained an eternal thought. Therefore, if we ignored the problem, it would eventually dissipate and disappear forever.

If by chance, the house did come unglued and divided against itself, the problem was easily reconcilable. We simply broke out the rolling papers and stash instead of the gavel and gauntlet. The idea of escalating pointless vociferous banter, leading to disagreements and discord was minimized, thus allowing us to cohabitate and coexist. This simple philosophy of non-intervention actually worked. For the most part, we instinctively knew when things needed to get done. It didn't take an ex-Nazi rocket scientist to organize and disseminate responsibility. We all chipped in.

There were, however, times when a concerted, united front was needed. This occurred when our very survival hung in the balance, usually due to an actual, rather than perceived threat. Our collective consciousness allowed us to work together with the sole intention of eliminating the problem. I can count these occurrences on one hand and only have to amputate the thumb.

1. The idea of the police cordon, blow horn, battering ram and drug sniffing Alsatians was our worse fear. So we decided to eliminate or at least minimize collateral damages by attacking it at the source. It's an obvious advantage to have an informant on the drug squad. It's even better when the individual in question relied on you to supply the rest of the squad with the best dope.
2. The idea of being awakened before 1:00 p.m. by a throng of renascence religious renegades, allowed us to mandate our position by answering the door in full battle gear. Our coordinated reception berated the intruders with a besetting array of blaspheming expletives betwixed a manly display of possible physical retribution.
3. The idea of 1984 and a Brave New World approach, introduced a plethora of cameras strewn across the city center, including all the main round-abouts. This actually amused us. It was however, the methodical meddling provided by the BBC and their countermeasures, including cumbersome eaves dropping trucks. That really blew our minds. Since we had no viable TV license, it was to our advantage to have a neighborhood watch committee that gave us a one-city block leeway. By the time the truck, complete with massive radar, appeared outside, we were innocently playing cards and listening to radio Caroline.

4. The idea that by tampering with the delicate vale that separates the normal from the incongruous and very strange could bring forth a new version of bizarro world. I am utterly convinced by using neither Hoover nor brooms, we allowed new life forms to spontaneously generate, evolve, mutate and procreate. We had in fact, sowed the demon seed.

The kitchen, besides being home to hearth and the occasional meal, became the focus of our attention for something far more nefarious. It was poorly illuminated by what seemed like a ten-watt light fixture. I'm sure this was due in part to years of negligence allowing the grease and grime to collect in stratified layers. I do believe three strategically placed candles would have better served us. This, coupled with the inconvenience of the all too familiar power outage, encouraged cockroaches, mice and even the bubonic prone rat to live and maintain quite a comfortable lifestyle.

It had been more than fortnight since one of us, perhaps Pete, had the insight and strength to maneuver the dustbin to the curb. Low and behold, the great discovery; that if passed onto either the *Lancet* or *Nature* magazines would have rivaled Alexander Fleming's research forty years earlier.

It stretched like a mangrove tree, the length and breath of the corner. A monstrous display, spreading it swings like Count Dracula. A shared presence incorporating the best elements from classic Hollywood horror films with the contemporary imagination of Steven King; an ominous engraving of camouflaged green and brown and an eerie serenity that slimed and clung to the house.

What was it? Mold, algae, fungus or an amalgamation of all three? Maybe a totally new life form taking root after that meteor shower from the month before; all I can say, we prodded it, studied it, discussed it, but for the most part, simply ignored it. Since we were unable to locate any surplus military biohazard suits, there was only one logical answer. The next time poor wayward sods needed temporary digs, we would indeed agree to comply with the usual customary request before leaving; "Is there anything we can do to repay you for you hospitality?" Our response, easy, a well rehearsed reply playing to their guilt…"No, well, maybe, well on second thought, do you think you could wash the dishes and perhaps scrub and disinfect the wall just behind the dust bin?"

The Squat: London Calling

No job,
  No hope,
    No school,
      No dope.
Can't wander, or squander,
  Need a roof, just to ponder.

Inspired by:

You Never Give Me Your Money
The Beatles

From the shadow of St. George's Hill lifted by spirit and eventually action, the throwback to the original "English Digger." They were ready, true to form, doused in conviction and principal to wreck havoc on the system. The only problem, it was basically the same system they failed to change over three hundred years earlier. So from the ashes they rose, reeking of desperation, yet poised to strike against a corrupt bureaucracy. They came from across Britain and Ireland, bearing only the clothes on their backs and the occasional rucksack. Dubbed the "scoundrels of society," this infestation became the latest in search of affordable housing. The twentieth century squatter!

They say the grass if always greener on the other side of the hill. Well, in our case, it didn't matter which side of the hill, it all looked so familiarly the same; a building block mentality where urban sprawl littered the landscape. Row houses and terraced houses snaking over and around the hillsides draped everything in view, the monotony being broken by only silky strands of white smoke, lazily arching toward the gray unfriendly sky.

Nick decided to take the road beyond the hills of block, brick and mortar. He possessed a voracious appetite for adventure so it only seemed proper that the road he chose would lead to London. Over time, the same road would be trekked by others. Once there, home would be a rundown condemned four-storied terraced house, long vacated amidst a watershed that saturated a large section of Camden Town.

Shangri-La

Remember me, steadfast, ne'er to change
Forever free, my home, akin the open range.

Inspired by:

Free Bird
Lynyrd Skynyrd

The first time I laid my eyes on the soot stained structure, I realized those inhabiting would probably be better off residing in one of the many shanty towns converging on and around Rio De Janeiro. It was missing not only a livable ambiance, but many parts and accessories, most of which either helped keep the house standing, but also which prevented the elements from entering. A sight for sore eyes since mine refused to stop watering once I entered through the front door, which incidentally balanced precariously on one hinge. As I rubbed my eyes profusely, I noticed the staircase suddenly ceased to exist at the beginning of what I assumed was the third floor; interesting I thought, the fourth floor must be a large "safe room," just in case the house is raided.

In any case, the whole mess was like taking a trip back in time, each step being the equivalent of a century or so. I was convinced by the time I made my way to Nick's hovel I would be back in the Stone Age. Ah, there it was; a large number three stenciled in fresh black paint.

I knocked; there was no response. I knocked again, encountering the same silence. I put my hands in my pocket, tapped my right foot and started to whistle. That's funny. I know he was expecting me. This time I kicked the bottom of the door, which gave way slightly upon impact. Still there was nothing. Like a thief, I looked right and then left, catching only the wall, which was badly in need of plaster and paint. As I reached for the doorknob, the door opened. So I nonchalantly walked in. I rubbed my eyes, this time because I couldn't believe what I had just walked in on.

It was like a builder's model proudly on display for all to see at a "Better Homes and Garden" expo. The bed was neatly made and strategically placed. It provided a view of the patio doors, which were adorned with linen like curtains. The hardwood floors had been recently stripped and freshly stained. A small oriental rug hugged the bed frame. The walls were alive and smiled back, revealing a peach texture that seemed to welcome the onlooker. There was a desk with a lamp and shelves containing a turntable, sound system, TV and a hot plate. Next to the easy chair was a small frig. It was perfect! The complete bachelor pad; a four star suite, thriving in the middle of urban squalor, more known for its perverse pernicious pauperism than images of grandeur and revitalized optimism.

The sun's penetrating presence made the room hot especially for a March day. I walked over to the patio doors, drew the curtains and opened one, just enough to feel the rippling effect of a cool breeze. The view was enough to prompt me to open the door wider and walk out. I was immediately captivated by a neatly laid and contoured stone patio. At each corner a large red clay flowerpot, trimmed with fresh geraniums stood aloof, yet ardent, accenting the perimeter. It was where Nick's world ended and everyone else's grating, degrading helter-skelter existence began. Between the end of the patio and the wall stood one lonely and for the most part, dead Larch. About half way up, leaning as though begging for help, one large branch hung over the patio. There was evidence of new life and at a fork, the beginning of a nest. I broke a smile, brushed my hair from the corner of my mouth and watched as a white dove, carrying a bit of broken twig, glided down, landing between the two branches.

"Hey kid!!" I turned and Nick stood poised, carrying only a newspaper.

I extended my smile, walked over and hugged him.

"Been waiting long?" he questioned.

"Nah, just a few minutes."

"So what do you think of my pad?" he proudly strutted.

"Not bad,....Not bad at all." I answered, nodding my head. "Typical you, let me rephrase that, only you."

He laughed, "Come on, I want to show you something." I followed him inside,. He pointed to the chair, chiming, "Please sit."

He backed up, and bounced onto the bed, which gave forth a squeak as though startled by his action.

He smiled, seemingly probing for my third eye. "Are you still interested in going with me?"

I bit my lip, hesitated and then replied, "I don't know? I haven't made up my mind."

He quickly opened the paper as though he had the page marked. He tapped his finger repeatedly against the page. "Baltic Schooner, needs work, must sell 19,000 pounds or best."

I took a deep breath, exhaled and fired back. "Listen man, that's a whole lot of bread. Where are we going to get that kind of backing?"

"Oh my longhaired freak of little faith, leave that one to me. Hey, tell you what. Martin owes me a fiver. Why don't we head to the pub and talk about this over a pint?"

I reluctantly nodded and said, "Why not."

Nick jumped up; the bed moaning again as he bolted past me, playfully jabbing his fist against my cheek.

"Back in a flash with the cash," he giggled, disappearing around the corner.

I knew I had to tell him I was a land lover, not a seafarer. I mean for the longest I thought the poop deck was where everyone went to take a dump. The head was where, on those long voyages, lonely sailors could release pent up semen, on other seamen. Ah, but at least I knew what a galley was. Funny, the last time I was on a cruise ship I spent the best part of three days looking for it. No matter where I looked, I couldn't find a room large enough to house one hundred slaves, chained to benches and grasping oars in the feign attempt to match time with a burley fellow pounding out the tempo on a kettle drum.

As I stood up, I looked down at the newspaper lying upside down. Instead of reaching for it I turned my head in order to decipher the headline caption. And there it was! Finally!! "US and North Vietnam to sign peace accord."

High Ho, It's Off to Work We Go!

If life's a dream, then why wake?
Only to struggle, the nightmares take,
all my strength, just to start the day.

Inspired by:

A Day in the Life
The Beatles

The 60's, the decade that brought us the Beatles, also wrought an over oppressed existence, featuring the tax man and the levies imposed against all—especially the working, with no boundaries; it held back nothing and managed to collect just about everything. You were taxed at work, going to and from work, when you weren't working and everything in between including that long deserved and anticipated pint after work. The 70's still taxed even the imagination, but also brought forth manna, long lost below the irascible forces of the North Sea. Who would have thought that from the moonscape bottom, in itself a watery desert, far below the sand, a hidden bounty lay? The assets of which, was a windfall producing both prosperity and new capital for the affluent few. This treasure-trove lay claim to a brighter future, housing the black gold, Texas T or more appropriately the North Sea "C"—for it was from these depths that pumped new life blood into an economy teetering on the brink.

I guess in a nut… shell oil, British Petroleum, Mobil and other capitalized on the fervor. What a boon, what timing and oh what luck! So, oils well that ends well! Since even oil and all that comes from it, eventually trickles down, reaching finally as a few droplets, the bottom of scarcely a bucket. Here, if used properly, it lubed even the rustiest of hinges, opening the doors to a better life for all including the bottom of the food chain or in this case, barrel.

It allowed even the hippies to kick back, relax a little, vegetate, well, medicate, get stoned, think…hold on, let me rephrase that, replacing think with dream and dabble. Dabbling to a hippie was a form of exercise or a practice involving a series of mental workouts. Here the intellect was exposed to a collection of cognitive calisthenics, each of which strained minimally, the desire to either focus or perform manually dexterous improvised tasks, such as anything to do with hand eye coordination with the exception of course, involving the loading and lighting of the bong.

In retrospect, since rarely anything of substance ever emerged from this often misunderstood art form, the observer could in effect, group both dreaming and dabbling together. In layman terms, it was just a variation of daydreaming taken to a whole new level. There were exceptions of course, such as the wishful entrepreneur engrossed, stoic to the world, in the tinkering or I should say, more often than not, resembling the tinker in the repair of the by-products of his or her craft. This took shape by way of primitive metal works consisting of molds, nails and chains, casting by definition ornaments which often evoked images of sacred Celtic symbols or the ever present Egyptian Ankh, bearing forth and embodying everlasting life. I'm sure upon reflection, representing the afterlife more so than a trivialized existence involving the repeated reproduction of this ancient symbol.

Of course, the Bohemian spirit derived its sustenance from the artistic flare of the few that congealed its imagery onto the weave that became an overnight-commercialized sensation. The Tie-dye T Shirt, besides the peace symbol, became the circular pattern, no two being quite the same, which as a psychedelic paradigm of elaborate color, patented as a collection of thought waves, mimicked the spirit of the hippie aggregation.

The center of this world became the stall or a street vender. It first appeared in the village of Woodstock, New York, spreading like a peacock's plumes to Greenwich Village, San Francisco and even as far as London's Portobello Road.

Living in the rather back woods equivalent, we felt no strong desire to emulate our cousins in London. Hey, life was rather grand. As long as we could march or even crawl to the local dole office, we did. The problem was once we grabbed or should I say, politely received, with all the familiar hints of gratitude, our allowance, we had to then walk, or I should say, crawl home again. This was the typical rag-tag melee that followed since by retracing our steps, we had to pass at least twenty pubs!

However, the allure of leaving the sanctuary of home and hearth, by way of a few well-deserved days off as holidaymakers, changed the equation. To do this, we would actually pool our resources, draw straws and force the losers to submit to the grueling ordeal of hard labor. Thank God for North Sea crude and the building boom!

Nonetheless, there were two problems. The building site was right smack in the middle of two pubs, long associated with the availability for the devious of hand, to lay their hands on, contraband and the local female gentry, including women of the night who by the way, had the nerve to work during the day. The combination of illicit substances that could be smoked and or eaten in lieu of the traditional ploughman's lunch in concert with a tart, spelled disaster. This lollygagging display of over indulgence, unwrapped before the transfixed foreman, who was somewhere between now and then, face down on the bar. Happy hour had become a loose clumping together of time, more aptly referred to as "Happy Daze!" This continued daily until the local council realized that the building site was a bit undermanned, resulting in the immediate demand for our sacking. Needless to say, we retreated, but before we returned to fight another day, had the foresight of mind to take that long needed vacation.

City of Plymouth

12th April. 1976

Dear Hippies:

BUILDING MAINTENANCE WORK (Site: Between the King's hands and the Queens Neck)

As the result of a call from Charles Cross Police Station, a member of my staff was requested to immediately visit said site due to the danger caused by your building operations.

At 11 a.m. on the 11th April, 1976, my representative, Mr. Loveknob, in attendance with the Assistant Traffic Warden Supervisor discussed the hazardous situation with your Sub-contractor. Your works were in progress without application of any basic safety standards. WORK WAS IMMEDIATELY SUSPENDED.

My observations on your works are as follows:

1. The footway was completely obstructed thereby forcing pedestrians into the roadway.

2. No temporary footpath was set out to accommodate Item 1.

3. You were using 2 no. parking bays without authority.

4. The defective plaster was removed from the wall and the debris was dropped/stored on the footway. The correct procedure in these circumstances would have been for your operatives to bag the debris as work proceeded and manhandle the bags from the scaffold.

5. The method used in Item 4, caused considerable inconvenience to adjacent shop owners. Due to your inconsiderate action, shop fronts and footways were covered in dust particles thereby placing the adjacent restaurant owners at risk in contravening the Health Act as it affects the preparation of food.

6. Against you scaffold permit/permission, Special Condition No. 3 instructed that debris netting be fitted to the scaffold structure. It was noted that plastic sheets were used instead. During high winds this form of covering can cause the structure to become unstable. I have therefore instructed the scaffold erector to replace these sheets with the correct type of safety netting. This work will be carried out by 5:00 p.m., on 12th April 1976. From the above it is quite clear you did not control your Subcontractor or give him guidance as to his method of working and or any safety precautions he should employ whilst carrying out your instructions.

Seeing your work would disrupt the adjacent business activities, it would have been politic for you to have contacted the owner of these properties and informed them of your work program.

The following instructions were given to your Subcontractors:

Work to be suspended until the following instructions are complied with.

a. Vehicles to be removed from the adjacent parking bays.

b. Payment for 3 No. Parking bays to be arranged at the D.C.C, offices at Treverbyn House, Plympton.

c. All debris is to be loaded away from under the scaffold.

d. On completion of (c) footway areas to be swept and washed down.

e. Free standing barriers and cones to be set up to form a temporary footway.

f. Scaffold and barriers to be lamped at night.

g. During the progress of further work, full consideration to be given to the safe passage of ALL highway users.

I hereby instruct you to closely supervise/monitor this site and comply with the safety rules/ instructions as laid down within various sections of the Highway Acts, and adhere to the guidelines within the Safety at Work Act.

Failure to do so will give me no option but to involve the Health and Safety Executive in respect of your operations.

Yours faithfully,

B.J. Smegma
On Behalf of the City Engineer

The Ranch
Clairemont
Plymouth, Devon
PL6 5B4

c.c. The Chief Constable, Devon Cornwall Constabulary.
For the attention of the Traffic Warden Supervisor
Charles Cross, PLYMOUTH.

A Royal Flush

A time for change, some will say.
To eat cake, will only make,
those fat,—fatter

Inspired by:

Sympathy for the Devil
The Rolling Stones

For hippies in general the royal family was viewed as "high society" hippies. Lets face it, except for their propensity to adhere to a superficial unabashed outdated birthright, our everyday routines were very much in sync; neither side did much of anything.

Ostensibly, the financial gap that existed between them and us was empirically equivalent when equated to distance, to a swallow migrating from Greenwich to the center of the Milky Way. Let's face it, the royals were worth millions and millions of pounds, most of which were ill got from a drought resistant tax reservoir. This concept was foreign to most hippies, since most hippies professed a perverse indignation toward any government quest to keep the Royals coffer full. It had come to my attention that we, the tattered trailblazers of scant and destitution, retained no tangible wealth. Collectively speaking our net worth was slightly less than the gross national product of Chad.

Be it as it were, the Royals were able to sashay through an existence steeped in both pomp and circumstance while the hippies scrounged an existence rich in survivability and sense of purpose. However, each vocation still managed to share a commonality on two additional fronts.

First, both were by definition on permanent vacation. Secondly, both loved to take a holiday whenever possible.

The aristocracy jet-setted to the south of France, the Bahamas or frolicked on the white beaches of the Caribbean. On the flip side, the hippies would hitch hike to the Isle of Wight and any free festival, or simply sanitized their senses during the summer solstice at Stonehenge.

However, to us this calling spelled a country retreat. A simple thatched cottage hugging a rolling hill, exploding onto a dew drenched Cornish down.

Laying Down Some Jiak

From its cocoon, its hanger I see,
the flight from bramble, and ready to flee.
I hope it doesn't stop, just to sting me.

Inspired by:
Woodstock

(Joni Mitchell)
Crosby, Stills, Nash and Young

The view was breathtaking. The picture window allowed me to scan to the far side of the Tamar. The prodigious river appeared majestically between the trees, crowding the bottom of the garden. The blue green water lapped from the cove, teasing the beach, which hung like a hammock between the branches. Just beyond, catching the late morning sun was Davenport. This was the Royal Navy's thumbprint, creating a hue of gray; a montage of radar and the occasional super structure toyed with my senses. I could just make out two frigates, a cruiser, what appeared to be an assault vessel, complete with two sea king helicopters, and the dark shape of a nuclear powered attack submarine,. This lethal representation was contrasted with a rapid flickering of many flags of color, which danced poetically between the motionless ships.

It was her majesty's Navy Days and the fleet stood resolute and replete, echoing an age where she once ruled the seas.

I felt somewhat awestruck, however I was trapped in my own presentation, depicting a scene from a theatre of the absurd production entitled "Hippies on Holiday," except I wasn't waiting for Godot. I was just waiting for something to happen and I didn't have to wait long.

Boom, a short pause, and then boom again, *what the hell!* I lounged forward, catching a glimpse of what appeared to be a Buccaneer as it streaked across the sky. Just then Rob carrying Denver's shot gun, darted past as though in hot pursuit.

I got up, ran to the window and in gopher like fashion, wedged my head out through the little opening. There he was watching enthusiastically as the plane dipped and then banked, angling into a turn that would take it back toward the rolling hills. I didn't even say a word, grabbing my shoes, which I struggled to put on as I galloped to the back door. I tripped as I passed through the opening. Rob, appearing a little startled, turned, still reloading, as the smell of gunpowder flooded my nostrils.

"You scared me!" he said.

"What do you mean, I scared you? What the hell are you doing?" I fired back with a quick volley.

"What does it look like? Since there are no clay pigeons, I decided to do some, uh, bird hunting," he retorted calmly.

He reached down, extending his hand. I smiled back as he helped me to my feet. As I brushed myself off, he pointed to the hill, which rose just to the left of the trees.

"That's where the next one will appear," he said with almost child like anticipation.

Just then, amidst a crescendo of sound, a large 'V' shaped aircraft appeared.

"My God! It's a Vulcan bomber," he exclaimed as he placed the fire arm firmly between his right cheek and right shoulder, seemly oblivious to any possible recoil.

I said, "You're not going to fire at it are you?"

He replied with a serious whip, "Just watch me. I'm going to put one right in the center of the target on its right wing."

"What target are you talking about," I replied with a curious undertone.

"That," he pointed as the bird of prey grew closer.

It was the red circle within a larger blue one, the British Insignia that dominated the triangular segment that made up the impressive wingspan.

I remembered from the movie *Thunderball* that the Vulcan was capable of carrying two hydrogen bombs. I prayed at that moment the ground crew wasn't stoned when they prepped the huge aircraft and inadvertently forgot to remove the strategic nuclear weapons.

If Rob inflicted a direct hit and ruptured the main fuel tank, it could set in motion a series of explosions culminating with the detonation of one or both bombs. At least Cornish would get his wish, as indeed Cornwall would be a separate landmass, surviving as a small island adrift in the Gulf Stream. Alas, his second wish would come to fruition, allowing him to retire to a tropical island as Cornwall finally came to rest somewhere off the Canaries.

I suddenly resumed contact with the real world as the huge bird rose to hover briefly above the wall at the bottom of the garden.

Rob turned and inexplicably handed the gun to me.

"Here, you have a go."

I shrugged my shoulders, thought for a mini second and rubbed my hands together as I gleefully reached for the weapon.

I'm truly amazed, the House of Windsor due to the sedating effects of their sedentary lifestyle, found time to cavort with the crème de la crème of society. Thank God for the luxury of the chauffeur driven limousine, to transport them between Wimbledon, Ascot and their weekly ribbon cutting ceremonies.

Give me fifty pence and I'll purchase a pair of scissors from Marks and Sparks. Pay me enough and I'll even fly to Scotland. Here I can take part in a soiree in Stirling celebrating, the new sanitarium from the society for civility through snobbishness for the areas suffering syphilitic sheep shearers'.

Upon examination, you would think British aristocracy would present with prominent prodigious backsides, to accompany their already swollen heads. Evidently the exercise garnered from both fox hunting and polo has paid dividends. Just think, if they consolidated these two humdrum activities, these blue bloods just might find enough time to mingle with the common folk.

Talking about blue blooded, legend purports that the term came into the everyday vernacular after one of the princes being held in the tower threatened to hold his breath, if he wasn't promptly released. Well, the rest is history.

Due to a very limited and for the most part, well drained gene pool, hemophilia and various forms of madness have plagued Europe's gentry for generations. By unique design, they also possess a rather peculiar affinity to resemble either their pets or each other. I'm not trying to imply sexual deviant behavior or a primitive form of cloning, but I once heard that the Duke of a little known Duchy from the far flung reaches of the Outer Hebrides looked remarkably like his pet Walrus, Waldo.

On the other hand, I remember this photograph of Queen Victoria's grandsons; the cousins, Kaiser Wilhelm, King George and Czar Nicolas looking rather regal, and flaunting their military regalia, they appeared staunchly stoic and identical down to their neatly trimmed beards. The only way one could discern their identities was through close scrutiny of their tunics. The Kaiser bore for all to see, the Iron cross. George proudly displayed the Victoria Cross. Poor old Nicolas looked extremely cross, since he had nowhere nearly as many fake and ill got badges, insignias and medals as the other two.

If the allies had only used this likeness to their advantage, they could have used deception to shorten the 1st World War. By kidnapping and doping the Kaiser, substituting George in his place and then removing the Czar and replacing him with the Kaiser, the whole face of Europe would have been changed forever.

Just think, the Kaiser would have been executed instead of Nicolas, George would have sued for peace in the Kaiser's stead and Nicolas could have waved majestically to the cheering throng safely from the security of his balcony at Buckingham Palace.

George as the Kaiser would have abdicated incognito to the jungles of Paraguay, never to be heard of again. After a short stay, and covertly returning to England, George would have replaced Nicolas who would have returned to Russia. The peasants, witnessing a miracle rivaling the resurrection of Christ, would have risen up, revolted and deposed both Trotsky and Lenin, thus returning the throne to Nicolas.

Hitler may never have come to power. Stalin in all likelihood would have become a poor Georgian goat farmer and Communism would have remained a footnote in Karl Marx's manifesto collecting dust in the basement of many of the world's libraries.

Just think, world peace, no cold war and no Vietnam War.......

Wait a minute! If this were to take place, then there would be no need for hippies. If there are no hippies, then why am I wasting my time writing this book? Oh my God! I've created my own version of a time paradox.

If the next page is blank, I've done a terrible injustice to all those reading this book. Hold on, I'm just going to take a little peek... It's blank. I can't believe what I've done! Wait minute, its blank because I haven't written anything yet.

I think under the circumstances I should write as quickly as possible to fill the space that still exists, hoping at the same time to maintain a sense of semblance without loosing my train of thought. Well, too late for the latter. Let's just say the royals and the hippies for the most part, shared one indisputable quality. What to do with all that free time? Ah, the concept, as absurd as it rings true, promotes the idea of taking a vacation while on permanent hiatus, or going on a holiday while enjoying a relaxing lifestyle conducive to living an already vacation like existence. The birth of yet another probable paradox!

Communication Breakdown

Hey there groovy dudes, our lingo is our scene.
If you're cool your in.
If you're square beware, cuz if you can't score,
    Hey man, you're a bore!

Inspired by:

Wink Dinkerson
Cheech and Chong

Earlier Bohemian movements such as the era of roar, though unique, predicated the hippie lingo, where the lost generation of writers screamed a concern for an age lost in decadence. Words like "baby," "cool," "crazy" and "man" were probably exchanged in conversations in back rooms of dimly lit and smoked filled bars and speakeasy's. Patrons like Hemingway and Fitzgerald may have even convened over boilermakers and bourbon.

Early beats frequented Black Jazz night spots, starting in Harlem and later on the road, where in those same dimly lit and smoke filled parlors Kerouac and Ferlinghetti exchanged ideas, developed a style which included such switched on words as "bread," "cat," "chic," "clyde" and "dig it."

The vocabulary remained relatively status quo until about the time President Kennedy was shot and the Beatles made the scene. (Oops! There's another one of those typical Bohemian words).

Surfing was now the craze and with the introduction of basement LSD being the innovative sideshow of the Grateful

Dead's soundman, Owsley "the Bear," things quickly got out of hand and into many a mouth. The over-abundance of the drug forced the numerous to stand back and watch, including the black fringe elements. Most of the excess, at least the remnants that weren't ingested by the Dead and their pals, found its way to many a clambake or beach party bingo session involving the surfer crowd. I guess the most appropriate surfing phases and / or words would be "wipe out," "far out" and "crash." I'm sure while tripping, many of these surfing aficionados ended up "braving the wave," "kissing the sky" and, as they "crashed" head first into the break wall, realized if still living, it wasn't as "far out," but a hell of a lot closer than it first appeared.

With the now widespread availability of acid came the Merry Pranksters and both the Hell's Angels and the Electric Kool-aid acid tests. The trademark Kool aid pitcher, with the classic smile, became a hideous henchman with reptilian appendages and claws, wrecking havoc, as the dose of the hallucinogenic remained unchecked. But from the wasteland, a fragile alliance existed between the new court jesters and the biker brigades. Each had something they didn't have before. The early hippies now had muscle and the provider of this potential deterrent gained a foothold, giving them a whole new source of earning power.

This marriage between the strangest of the strange in terms of bedfellows was about as meaningful as the handshake between Molotov and Ribbentrop in 1939, sealing the fate of not only Europe, but ultimately Germany as well. Just over four years to the day would be its undoing, culminating with the stabbing at the Altamont free festival. Upon reflection, the movie *Easy Rider* depicted this tenuous alliance, showing the hippie persona riding aloof atop chopped Harley's. They carried their illegal bounty concealed in the gas tank of Peter Fonda's Captain America; the ultimate riding machine. The jaunt across country characterized the symbolic gesture of just how easy it was to saturate the American mindset with this new wonder drug.

With the merging of sub cultures came the inevitable exchange and consequence centered around languages. Words like "bro" and "bummer" were now part of the hippie linguistic manifesto. I'm sure on more than one occasion; a biker apologized to a surviving hippie for cutting the throat of his unsuspecting mate.

Biker: "Geez bro, I know it's a bummer, but he shouldn't have called me a prude."
Hippie: "Hey man, he said, hi dude."
Biker: "Ops!"

Tom Wolfe's *Electric Kool-aid acid test* painted a vivid representation of just how the psychedelic rage of the 60's gave much to the hippie coterie. New words, described a phase shift into a new age, which captured the rapture of mysticism through philosophy shaking hands with theology.

The San Francisco Diggers were the first true hippie activists. While the flower children wallowed in art, the Diggers' social agenda included the creation of a free city where everything was free for the taking. They coined many slogans that slowly oozed into the counterculture and eventually into the mainstream. Phrases like, "Do your own thing" and "Today is the first day of the rest of your life," became commonplace. This was a trigger of sorts, giving impetus to our credo.

"Put off today, that which can be done tomorrow" and "let tomorrow be the first day of the rest of your life," and since tomorrow never comes… well, you can remember the rest. Here's the list of 'my dirty dozen', or the words that filled me ole bucket with synthetic syntactical shite.

1. **Acid** LSD, Lucy, mikes, Mr. Natural, specks, sunrise, blotter, blue cheer, microdot, California sunshine, dots, Electric Kool-aid, haze, fields, domes, purple haze, pane, pearly gates, strawberry fields, window

pane. There are more, but this is all I had a chance to try.

2. **Axe** Guitars, any tool used to do art. Weapon (part of the Blade's arsenal.)
3. **Bad Scene, (trip)** Bummer, Atmosphere due to bad vibes. See #9.
4. **Bag** A quantity of drugs, usually pot; a done deal; work (job—heaven forbid, or when applied to us, a bird or a chic, picked up at the Pub as an after thought.)
5. **Bread** Money (ya need a job to earn it) or (the government gives it to you so you don't have to work). We chose the latter.
6. **Cool it** Relax, calm down. (A word that often was spoken by anyone engaged in conversation with me).
7. **Fag or Faggot** Male homosexual, cigarette, sausage.
8. **Getting Off** Feeling a drug starting to work; satisfying a craving.
9. **Split** To leave; to crack a skull (the word was commonly used by the Blade or Big John when describing a typical evening on the town.)
10. **Head** Hippies, freak, blow job; wasted; John/WC or prefix added to denote what type of head—e.g. pot head. It becomes more evident when used in a sentence. "While in the head, I got head, from a head, who was out of her head."
11. **Heavy** Depressing, a tense or stressful situation. Any every day endeavor that required the moving of an object weighing more than a tightly packed bong. If applied to me, escaping from a pub, after a brawl, sandwiched between two bodacious tarts, acting as human shields,

rather than paid escorts.(in this case, heavy refers to the size of the chics instead of the actual scene.)

12. **Crash** To sleep, which was done by synchronizing the biorhythms with the movement of the sun. e.g. sunrise to bed, sunset to rise. However, when dealing with a three-day acid trip, hopefully coming down from the experience before totaling the car.

It's amazing how language can change subtly by traveling regionally, or in some cases by literally walking across the street. Dialectal differentiations and variations in diction can affect how one is perceived or more importantly, when communicating how one is heard and understood. Britain, especially England, is made up of a disturbing variation of seemingly non-pragmatic hyperbole, intonation, jargon, gibberish and syntactic slang. This forms the basis for the plentitudes of dialects that spill into each other causing many to shake their heads in disbelief when asking for simple directions.

For an English hippie born and raised in Cornwall of a Cockney mother and Geordie father, the copious over-use of the language, especially when high on speed could and did cause the listener to appear as though the barber had been the previous pit-stop before encountering the "I wish he would pause and take a breath," orator.

After finishing the act of removing all vestiges of hair, the listener could then opt to either pull out the talker's locks, or shorten the entire process by simply cutting out his or her tongue. At least with a straight forward, stereotypical superlative hippie of upper class stock, it was easy to substitute or even supplant the over use of descriptive nouns, such as man, pad and stash, and still effectively understand the statement, question or request. Now try and do the same thing when listening to a hippie from Newcastle, Glasgow or London's east end. The best response; say nothing. Instead use body language to show interest and approval by smiling and nodding a lot. This should be done in conjunction with the age-old practice involving the introduction of the token. Hey, it worked for the explorers and missionaries when dealing with the new world savages. There's no reason to think by suddenly producing a pack of cigarettes and offering one to the speaker, that the lull caused by either the acceptance or rejection of the token, just might allow you to gain the moment, to effectuate change. Switching topics, excusing yourself, or innocently redirecting the conversation to the total stranger next to you best accomplishes this. It's a bummer when you discover by opting for the third choice that the bloke is fluent in only Lithuanian and Dutch.

Our situation, besides the potential for any gabfest to become a geographical semantic gaffe, introduced the linguistic double-entendre. Certain words or phrases, usually American slang, being misinterpreted by an English listener, or for that matter, the other way around, where myself as the listener would take the English word or phrase and put it in the context of the American equivalent. Words like "pissed" and "bloody" can and did initially cause some difficulty. The English might say, "Hey, let's go to the bloody pub and get pissed." After thinking about it, I guess I would be pissed off if I walked into a pub after a serial killer with an AK-47 had just strafed the bar. Or if I said, "I'm pissed that the pub is closed due to a bloody mess," an Englishman might conclude that I was already drunk and had been kicked out of the pub for causing or taking part in a fight. Now, if either one of us said, "I have to take a bloody piss," then one might conclude that we were suffering from either an acute kidney infection or a really bad case of the clap. Clap, now there's another one of those words. I remember when I found out I didn't have VD, everyone especially the chics, clapped.

But my favorite word was fag or faggot. The English insisted on either smoking them or eating them, depending on what they had just smoked. To me it meant queer or gay. My worst nightmare was being approached by a total stranger, asking me if I had a light for his fag. I mean, the idea of holding a flashlight over two homos engaged in buggery before I had a chance to fully appreciate the faggot I had just consumed was, to tell you the truth, a bit hard to swallow.

So you see, the list could go on at infinitum. But with Cornish around, you never knew what was going to be said or when it was said, exactly what he was attempting to say. Steve was a combination of slang, innuendo, and Chaucer nicely packaged as a new form of the King's English with just enough emphasis provided by inflection and a touch of pig Latin for good measure. He was our brand of Digger, not because he loved to raid with shovel in tow, the occasional spud patch, but because he introduced many a phrase that hung around us like the mildew in our kitchen. "Ya boy, how r ye." Or "Ur me hearties." But the one that did it for me, because I was usually the culprit, even though Steve was the one who actually did the deed, "Ya know what ya done, didn't ya." The point being, it's very easy to pass the buck, especially when everyone else has no flipping ay dear what the fuck yer talkin' 'bout.

A Cunning Linguist

I'm talking, and no one cares.
I'm talking, so frigid their stare.
I'm talking, full piercing their glare.
They're talking, a freak to their fair.

Inspired by:

My Generation
The Who

The noon sun was deceivingly hot even though my watch indicated the time was closer to one o'clock than midday. I looked down at the protracted pink prize; the jumbo elephantine monstrosity that leisurely dangled as it undulated slightly, dipping just past my knee. The giant Cyclops seemed to chastise the ground as its slithered toward it. I held the flaccid flute with both hands, darting from behind the protection of the large Oak as unsuspecting motorists innocently inspected the Cornish countryside. Even though this titanic tubular trunk produced no sound, it managed to create a melee of responses including the high pitched screams of shocked women who either shielded their eyes as though exposed to a Medusa or instinctively turned with mouths aghast, catching me waving as they pried themselves up, using the seat, thus allowing the moment to linger just a little longer.

I felt a tap on my right shoulder catching Rob looking impishly over my left.

"Wow! I'm drooling at the sight of it. It's so big, so succulent and I'm sure, as God is my witness, it tastes as good as it looks.

Ummm! I just want to put the whole damn thing in my mouth and let it tease my pallet."

"Yes, I desperately want you to devour this soon to be hot, throbbing elongated mesh of raw meat. Now, sweetie, now! As I overemphasized the "S" for a more pronounced effect."

Our hands met halfway as we exchanged the phallus prop, the phantom penis, and the phantasm that was—hopefully at some point still going to be our supper.

The one piece, Polish Kielbasa danced the Polka as Rob waggled it back and forth; it remained however, unsoiled and therefore still edible.

"Dude, tell me when the next car's coming,. He was almost panting in anticipation."

As he fumbled about, back toward me, but still shrouded by the tree, a large, black estate wagon turned from behind the thicket, meandering with the road.

"Here it comes." And as it rambled past, Rob, like a daring highwayman, jumped from behind the tree.

"Christ, it's a car full of bloody nuns!" My reaction distorted by a feedback of laughter.

Rob, hysterically swaggered from side to side, stopped momentarily, dropped the evidence and arched forward, placing both his hands on his knees.

Jimbo, who was at least thirty yards ahead, had turned to witness the prank, but now watched as the car braked, then veered as it crossed the double white line. The sound of angry rubber cried in defiance against the persistent braking, as the car sneered, producing a hue of gray smoke in its wake. The vehicle continuing to weave disappeared around the bend.

Still reeling with uncontrollable laughter, I fully expected to hear the anticlimax being a catastrophic impact, producing one lone tire, rolling back into view as it navigated the same curve before coming to rest like a gyrating coin on its side. Jim sprinted back, offering his rendition of what had just happened, savoring the moment and inducing further laughter.

I recovered not only the sausage, but also my composure as the other two remained in stitches, still dousing themselves with tears from the sidesplitting high jinks of perversion.

I blew any remnants of organic matter off the outside casing, which brought a smile to my face. Up close it looked like a mammoth severed member minus its Rocky Mountain oysters, still contained within a large jacket-like condom. The jocular mania continued next to me, uninterrupted as I rejoined the giggling which continued unchecked for the next few minutes.

From the direction of the mishap, a car suddenly appeared. I looked for a moment, squinted, bringing my hands up to act as a visor, "Guys, I don't want to bring you down, but we've got company!"

The two tone Panda car pulled up immediately announcing its intention by initiating the rapid flickering of the red cherry adorning its roof.

He appeared young, not much older than the three of us, a gunslinger without a gun, where his peacemaker was going to have to be his wit and hopefully, not his truncheon. He was indeed relaxed as he slowly extricated from the car. He closed the door gently, putting on his cap as he reached into his pockets losing the keys, but finding a small pad containing a pen. His gait was cool, his demeanor cooler as he laggardly strolled toward us avoiding any eye contact by seemingly gazing toward the tree line, which rose like a Roman legend just behind us. I swallowed, feeling more like a vanquished foe than Julius Caesar.

"Afternoon gentlemen," his voice deepened, obviously forced to gain the advantage.

"Hello officer," Rob interjected before either Jimbo or I could find the words. "What seems to be the problem?" he continued.

The officers bit down on his lower lip, turned his head toward the corner where now I hoped four nuns were not attracting vultures from across the length and breadth of Britain. He seemed to be rehearsing what proved to be a short dissertation.

"Well lads," he barked, and then paused. "I was headed toward a previous call when I came across a group of hysterical nuns. The driver was slumped over the steering wheel. The other front seat passenger was grabbing at her rosary and speaking in tongues."

Rob raised his hand to cover what was becoming an obvious Clock Work Orange smile. Jimbo looked across at me as though telepathically prodding me for intervention. I attempted to communicate using my eyes. Jim broke the silence.

"Excuse me sir, but what's this got to do with us?"

"If I can finish, it will become painfully clear!" His tone changing as though frustrated by Jim's ill-fatal attempt to divest us from what was rapidly becoming a criminal matter.

Jim sighed but refrained from further fanning the potential for escalation. The officer momentarily lost, picked up where he had left off, "Where was I, oh yes, the two remaining victims. Both in the back, the one behind the driver had obviously been sick and the other though catatonic, was smiling into thin air. Other than that, all seemed pretty normal," stressing the last sentence with a pronounced quip.

"I did however, manage to decipher something about Satan and fornication."

He paused and then quickly scanned us for any evidence of twitching or other body language that might just incriminate us.

"Okay, who's the bloody pervert?"

"I don't know what you're talking about," glancing over at the other two.

Rob began to kick at an empty cigarette pack. Jim started to blow air and then began to whistle.

"Listen gentlemen, I can arrest you for indecent exposure, lewd and lascivious behavior, public urination and the like. Now, stop fucking about and tell me who the bleeding perpetrator is!"

I looked through him, realizing that he was indeed dead serious and no doubt, would take great pleasure in running us in on trumped-up charges so to gain brownie points with his superiors. All of a sudden, our salacious activities could become fodder for the evening press, implicating three hippies for sexually assaulting four harmless penguins all on the anniversary of the Manson murders.

I quickly managed a forced laugh. "Oh, now I think I know what you're referring to! You see officer, my friend here," pointing at a surprised Rob, "was well…." I bent over and picked up the white disheveled piece of wrapping containing the wax paper and as the sun touched it, the most strapping specimen of glistening sausage I have ever seen. "You see, the package, this package, exhibit A," sounding more like a solicitor than a long haired freak, "came unwrapped and while he, I mean Robert, was simply attempting to rewrap it."

I proceeded to place the evidence at groin level. "As you can see by its proximity to my, well, manhood, it could easily, very easily, be mistaken, especially if it came loose, and well, momentarily presented to an unsuspecting group of onlookers, as a semi-erect, well, well endowed pecker."

I took a breath, fully expecting my audience to shake their heads, clap in unison and shout bravo, bravo, forcing me to bow!

But Rob, looking for an entrance, found one. "Yes, sir, that's exactly what happened and I'm truly sorry if I frightened those poor sisters of mercy! I truly feel their pain; I'll just walk over and…"

"Not so fast. ID's please." Both Rob and Jimbo obviously had been in this predicament before, presenting their ID's before I had a chance to remove my old international student identity card from my wallet. By the time I located it, the officer had made the necessary inspection and proceeded to scrutinize mine. As I was placing the wallet back into my inside pocket, a small piece of foil dropped. It hit the ground with the devastation of an errant asteroid smacking the earth. The impact could not be ignored.

"Well, well, what do we have here then?" he drooled like a

bulldog being left alone in the back of a meat wagon. He proceeded to pluck it from the ground with a one handed motion that swooped it into full view. My world suddenly closed in on me where I was now not the insignificant speck in the vastness of all that is, but the center of everything that was about to happen.

Shit! I thought. Hurry think, do something, point behind him and say look, there's Lady Godiva riding a stallion, and scurry, but he might arrest me for resisting arrest and promoting the virtues of bestiality.

Christ, I'm busted. I'll be found guilty of helping keep the Moroccan balance of trade in the black and deported to the Australian outback.

By the time he unwrapped the three layers of foil, for I was a firm believer of keeping my stash as fresh as possible, there was a small piece of hash that rivaled the head of a pin.

"Busted!" he proclaimed an edict that saturated the landscape echoing across the street through the wheat field and beyond, stopping just short of the village square, located by way of the forced march slightly less than two clicks due east of our current position.

"You've got to be kidding, right?"

"Sorry lad, you're done."

Just then a pushbike, struggling to hold its cargo, parlayed the curb negotiating a position, allowing the passenger to disembark.

It was Cornish, like the lone ranger, here hopefully to save the day.

Rob looked at Jim, who proceeded to look at me. None of us uttered a word.

As the officer turned, Steve already primed, started, "I thought it was you! Kevin, right? You're Jeremy's older brother." He attempted to speak, but Steve wouldn't surrender. "How's the little wanker doin'? You know we were mates, real good mates, when at school. Remember me then? I used to live at the top of the 'ill, not too far from Rupert Turnipseed's farm. It's been a while, aye, a long time," he paused and started to laugh, drowning out the flabbergasted copper's feeble and passive attempt to recapture the high ground.

"I don't suppose you recall that party? You know the gala they threw ya, just before ya left for the academy in Bristol? What a blast! And you got pretty toasted, didn't ya. I heard they found ya wandering the fields in only yer knickers. Remember now?" The cop just stared, an unmitigated frenzy of paralyzed containment, totally numb to the situation that continued to unfold. "Remember me now? I'm the bloke you scored from. By the way, you still owe me a tenner. But I bet ya it was worth it and everything that quarter ounce of Lebanese."

The tarnished officer, blemished red, head bowed, nervously placed the minute sample of contraband into his trouser pocket. He fought the words, but managed to string together, a broken sentence, "do you," he paused and coughed, nervously continuing, "do you know these three," speaking more from the position signaling submission, than one mounting a new offensive.

Steve shook his head and said, "These blokes, yeah, they're harmless."

"Listen you three, I don't want to catch you loitering around here again. Take this as a warning, you're only warning. You're free to go."

Steve walked with the policeman, not sharing in his embarrassment, but more consoling. They talked briefly before bidding farewell. Steve stumbled as he turned, briefly losing his balance, just leaning into the now repenting officer. He apologized, turned, and walked toward us, winking as he smiled.

"Here, I believe this is yours." Handing me back the small round piece of foil. "Never put it in ya wallet; always in your knickers or your bloody boot, but never in yer wallet, okay boy. I'll see you varmints back at the hide-out then, cheers."

As he turned, Jim's flare for the dramatic pounced on the moment, "Bro what were you guys talking about!"

Steve looked over his shoulder, stopped, grinned and twirled his tongue, "Ah, he asked if I knew of anyone discharging a firearm during the flyover. So I told him!" He pointed quickly to the shop and rejoined the conversation. "I thought the shots came from the farm behind the post-office; never liked that prat anyway."

We all chuckled as we initiated, as though programmed, the thumbs up in celebration of our victory

Cornish mounted his bike, pushed off, synchronizing the whistling of "Won't get fooled again," with the squeak that emanated from the rear mud guard.

Beyond the Fringe—Europe

NEPTUNE'S NIMROD

They say the grass is greener, but the hill is steep.
And to slip, the fall, a hell of-a-lot, meaner!

Inspired by:

Sea and Sand
The Who

We both watched nonchalantly as it bid us farewell while suspended momentarily like an osprey, before kamikazing into the cascading waves of the North Sea.

"I'd hate to be that bugger." Nick laughed as he pointed to the tent which by now was acting more like a ladle, bobbing briefly, before plunging as though in hot pursuit of black pearls.

"You know dude," he paused and giggled again, "It's supposed to rain more often than not during the next fortnight."

As he leaned over the railing and looked toward the stern, I realized his rucksack was untied and doing about as much flapping as his gums.

I reached over, grabbed the canvas tie down and peered inside. I rolled my eyes in total disbelief and while wiping away the salt-water remnants from my cheek, had this overwhelming urge to push him over the side.

"Nick, you twat! You know that tent you waved to as it disappeared?"

"Yeah, bloody shame, really," he sarcastically whimpered.

"Well, you idiot, it was our tent!"

His jaw dropped, just missing the railing as he turned and ran back to be swallowed, like Jonah, into the safety that was the ship.

Oh, the French would tempt us with casks of beer and fine wine.
But, the Germans did threaten us if we dare cross the Rhine.

Inspired by:

Postcard
The Who

The continent was only a hovercraft or Ferry away, yet seemingly a world away; historically, a clash of cultures, ideals, and ultimately nationalistic fervor that led to imperialistic intention, and many a conflict.

Still today, an uneasy feeling permeates the strata that provide the unstable foundation where East meets West, separated by only Churchill's iron curtain.

But now, Britain was part of the European neighborhood, much to the disdain of the French. Ah, the French. You see, I have this bad taste that lingers every time I think of France. Partially because the French have been traditionally a British foe, or should I more aptly say, foil.

I think, over the ages the French developed an inferiority complex first with the English and later with the British. I believe it started five and a half centuries earlier at the battle of Agincort. Here the English, though outnumbered on the battlefield four to one, still managed with the long bow, to exercise with surgical precision, the removal of the Fleur-de-lis from Frenchee's sorry red derriere.

The French were constantly spanked through the ages, reaching the ultimate waxing at Waterloo. After Wellington tanned their hides, John Bull for good measure, left his indelible boot print tattooed for all to see, on their turned tailed heines.

But for me it was more personal. After eyeing and then drooling at the menu from the roadside café just outside Calais, I insisted on ordering the house specialty. From the first bite of le bifteck extraordinaire, I sensed some thing was wrong. Not only did it require a chain saw to cut, but it tasted remarkably like the bottom of my shoe. Not to say I customarily lick the bottom of my own footwear, but I do shamefully admit that on more than one occasion, I have licked someone else's boot. How do you think I managed to afford to take this vacation?

The coup de grâce became painfully clear, as I walked to the cul-de-sac behind this culinary boutique, looking for a bouday to extinguish the three alarm blaze lapping at my anal sphincter. Here I witnessed first hand what I thought were rhinestone shrouded leather belts. However, upon closer scrutiny, my self imposed cataracts, the ephemeral barrier that allowed me to see what I only wanted to see, vaporized, revealing to my horror, a bovine buffet. It was a Mardi-Gras extravaganza, featuring an insectoid smorgasbord where a rather large horde of overly enthusiastic French bleu bottle flies smothered the sisters and brothers that remained from the choice the chef had made for me. Since it was located right next door to the latrine, I could only imagine where this voracious mob had congregated earlier in the day for breakfast.

Yum!!! I spent the next three days doing my best impression of Toulouse-Lautrec, as Doctor Colon's monster hunched over, retching, heaving, making oodles of cookie batter and fertilizing much of the French country side between Calais and Paris. But it was the illuminating presence provided by the nightstick and flashlight that gave new meaning to the *City of Lights*. It was while lying in a pool of my own vomit I tried to ascertain whether the spasms in my gut were worse than the pain I now felt in my lower back. The local gendarme had a way of knowing just where to jab to inflict the most discomfort. It was here I found a slight respite from the constant spasmodic twitching that tightened its hold on my abdominal cavity, which was by now truly empty. I likened the ordeal to the throes of childbirth, where a nine and a half month pregnant French milkmaid was being punished for witchcraft by having her legs bound tightly together by wet rawhide.

Thank God for the consideration of the gay Parisians for planting such large shade trees along the Champs-Elysées, though originally I must say to keep the hot burning sun off the goose-stepping German army, who had a habit of marching along these same streets about as often as my peristaltic eruptions attacked the lining of my gut. During this trip to hell, for I had been there on occasion before, I actually contemplated staying this time by perpetrating a capital crime. But the gendarme had now given up, presumably thinking I was dead.

Maybe if I did succumb, the French government out of fear, taking into account the American's propensity to sue, would instead bury me next to Napoleon's tomb. The only problem, myself being slightly less than six feet tall, would if, entombed, dwarfed by comparison, the emperors eternal resting place. Can you imagine just how small his burial chamber would have been if they hadn't insisted on burying him with that bloody hat! History might have been better served if they had put him in a matchbox and buried him under a smaller version of the Arc-de Triomphe.

Here's a bloke who not only possessed an inferiority complex against the British, but one against anyone that stood over four feet tall. Based on his vertical handicap, I'm convinced he devised the metric system. I'm sure if one were to examine closely all the supposed love letters from Josephine, a metric conversion involving centimeters rather than inches would be apropos when dealing with his 'Grand Pierre.'

Weight loss for a hippie is a very serious problem since most hippies have no extra poundage, ops! I mean kilos to flaunt. So after buying a real belt, not some beef jerky imitation to hold up my jeans, we set off for Amsterdam.

A true hippie paradise! This is where the world wide congregation of Hippiedom had their yearly convention. Conventional wisdom would have me say it was really a year long convention, spawning no beginning and as a result, proclaiming no end. Everyone converged, moving from Vondel Park each and every morning, like a large school of tuna, to spend the entire day in unison, forming a circle around Dam Square. Here the group manifested a semblance to sculpture, reminding the onlooker of two thousand impressionists or mimes acting out in concert, two thousand slightly different poses of Rodan's 'The Thinker.' I would look in amazement at all the different 'freaks' contemplating in an almost ritualistic stupor. I wonder what each one is thinking! This self-imposed mind game played out over the course of the day, pounded my brain with two thousand different scenarios, each unique to the individual. At just before 6:00 p.m. I would pause, stand-up and walk nonchalantly to the other side of the street. I would proceed to light a cigarette and watch with a fiendish glee as the remaining one-thousand, nine hundred and ninety-nine poor souls were hosed down by an overly zealous battalion of Amsterdam's finest.

Dam Square

(Reopening the Doors of Perception!)

Swedish, blonde hippie chic—"The Saab on my Volvo really hurts, especially when I walk."

Russian Hippie—"The greatest heroes of the fatherland are Marx and Lennon. You know something, Groucho was right, I wouldn't want to join any party that would have me as a member either."

Irish Hippie (*Looking down*)—"I wonder what's up with that bloody snail? Doesn't he have anything better to do than follow me around all day!"

American Hippie—"Christ, I'm so sick of youth hostel food. I wish I could look across the street and see a pair of golden arches in front of the main entrance into the Heineken brewery."

Canadian Hippie (*Pointing at the American*)—"I'm thinking what he's thinking."

German Hippie (*Wiping the sweat from his brow with a bandana*)—"Achtung, it's so very hot, and there's no shade trees. Why couldn't the Dutch be as hospitable as the French and plant them. Ah, maybe the next time we invade."

Polish Hippie (*Rubbing his head*)—"Thank god there's no shade trees. You know, my head still hurts from falling out of that tree in Paris while raking leaves."

Italian Hippie—"Mama Mia! All these beautiful women, and they're all sitting down. Now I have no choice but to goose myself. But what if I like it?"

Spanish Hippie (*Head leaning forward*)—Zzzzzzzzzzzzzz

English Hippie (*Looking perplexed as he scratches his head.*)—"When does a square become a circle? Oh sod it, damn that bloody square."

French Hippie (*Scratching his balls*)—"This is ridiculous! I wish they would only hose us down on Saturday night!"

And oh yes, a...

Dutch Hippie (*Looking at a half smoked camel*)—"Who was Peter Stuyvacent anyway?"

The German youth, particularly the hippie, seemed far removed from both the horrors of yesteryear and the blunt cold war realities. Their motto borrowed from the archives of Alfred E. Newman, hinted, 'What me worry!' The movement seemingly screamed in silence. Nevertheless, the pain was apparent especially if you journeyed into the emotions that remained dauntless, but provocatively removed in the form of delicate tears that covered each eye, but rarely spilled.

"Listen dude, please separate me from the evils perpetuated by the likes of my father."

Both Germanys stood for different ideals, but each remained as the potential for flashpoint, if the Godfathers so deemed. As a student I remembered being totally immersed in the works of

Heller and Vonnegut, thinking, where did they draw their inspiration. After living the German experience, I began to slowly understand. The German hippies bulked at the idea of having their individuality removed and so too, their lives controlled. The total absurdity of living under a nuclear umbrella, shielding them from the horrors of total war; any war, and the front lines became their front yards and for that matter, their back yards too. Christ, differences in doctrine came to symbolize the largest Portabella mushroom imaginable, rising from the ideological mumbo jumbo that raged in the hearts and minds of men. Once allies, committed to ridding the world stage of heightened evil that had congealed in the mindset of a people. Now we had come full circle only to have the definition of evil changed to suit the suitors, as the U. S. and U. S. S. R. epitomized the classic "Mexican standoff."

Maybe the notion of total war equaling total obliteration prompted the higher ups in the military industrial complex to design, promote and implement deployment of the Neutron bomb. Certainly all life would be extinguished. However, the gothic cathedrals, Bavarian villages and the Prussian monuments would be preserved for future generations to enjoy; sort of like visiting Athens to see the Acropolis and Parthenon. The only problem, the tourists won't be our descendants, but visitors from Zeta Veticuli who unfortunately have minimal interest due in part to unbelievable saucer lag.

Ah, but behind all the doom and gloom there's always the solace that is "OKTOBREFEST." Here everyone, including CIA operatives, KGB informants, MI-6 double naught wannabees, red army faction renegades, neo nazi extremists, serial killers, rapists, wife beaters, manic depressives and ah yes, the odd war criminal could converge.Together this collection of plotters, misfits, traitors and the hunted and gathered could forget the world and its problems, mingle, sing and toast each other as they shared a good time and occasional joke with the peaceniks, green peace fanatics, anti-nude demonstrators, draft dodgers, yippies, drippies and even a few dislodged "I can handle a couple of pints, but would rather smoke a joint—hippies."

As long as the beer flowed and the bands played, all differences were forgotten and though temporarily buried in a sea of swaying flesh, showed a level of cooperation that could not be duplicated anywhere.

Maybe the UN should take notes and incorporate this theme, including the voluptuous, curvaceous, blonde braided, buxom and very naughty but ever so polite beer maids when entertaining thoughts of simply window dressing world issues and hot spots instead of rendering mandates and resolutions that actually have substance.

Munich, a grand city steeped in history, contained a storied past that occasionally knocked fervently on disaster's door.

1. It played host to Hitler's rise to power beginning in the early 1920's. In the shadows of his legionary drunken bashes with those party animals, the brown shirts and the 1923 Beer Hall Putsch, were his clandestine encounters with the soothsayer Hansussen and his resulting obsession with the occult.
2. The Munich air disaster of 1958, The Manchester United Soccer Team teetered on the verge of being eliminated from all future play.
3. The Olympic massacre of 1972 and the death blow to Israel's Olympic team. Organized sports had become little more than the gladiator spectacles of old. Maybe that's how civilized war should be fought between opposing Generals in the arena.
4. The day Nick had managed to temporally forgo ownership of his passport to a EWIB, or mysterious elderly woman dressed in black.

I remember her riding up on a moped. She appeared gender exempt. Her cunning demeanor, "Please, I see your passport now," still echoes as Nick, playing jolly old Nick, captured in the haze of St. Pauli Girl, simply handed it to her. Her android reflexes and black frock gave her a nefarious quality; something hauntingly reminiscent of a character straight out of a Fritz Lang classic.

With Nick in hot pursuit until his third step, which rendered his steeplechase useless by placing him face down in a puddle of trouble, I decided not to tempt Murphy's Law by having another beer. It was here I was joined by a group of blond, blue eyed Aryans who proceeded to point out the potential pitfalls of wearing a US Army jacket with the stars and stripes boldly displayed on the right shoulder. This is where I was schooled and learned first hand, of a potential nemesis, a regional representative of the Baader-Meinhoff gang that locals with almost cold reverence referred to as the Red Army Faction. This was another terrorist group that I mentally aligned with the likes of the Popular Front for the Liberation of Palestine and the Irish Republican Army. But, after listening to an impromptu rendition of their history, I realized that I, and perhaps many hippies, had more in common with these freedom fighters than I originally thought. These guys (there were a few chics as well) were tough. They were young, survivalistic, energetic and committed, and like us, still considered students. As University interns, many copped attitudes, which like the displeasure we harbored, entrenched their position against the old guard or establishment which refused to change to keep pace with the ever changing demands of society. However, this is where any similarity ended, for their resentment had boiled over, in effect cooking the chips that balanced unsteadily on our shoulders.

They presented a united front based on reckless abandon, munitions and bombs. They perpetrated acts of violence, kidnapping, extortion and murder, while we simply had trouble getting out of bed in the morning. If we did manage to eventually roll out, it was time to roll up and of course, any issues that might affect this early afternoon practice were soon put to rest. Instead of the debilitating technique of raising a clenched fist in defiance, it proved much easier to crawl back into the safe haven of the bedroom where a simple pillow over the face proved secure enough. This was our form of collective anarchy; a state of mind that never really made it out of the house. So you might say anarchy only enveloped our existence in the hallway that joined the sitting room to the bedroom. This is where the likelihood of a burned out light bulb presented the possibility that anything could happen, which unfortunately did, especially when the bodies started to pile up, just short of the bedroom door.

Let's face it, society isn't perfect, but to bring about complete change, I don't think so! I suggest if Misters Baader and Meinhoff want to create a utopian worker's state, they just have to convince everyone, including the hippies, of the virtues of work. In order to achieve this, they would have to travel to the USSR and conduct a worker's satisfaction poll. Once they are released from a Siberian worker's rest home, or gulag, assuming they survive the forty year sentence, they can tabulate the results of their poll, and release them to the same group of people they originally convened, who by now are mostly retired and living contented lives along the various Rivieras' of Europe.

Needless to say, I still, without hesitation or reservation, removed "Old Glory." As I placed the insignia in my pocket, Nick, the madman or should I say, the mudman, returned with passport in hand. You see, he had been detained, interrogated, stripped, searched, probed and threatened, all because he bore an uncanny resemblance to a German fugitive.

You know something; it really wasn't the quandary that shaped the lives of the young Germans, whether hippie or aspiring terrorist, that bothered me. It was really the uncertainty that shrouded the past lives of the everyday German over the age of fifty. I found myself totally engrossed in playing my own version of *What's My Line* as I scanned the sidewalk congestion of Germans marching in general chaos. It was from this enduring sight I tried to pinpoint the SS snit, Gestapo thug, or panzer protagonist.

The Fatherland and the Motherland:

A Nation of Three

He fought in wars, the glory and the sins.
He fired, his orders, a soldier, never wins.

Inspired by:

Oh, What a Lucky Man
Emerson, Lake & Palmer

It was still spitting just enough to be an aggravation. I was struggling with the last of my dry socks when I noticed the dark figure of a man carrying a black umbrella. The scene captured the spirit of a 'film noir' classic. He looked like Robert Mitchum as he strolled closer, stopping momentarily to light a cigarette. I began entertaining offers, gripping the imagination. Were we standing in an electromagnetic vortex, capable of penetrating the space-time continuum, taking us back to the Germany of Hitler's Reich?

My heart pounded faster as he grew closer. All I could think was, *Christ, I'm glad I'm not stoned!*

As I put my boot on, I stood up and like a German soldier, stomped hard, not once, but twice. I could still feel the cold and damp as I looked up. He was imposingly tall, standing well over six feet. He appeared to be in his mid fifties.

He opened his mouth and surprisingly, nothing came out. As he struggled, his eyes flickered rapidly. Before he could utter a syllable, I chirped. "Hello."

He smiled, adjusted his glasses and in broken English said, "Bad road for hitchhikers, come with me."

In one motion he turned and pointed to a block of apartment houses and said, "Follow me please."

Nick looked at me, shrugged his shoulders and replied, "I'm too fucking wet to argue, let's go."

I picked up my rucksack and gingerly started to walk behind Nick who was easily fifteen yards ahead of me.

We crossed the street and by the time we reached the opposite curb, my right sock was soaking again.

"Damn!" I thought to myself. "I'll never dry boots over an open first again."

The tall German turned sharply and proceeded through a gate and down a cobblestone path. He turned back to see if we were still behind him, smiled and again motioned us to keep following.

Instead of marching to the apartments beyond the far fence line, he suddenly stopped. He popped his umbrella, shook it and smiled again.

Nick and I stopped in unison. Neither one of us said anything as he opened his mouth. This time, without hesitation, he introduced himself.

"My name, Erik Mueller. What is your names?"

Nick turned, glanced at me and as he turned back toward our host, replied, "Hello, my name is Nick and this is Ian."

"Do you like to eat?"

Before either one of us could answer, using his hands like a steam shovel, brought them up in a alternating motion toward his open mouth.

We both nodded, almost drooling at the thought.

His garden chalet was very quaint. The window boxes overflowed with various annuals in a rainbow mosaic. The roses and dahlias were robust, but pushed down by the canopy of rain.

When I walked toward the front door, I noticed it had

stopped raining as the sun began to peak shyly from behind a wall of cotton like clouds.

As I searched for a place to sit, I heard the familiar presence of a cuckoo clock. I couldn't actually see it as it ushered in the new hour. However, I imagined an elaborately decorated timepiece, resting solely on the mantel above a fireplace. The sound of a train in the distance muffled the original sound, creating a resonating clamor, undiminished in scope, yet characteristically familiar as in a cheering throng, punctuated by a distorted barrage of animated Sieg Heils! I closed my eyes and visualized a small statuesque figurine of the Fuehrer with his right arm fully erect in place of the cuckoo bird.

My brush with National Socialism was interrupted by a strong German dialect sounding more like an order than a friendly gesture.

"Please, you sit down now," pointing to a recently wiped down white wooden chair.

As I sat down, I noticed his eyes, which seemed like large menacing saucers through his thick spectacles. They appeared sad, laden with guilt and pain. It made me think, *"I wonder what the hell he did during the war?"*

By this time, he and Nick had struck up a conversation and Nick, as only Nick could do, was actually conversing with him. I watched intently as Nick reinforced his banter with body language and hand gestures. I began to look into our host's eyes again hoping to catch a glimpse of a hell frozen in time.

Was he Wehrmacht or Waffen SS?

Was he a member of Goering's Lauftwaffe or Dornitz's Kriegsmarine?

He could have been a bombardier in a Dornier or Heinkel, aiming his blanket of destruction over London, Coventry or even Plymouth. Maybe he fought with Rommel and the Afrika Korp in the desert, surrendering to the British at El Alamein, remaining interned for the remainder of the war?

He might have been a tank commander at Kursk, fighting the

rest of the war in retreat as the Russians pushed the Panzers back toward the Fatherland.

He may have been peering through binoculars seeing through the thick haze of June 6th, the largest flotilla every assembled.

My mind kept surveying every possible scenario from a U-boat commander smiling as he gazed triumphantly through his periscope as a liberty ship burned feverishly, a beacon in the ink, a honing device to the wolf pack of the night. I saw him for a moment as a German guard at a railroad station in Holland, assisting the loading of innocent men, women and children into the Auschwitz bound cattle cars.

As I drifted further and further away, a voice suddenly interrupted my train of thought.

"Would you care for beer with bratwurst and sauerkraut?"

"Uhmmm," I hesitated, "sure, please, that would be nice," I replied.

I began to devour the meal as soon as he placed it in front of me. Even though my voracious appetite superceded the moment, it was brief at best. I was soon entrapped in the man again, dueling with his soul.

Yet, he was kind, considerate and epitomized a sensitivity that made me think of myself.

Maybe vicariously though Nick and I he was experiencing a chapter in his life, one he was unable to fulfill. If he had been forced to join the "Nazi Youth," the chance to travel and see Europe as a tourist, instead of a goose stepping conquistador, was lost forever.

As I reached for my beer stein, Nick leaned over my left shoulder and whispered into my ear that as soon as I was finished, our host would escort us to the proper road that would take us to Denmark. I nodded as I brushed away the froth that had collected over my moustache.

Within twenty minutes, I was again dragging behind the two of them. A stark contrast in every way! One tall, one small, one old, one young, one so mysterious, only my infatuation with the past held his character in question. My friend, my comrade, he appeared so innocent, yet so naïve, but alive nevertheless with the inquisitive passion of a forgiving human being.

As he bade us farewell, I smiled and reached for his hand, which grasped and held mine without trepidation. His eyes met mine and I felt an intense reckoning, knowing he knew but didn't care.

He turned and walked away. There was a certain harmony in his gait, a merging of the physical with the spiritual. He was happy and at peace.

I turned to Nick and asked without reservation, "What do you think he did in the war?"

Nick looked away; by this time the man had disappeared. He glanced back and put his arm around me, patting my shoulder gently. "Funny thing, he didn't serve."

"What!" I exclaimed.

"Yeah, he had a medical deferment, flat feet, I think."

"Well, what did he do then," I responded quickly.

"He ran a cabaret in Berlin, and when the bombing got too bad, moved to Bavaria, and helped his older brother run the family farm."

I closed my eyes, shook my head and started to laugh.

Chapter Three

Of Mice, Men and Supermen

The best laid schemes o' mice and men
Gang aft agley (often go wrong)
And leave us naught but grief and pain
For promised joy!

Robert Burns

The House That Yawned

The mines are all closed,
    the country bends, but won't break.
The candles burn,
    the wicks flicker, as the Whigs bicker.

Inspired by:

The Dirty Jobs
The Who

During the 60's the British political arena was crushed by a series of scandals that in Vaudevillian like fashion, almost brought the house down. For over three hundred years this pish-posh parliamentary system had caused many a member to suffer involuntary spasmodic dilations of the oral cavity. I'm certain that Guy Fox's ill-fated attempt to pulverize parliament was indeed, simply a display taken to an extreme, with the sole purpose of rousing all from a deep sleep.

As a result, politics rarely if ever, became a topic for discussion at the dinner table, at least from my standpoint. I was usually too preoccupied, hoping no one would find my secret stash of pastry delights hidden over the water tank in the Looe.

The idea of exchanging political jabs or debating the issues was something reserved for late night theatrics, akin to the image of an insomniac counting sheep to induce sleep. I personally would rather watch uninterrupted, a five-day cricket match between eleven catatonic-crippled cricketers from Croydon, playing host to an all star team of eleven blind paraplegic Alzheimer's patients from High Wycombe. To say the least, more would get accomplished by these twenty-two pathetic brethren than the entire house of yawns—sorry, I mean the House of Commons on amphetamines.

Look at current events, whether it was images of Black September and the BOAC VC—10 vaporizing in the Jordanian desert, the kidnapping of the OPEC ministers in Vienna, or car bombs rocking Londonderry as a postscript to Sunday Bloody Sunday. The early to mid 70's set the world's stage for the threat of organized terrorism. Such groups as the PFLP, the IRA and the RAF were all well schooled, graduated malice Cum Laude from such international feared institutions as the UDDD, or the University of detonation and demolition at Damascus.

Detante and the SALT treaties only meant the world could be destroyed more than one hundred times over, using the logic supplied by MAD, or mutually assured destruction. Yes, an appropriate acronym, since those responsible for drafting this doctrine were at the same time, feverously building nuclear blast resistant bunkers.

We tended to ignore the fact the world could end with the blink of an eye, or by President Nixon simply mistaking the launch button for his new VCR remote control.

It was issues closer to home and hearth that undoubtedly affected us more, such as suddenly finding ourselves without either electric light or the ability to stay warm. This did however, help us psychologically since wearing an additional five sweaters perpetrated the illusion that we were actually putting on weight while continuing to eat brown rice.

But a country that was being held by the short and curlies while the government and the miner's union bickered over wages and benefits almost brought an entire nation to its knees. I'm not taking sides, but this pathology created by this indecisive ineptitude fostered pathos for the suffering masses rather than two stubborn participants.

It reminded me of two prepubescent boys fighting to establish turf and territory. No holes barred, ready to go the distance spurning any possible ramification, based on premature action without sufficient in-depth analysis.

The atmosphere reflected what we felt, a cold front. The hours of frigid debate only created inexorable permafrost. I remember feeling not only numbingly cold, but a genuine ire toward both parties. It was a toss up who deserved the tag, "Mr. Freeze." Both Mr. Heath and the head of the coal miner's union, Joe Gormley, displayed a flagrant thick-skinned insensitive attitude worthy of the label. They seemed to be cut from the same cold piece of hardened granite. Stone-hearted with ice water coursing through their veins.

The hippies, if given the green light, would have taken these two pretentious political pundits and in only their skivvies, perched them on a precipice protruding from a parapet at Bamburgh Castle. This panoramic breathtaking view of the North Sea would have supplied just enough of nature's wrath, as a cool hyperborean burst of Artic bliss, to take their breath away. I can guarantee you before a cryogenic transformation occurred, these two paltry pansies would have agreed on something.

Brown Outs and Carry Outs

Light dimmer to shine, orchestrates my sight.
Darkness simmers the whine, architects my plight.

Inspired by:

Spiral Architect
Black Sabbath

As I paused at the Zebra Crossing, Clive motioned me with a cigarette pack. I thought for a moment, looked at him and shook my head no.

Clive reached for the button and as he did, I noticed across the street an open window. It was the dry cleaners located conveniently next to Marks and Spencers.

I felt this huge one thousand watt light bulb, burning like a laser, a hole through my new darkening aura. Ah, the possibilities I thought.

The parcel containing two now, odoriferous mackerel, felt like two miniaturized petrified Egyptian deities. The idea of dinner curing over a hot fireplace at the Pub for over two hours, made my decision that much easier.

As I walked across the alternating black and white stripes, I took aim. The adrenalin carried with it the possible ramifications of this indecent act. I could hope that the accuracy of my throw would place the decaying filets into the pocket belonging to the frock, that I hope belonged to the Lord High Mayor of Plymouth.

This symbolic gesture would, with a little luck, lend credence to the inability of anyone in the British parliamentary system to find a quick and fair solution to the ongoing fight with Iceland over territorial fishing rights.

I could just see the Mayor standing pompously posed, ready to slice his audience with poignant flair. It would only seem proper for him, to then reach into his left pocket for the speech, to pull out for all to see, the remnants of the previous day's catch. What symbolism! And, oh what justice!

As I tripped against the opposing curb, Clive turned to witness an off balance throw that bounced off the upper window, slide down the glass and disappeared between two clothes racks.

"Hey, what the hell! That's our dinner!" he yelled with just enough distain to make me think my face just might be introduced to his fist.

"Calm down," I replied with the coolness I would typically associate with a con man. "The fish was cooked, if you know what I mean." I now took complete control ready to officially diffuse the situation once and for all.

"Listen, you know that Chinese take-away just off North Road, I'll treat you, okay?"

"Well," he paused, took a deep breath, exhaled and said, "I hope they're open."

"You worry too much," I said with a consoling demeanor.

As we walked, quickening our pace to coincide with the rumbling that had now begun to churn inside, I broke the silence. "Hey dude, you know something? Don't you find it a little peculiar that the Cantonese take-away is always open, even during the brown-outs?"

He turned his head and, without breaking stride or slowing down, replied, "To tell you the truth, I never really thought about it."

"I have a theory. Do you want to hear it?"

"Do I have a bleedin' choice?"

His voice was still a little agitated so I thought I'd placate him further.

"Don't you find it a little strange that after the city cut down all those dead elm trees that the Chinese take-away was able to remain open?"

"Christ, I have a feeling this is going to be a goodun'." His voice offering a freer spirited tone.

"Yeah, I bet they were able to get all that wood for next to nothing, build a large fire pit, construct a pyre, and top it off with the world's largest wok."

"You know something dude? You're outrageous, even when you're straight." He smiled back and as he slowed his pace, put his arm around me, initiating a march by synchronizing his step with mine.

I continued where I had left off. "Yeah, the fucking wok is probably the size of one of those Seti radio telescopes turned on its side. You know, like the one dish in ahhhh, where is it, ahhhh, Puerto Rico?"

It was like the parting of the Red Sea and without hesitation, Clive ambushed the segue, jumping the opportunity to blurt in.

"Arecibo, it's Arecibo, Puerto Rico, that's where Seti operates that radar radio telescope."

It was just enough to drift from the topic without actually losing sight of land.

I thought for a moment, "Arecibo," paused and continued, "Ah, yes, Arecibo, that celestial eavesdropper."

"Yeah," he responded, and I knew without reservation I had allowed the floodgates to open.

As he removed his arm, he slowed to almost a snail's pace, forcing me to do the same and without missing a beat, began the lecture.

"I recently read an article in *Popular Science*. I was amazed. It's the largest of it's kind in the world, truly remarkable. Christ, it measures over one thousand feet in diameter and was constructed in a sinkhole. It's so sensitive it can actually detect a signal from a point, a thousand light years away."

At that point, I felt almost a thousand light years away.

"Dude!" I screamed without hesitation or fear of consequence.

"What! What!" he boomed back.

"God it just dawned on me!"

"What!" his voice still reeling,

"There's no cats in the neighborhood." My ploy was working. He hadn't picked up where he had left off.

For a moment I had derailed his train of thought. But before there was a head-on collision, involving his energetic, dynamic locomotive of pure intelligence, ramming and then steam rolling my poor pathetic diesel of drivel, I continued. This time my voice deepened as I became cynically sinister in my delivery. "Yeah, even little Splif, the stray has disappeared. Coincidence?"

"Listen if you're trying to put me off so you don't have to pay, it's simply not going to work!"

He sounded a bit aggravated, but at least my simple act to run interference had worked. I just wasn't in the mood to play Sherman to his Peabody.

By now the sky was a combination of yellow and brown with just a hint of gray. The halogen street lamps at half power flickered, giving off a strange hum. The overall scene was eerily familiar, hauntingly captivating like a cheap Monet copy, holding London hostage during a Nineteenth Century smog.

As we crossed the street the red neon sign pierced the night. I knew then, sweet and sour or not, I better have the necessary dosh. As I reached into my wallet, I hoped I hadn't spent my last quid at the pub!

British politics was a political yo-yo. If it wasn't the Tories under Heath, it was Labour flying Wilson's flag. Edward Heath symbolized the Pinocchio complex. I'm sure I witnessed his already prominent proboscis growing during each and every address to the nation. On the other hand, Harold Wilson reminded me of Lt. Columbo right down to that dingy raincoat he wore. It's not hard to see his finger pointing, accusing the wrong suspect or I should say, blaming the opposition for his own party's ineptitude.

In the middle of all of this, I became a devout follower of the American Libertarian party. This is not to be confused with the all to familiar taunting most hippies were accustomed to. That being labeled a "bleeding heart liberal."

David Nolan's Libertarian credo emphasized a free market economy, civil liberties and a foreign policy with a cornerstone emphasizing non-intervention. I especially liked the whole idea behind non-intervention. It allowed me on more than one occasion, after consuming more than one beer to ignore more than one socialist.

A Matter of Fact; A Question of Faith.

Look across and see,
  a world, where boundaries cease,
  and war is no more.
Look across and see,
  a world, where religion bequeaths,
  —everlasting peace.

Inspired by:

Imagine
John Lennon

"Here is a door behind which,
  according to some people, the
    secret of the universe is waiting for you."

C.S. Lewis

For all of us, the philosophy concerning life and its meaning can be chiseled from two separate pieces of granite. The use of granite is preferable to let's say, pillars of salt, which tend to dwindle in both size and shape, when exposed to the elements, especially British "acid" rain. Though diametrically opposed, we tend to gravitate and queue according to our religious or spiritual beliefs. If you align with atheists, communists and some egocentric eggheads I know, the line forms to the left, where the universe is viewed as a random event, and life on this planet a matter of chance. Conversely if by chance you file to the right, the belief system evokes an intelligence beyond scope, giving the universe order and life meaning.

Hippies as a whole broke rank, and often tripping over one another, most, ended up bruised, confused, tattered and abused, lending to the mayhem, by joining the already swelling lines to the right.

Sigmund Freud insisted on padding the painful overuse of the phrase, "Why is there so much suffering in the world?" He developed the psychological arguments that the whole concept of religion is really an illusion, projected out of the childish wish for continued parental protection from the vicissitudes and sufferings of human existence.

This in itself was enough for many hippies to denounce "atheism," which acted as the foundry, whose flatulence produced the brimstone airing traditional religion as chimerical chatter or malicious malarkey.

With the exception of Freud's Libido argument, the notion of hippies promoting any form of parental control, would entice, I'm sure, the very tempting proposition of inducing Helter Skelter in the form of mass patricide. I can envision a rather irate Darwin cringing at the sight of well intended male hippies indulging their mothers in matrimony, only to produce offspring akin to a Dr. Moreau experiment, gone awry. However in my opinion a genius alternative to restocking the already depleted gene pool of Appalachia.

This in itself, kindled the spark, inflaming the passion to pursue religion from the confines of consciousness within the boundaries of spiritual enlightenment.

In time, hippies became hip when dealing with religion. Let's face it, we viewed Jesus as a far out dude who was both switched on and in tune. He was in a sense, the first true hippie. He certainly looked the part; the long wavy hair, the beard, the sandals, that strong sculptured Celtic, Nordic look. His doctrine of peace and love could have put him at the head of any class, standing resilient at least for the moment, at the front of any protest march. But the crucifixion, that sort of changed everything. If that is the logical result, then the crux of the matter indicated that most hippies, especially those with a propensity to challenge authority, better watch out.

As a man, Jesus embodied the spirit of tolerance, love and the ideal of selflessness. In the truest sense of the word, he was indeed a superstar. If he was terrestrial, he was the incarnation or maybe the reincarnation of some super-human specimen that coalesced a mutated mesh of tissue, skin and bone with a superior intellect; a superman, without the cape, if you will.

If he was extraterrestrial, he harbored within a tempered existence ripe with the genetic alterations to both mind and body.

If he was divine, then surely metaphysically speaking, he represented the power of an omnipotent celestial creator, or God.

If Leary could transform the Buddhist *Book of the Dead,* then surely the supposed children of God or more aptly the pariah might have done the same with the *Bible*. Come on, a burning bush, not consumed by fire, the chariot of fire moving across the sky and the parting of the Red Sea by simply waving a staff. Could these acts, long associated with the hand of God, be manifestations caused by an overly stimulated imagination? Hey, if a hippie can stroll across the Moors and pluck mushrooms that if ingested can take the consumer to the equivalent of middle earth, then isn't it possible that Mr. Moses added a little elixir to the vino he swigged to wash down the Matza?

Hippies down played the relevance of traditional religion, because it offered very little in terms of redemption. Just look at what was currently playing to packed houses on the world stage. Political intervention has brought forth a motif, based on the motive that "Onward Christian Soldiers," had spread the words of God by any means possible, including the testimony through testament, flaunting the over-use of the sword.

So when the Crusade became the battle cry, and the words "My invisible omnipotent, long haired, white bearded, robe wearing God is better than your invisible omnipotent, turbaned, white bearded, robe wearing God," it brought Christians, Moslems and Jews to pilgrimages involving wholesale slaughter. Its unfortunate that all who died were considered by definition to be infidels or sinners. What insanity, since our God and their God are not Siamese twins, or a deity sidelined by a multiple personality disorder, but the same Supreme Being or creator.

I hate to sound impious, heretical or even agnostic, but Biblical intonation captured the ear with a scintillating scintilla that overwhelmed the other senses. It denoted by association, the presence of myth, magic and allegory. All by which were arranged, surprisingly enough, by men in white beards and long flowing robes, to strike fear, reverence and control over lesser men.

Hippies wanted a personal connection or one on one relationship with the creator or divine spirit. Here intersection with the cosmic consciousness could be achieved without memorizing and reciting from the psalms. This was fulfilled in part, with the help of the Beatles and others who encouraged the inclusion of Eastern practices. Now the hippies had an alternative to prayer, by using meditation, yoga and even chanting to reach a higher plane.

It was so easy to look at religion, especially when stoned and down play or even systemically dismantle the rigid parameters that held it so traditionally fixed. It failed to change as society changed. It was in truth, outdated and so passé, that anyone with a calling could, and did take advantage to skew or even screw it to fit a passing fancy. The result, the birth of cults and sects, some so outrageous that even hippies became suspicious. So, maybe the Rastafarians had it right all along. It's not just that they looked cool with those dreadlocks flowing like the roots from a large Cypress, or for that matter the funnel shaped joint hanging like the horn of plenty from between the lips. But, I must admit there existed a certain appeal. It's more than religion; it's a way of life. Sound familiar? Rastafarians prided themselves on speaking out, especially against poverty, oppression and inequality and used the *Bible* for guidance, but not as a divining rod. Instead it was weed or ganja that became the spiritual and physical panacea or the essential component to their belief system.

"He causeth the grass for the cattle, and herb for the service of man."

Psalms 104:14

Christ, I sound like Billy Graham on drugs. Reality check; on second thought, its' too bad that the Rastafarians don't trust the white man. It's equally disturbing that the hippies who are predominantly white don't reach out with a more sustained and committed front to the black masses. Yes, it sounds all too familiar. Some things are destined at least for the moment, to remain stagnantly status quo.

A Matter of Faith: A Question of Belief?

God is eternally dead, cried the media.
Madness from the head, some of us said.
It can't be!
Just look at the world as it spins,
—out of control.

Inspired by:

Levon
Elton John

The road to the superman meant the destruction of both democracy and Christianity. In order to promote the latter, the German philosopher, Friedrich Nietzsche proclaimed, "God is dead." I believe all this did was piss God off! This is quite evident based on the sequence of events that unfolded since Nietzsche uttered those words almost a hundred years ago.

The Franco-Prussian War, the First World War, The Russian Revolution, the Stalin purges, the Great Depression, the rise of National Socialism, the Japanese atrocities in China, the Second World War, the death camps, Hiroshima, the cold war, Korea, the cold war, Vietnam, the cold war, the Middle East, the cold war, the killing fields and the cold war! Not exactly a stroll through Regents Park.

It's strange how history tends to repeat itself. *The New York Times, Time Magazine* and other rags of the era didn't hesitate during the turbulent 60's in eulogizing the Supreme Being. I guess, based on prophesies and recent trends, the next thirty years should be one big party leading up to the final days.

If God is simply to be mentioned in the past tense, how can some of these same liberal rabble-rousers condemn John Lennon for proclaiming the Beatles more popular than a now defunct and non-existent Jesus? If he indeed resurrected, leaving the controversial Shroud of Turin as proof, he too, ended up suffering the same fate as his father.

If God is indeed dead, then how did he die? Some believe he has no beginning and no end. Maybe the big bang is really evidence of God's demise. He may have become distraught after a series of early mishaps involving previous universes, which for whatever reason, failed to take hold and root. In one brief moment, well brief for God, he concocted a large cosmic ray gun, which infused the intensity of a billion galaxies, put it to his head... Well, I know it sounds a little but like a David Bowie song, but if he pulled the trigger it would account for the big bang and the seeding of what is now our universe.

On the other hand, maybe he was murdered; the motive being jealously and frustration. In a fit of rage, the holy trinity became the dynamic duo. I doubt a son would kill his father, but what about that Holy Ghost fellow? I've always suspected this part of the whole to be a little shady, you know, always lurking in the shadows and on the outside looking in. All this over time, lets say billions and billions of years is bound to take its toll. When you're God's henchman doing all his dirty work, Sodom and Gomorrah might have been the last straw.

Can you imagine the archangels led by Gabriel trying to find him? Not an easy task, when you can't be seen.

Hold on, it's raining. I've got to open the windows. It's not raining outside, but here in the house. I'm just going to gather...wait a minute! There's a bloody huge black cloud lurking over my head! Wow, that was close! That bolt of lightning just missed me! Ah, that's better! It's always warmer outside when a deluge is flooding your sitting room. I'll just sit down on this bench and pick up where I left off.

If we were created in the image of God, then surely he's able to put on a Groucho Marx face and enjoy a good laugh once in a while.

The idea of death scared the hell out of me! Maybe that's why hippies adhered to an existence where a change based on the life experience wasn't a curve, but a straight line. Here, by living as a hippie, you never really grew old because you, in effect, stayed at the same point and never left! Well, it gave the impression of not growling old, except maybe for the gray hair, missing teeth and foul smell. Hold on! Let's leave that one alone with the exception of gray hair. Since I knew a few freaks that met the criteria laid down by the other two and they were only in their early twenties.

Okay, so we all die! Having to atone after physical deaths for my litany of sins was worrisome. I could see myself standing in line after taking a number. With my luck, I'd get 6,432,114. But, if Drakes' equation was right, and the universe was teeming with intelligent life, then that number would increase exponentially to let's say, 643,211,412,001. Not a pleasant thought when the interviewing process ultimately involved a one on one with his divineness.

Based on this scenario, it only seemed logical to be triaged for reincarnation. It's interesting to note that the early Christian Church toyed with this feature only to decide, at the last minute, that the practice was a little far out to be included.

However, if given the choice, I was seriously going to consider taking it. I vaguely remembered my last incarnation, besides the bad diet, cramping and gas; the Western Front was a quagmire of blood and mud. As a British officer, I experienced the hell that was the Somne, resulting in my own miserable death. You see, I'm ashamed to say, I was shot in the back by either the Germans, as I turned and scampered back to my own trench, or by my own men, leading a suicide charge that nobody was really interested in partaking in.

I guess in the grand scheme of things, it really didn't matter what version occurred. All I knew was that I was definitely going to pay for it during this lifetime.

Next time I thought, I'll play it cool. I'll come back as a common garden slug. I mean, how many Hail Mary's will I have to utter in the slug dialect, waiting in the slug line for eating some poor Cornish farmer's cabbage patch?

Maybe religions incorporating the concept of reincarnation are on to something. The idea of the Hindu Vedes and the ancient mythology where sixteen invisible elephants hold up the earth really doesn't seem so far-fetched after all. If you think about this concept, it lends credence to the explanation concerning earthquakes. It's simply one or more of these elephants reacting to an invisible mouse as it suddenly darts past.

Thank the gods, Ghandi, didn't grow up in Vienna and attend University in Germany. All those poor cattle being forced into passenger train cars and taken to Cowschwitz and adding insult to injury, the coincidental opening of a McDonalds in Kashmir.

Buddhists too, have a cycle of life, death and rebirth. By combining the integrity of the Buddhist *Book of the Dead* and the monk dousing himself with gasoline and then setting himself alight, something is drastically wrong. I get the fleeting impression all would be better served if the book were revamped to include a special footnote denoting the art of fondue and fricassee.

The Chinese on the other hand, well, a very small minority, probably no more than let's say two hundred million or so, accepted the doctrine that everything, even inanimate objects possessed souls. This practice known as Animism really intrigued the hell out of me, especially during trying times, when my stress level was like a nuclear reactor during melt down.

For example, when the tele was on the brink. This unfortunately seemed to occur coincidently every time *The Old Gray Whistle Test* was about to air. The TV, as though it possessed a mind all its own, reeking vengeance no doubt for the last Tom and Jerry marathon, would predictably engage in a session promoting the virtues of white noise.

At about this time, I would grit my teeth, look toward the heavens, thrust a clinched fist in defiance and exclaim, "You bastard?" I would then swarm to the set with the fury of African killer bees and swat the side panel as hard as I could. Since this premeditated act never worked, life would have been better served if I had accepted the wisdom of this ancient Chinese philosophy. Instead, I should have simply strolled over to the set, whistling a few bars from "Greensleeves," calmly picked it up and innocently walked over to the open window. Here I could have watched with enthusiastic passion as the set plummeted two flights to the ground below.

Obviously the gang would have suffered through evenings without the luxury of the BBC but my God, the satisfaction gained by releasing a long trapped soul back to the ether world have justified the move.

As a hippie, I researched contemporary religion finding many examples drawn from ancient cultures.

Even Christianity had a link to the rich past. I found during my extensive reading on the subject, compelling evidence suggesting a connection to the Greek mythologies of old. Upon careful scrutiny, it became evident that the Spanish using the Mexican dialect pronounced Jesus as H A Y—ZOO –ES. If you took this phonetic pronunciation and related it back to the Plutonian Greek, it took on a slightly different meaning. Jesus, the Son of God or more importantly as the holy trinity represented, as God, now became the omnipotent leader of all the major and minor Greek deities; it became more apparent when used effectively in a sentence.

Example: "Hey Zeus, heard through the Olympian grapevine that you, Hercules and Pan, gangbanged Aphrodite!"

The Garden of Weedin'

The truth will be told
    from the tongues of elders, free to assist.
Deny the hidden wisdom damned the peril lost,
    souls that resist.

Inspired by:

Kashmir
Led Zeppelin

If you dissect the meaning behind religion and contemplate the intangibles, it's apparent there exists both a dichotomy of standard, as an oxymoron when evaluating ideology. There is an obvious fine line between love and hate. Due to this idiosyncrasy alone, the notion of religious persecution plays a prominent role whenever fanaticism operates as the fulcrum. By the hand of the religious zealots, more have died in the name of their God, than by any other means.

During the 70's, it was the Middle East; the garden that germinated forth Judaism, Christianity and Islam. Whether it was Protestants and Catholics, Jew and Arab, or Moslem and Hindu, the human element introduced both cultural bias and political differences, which further clouded the issues. Each worshipped the same God, but chose to continually be in conflict with one another. As a result, they were constantly undergoing change, being redefined to suit the cause or crusade of the moment.

The focus then was Israel, struggling to survive, precariously alone in a sea of sand, where each grain represented the undeniable hatred of the collective Arab consciousness.

I don't know what the hell Belfour was thinking when he introduced his declaration. There was a reason the area in dispute was referred to as Palestine! If he had just taken the time to study scripture, he would have understood that both the Jews and the later followers of Mohamed were to have, each a homeland.

Something went totally wrong. It was as though Jehovah, after setting the wheels in motion, decided to leave. I can imagine his voice echoing, but falling on deaf ears through the epochs of time.

"Listen I'm going away for awhile. If all works according to my grand plan, I'm investing in a large expanse of essentially nothing. It's just a vibration away, next to the constellation Pleiades. It's sort of a, well, a back-up universe, just in case. Oh, by the way, I'll send my only begotten son to look in on things, in, let's say…three thousand years or so.

"Remember, be good and trust in your fellow man."

The more I thought about this, the more I was convinced all listening weren't really paying attention, and thought God said, "Remember be good and thrust in your fellow man."

Don't you think this would account for all the hate and killing that had occurred through the ages?

We also ended up killing his son, because again we failed to listen. A simple mistake really, misinterpreting only begotten son, for only rotten son. He must have shaken his collective heads in disgust and thought to himself,

"Christ, what a stroke of luck creating that parallel universe!

"I just wish man understood fully his place in the cosmos. To think that I, God, would show favoritism by choosing one race over another or for that matter, holding dearer one life form over another. Each species has its place, even those hyper dimensional ionized plasmatic proton ingesters I created as an afterthought to inhabit the event horizons of black holes."

"You know, if that klutz, Moses hadn't dropped the third and most important tablet from the top of Mt. Sinai, earthlings would understand their place in my scheme of things. Oh, blimey, on second thought, who gives a fat rat's ass, hey—there's an idea. If they keep it up, I'll just let it rain rodents by the score."

Maybe God should have reconsidered sending a now fully recovered and well rested Jesus back a second time. The way the world was, I wouldn't have been surprised if a paranoid hippie on a bad trip ended up stoning him to death. If he looked at the mess, particularly the Middle East, it might have been be justifiably prudent to dispatch Abraham instead. For it's his lineage and the descendents of both his sons, Isaac and Ishmael that have forged this polarized hatred for one another. As the patriarch, Abraham should have been held accountable and given the indispensable task of defusing once and for all this powder keg of undaunted hatred.

It was easy to see why the group became both disillusioned and disenfranchised with religious affiliation. We chose instead to concentrate on the spiritualistic endeavors associated with the practice of achieving godhead. I however secretly possessed an ad hoc relationship with the God of the *Bible*. I professed to be an eclectic deist, being ever so careful not to offend anyone. However, this also allowed me to maintain a stake in the traditional belief system, just in case.

Beyond Godhead: The Synthesis of Self

Look back at your life, and see,
    all the things you hoped to do.
Look at your life, and dream
    of all the things you want to do.

Inspired by:

Breathe
Pink Floyd

Most hippies took pride in a personal association with an avant garde or controversial writer. By title, a laureate, whether given by peers or labeled by the hippies themselves, it didn't matter. Poetry or prose, the words and the meaning behind the words, held different in significance and substance when attached to the heart and soul of the reader. So, a close and personal alliance existed between a hippie and his chosen scribe. Whether beat writer or poet, philosopher or New Age fifth dimensional fourth estatist, it didn't matter. Others like Huxley, Salinger, Poe, Burgess, Thomas, Tolkien or Blake, as long as the experience held the spirit, passive interjection or simple quotes could guide or spice an innocent conversation. It was a religion, like music, a personal journey only to be enhanced by the drug experience. Given to self-discovery where meaning and the soul's third eye were essential in establishing this bond. However, for hippies "struck dumb" by stretching the intellectual playing field, and "tripping" just short of the finish line, there was always "visualmania." These were the challenges presented by the ever-popular, suggested for ages 8 to 12, Etch-a-sketch, etching to Escher, or painting by numbers using crayons, conceptualizing a can of Campbell's tomato soup with arms, strangling Andy Warhol.

I first gained insight into the mind of Aldous Huxley while away at school. I found it apropos that *Brave New World* was a mandatory read. Being filed away and type cast, everyone was easy prey to the manacles of a programmable regime. I guess in retrospect, this is where my early bouts with rebellion started. I didn't want to be a machine operating within the confines of a dehumanizing regulated system. The drudgery beginning with morning revelry and ending with the ritualistic "lights out," dimmed any hope of true independence.

I was different and found it befitting as a newly ordained drop out, to enter a phase of deprogramming. Life was, in a sense, a reform school and I took solace in people like Huxley, whose alter ego pranced through life as though it was a psychedelic garden. It was a delicate array of redolent blooms with splashing colors, hinting of a wider spectrum where the full potential of the individual could be tapped and exploited.

Through his *Doors of Perception*, I was able to find the key to unlock the imagination and here I stumbled into Timothy Leary and his psychedelic experience. This revised version of the *Tibetan Book of the Dead* turned the whole process into a fervent religious quest for both enlightenment and legitimacy. I must admit it offered a viable alternative to attending chapel twice a day, everyday. Talk about overkill, all this did was bring out the "great beast" in me where I became anti everything, including anti Christ.

With Leary's guiding hand, it was easy to "drop out," with the idea of establishing a more wholesome relationship with the world. However, I neglected to comprehend and accept the realization that the longer you remained outside peering in, the harder it became to initiate a reversal in terms of re-entering to re-assimilate, becoming once again subservient to the status quo.

In a sense, maybe this is what happened to Edger Allen Poe. It's still a matter for debate, whether the vivid imagination of this venerable poet extraordinaire, succumbed to the allure and hardened addiction perpetrated by the innocence of the poppy. This, like a flower in bloom, drew the user to its nectar, only to capture forever the soul like Venus, in a flytrap. He tripped and fell, tumbling through the "dark side" of life where expression and the mother load exploded in a mania that tickled the imagination of people like myself.

All that we see or seem,
Is but a dream within a dream

Edgar Allen Poe

These words pulsated through the empty warehouse that occupied the vacuum between my earlobes. The echo affect was strong enough to allow my creative side to drift without reservation; a lucid, transparent flight, on astral wing, feathered, gliding my senses to the steps of the Lincoln Memorial. Here, to capture forever the powerful, yet magnetic dialogue that drew forth a multitude; imprinting an indelible passion to promote freedom and equality for all.

I say to you today, my friends,
That in spite of the difficulties
and frustrations of the moment,
I still have a dream.

Martin Luther King, Jr.

Being an idealistic, yet for the moment forsaking my revised birthright and with it, the all-important American dream, I still managed to search the sanatorium that masqueraded as my brain with the hope of achieving some sort of personal victory. I hoped one day to string together a comprehensive semblance of both semantics and syntax.

It didn't take long. My first attempt at creative writing became more of an ode to self, where the loose prose loosened my grip, allowing all future attempts to flow with undulating grace, creating a flair for irony, sneering sarcasm and oh, yes, poetic justice.

J.C. Carella, famous underground guerilla leader,
was captured today,
on the south sides of Chicago,
for purse snatching.

Upon initial observation, it appears almost simplistic and very innocuous. But if you take the time to read between the lines, sadly, you'll still see nothing except wasted space. However, if you could tap into my creative sub-conscious, you'll soon realize my use of double entendre, though nebulous, hints at urban unrest, civil strife and crime. If you dig further, being careful not to scrape the inner portion of my skull, it becomes ostensibly clear; these subtleties ultimately lead back to the birthplace of the blues.

Boarding school not only stimulated my creative side, but also roused my spiritual curiosities awakening them to search for the pleasures of spirit. The most obvious occurred one Sunday while meditating during evening chapel. I was thrown into a state of total confusion. I was just about to fondle Raquel Welch's breasts when I was struck in the left temple by the collection plate. (I would have used the word tits, but for Christ's sake I was in church!) Being caught off guard and not wanting to make a fool of myself, I innocently reached down and removed a gold plated button from my Sunday blue blazer. Upon raising it to the heavens, I looked at the Chaplin, smiled and dropped it into the plate. Since the gusto of the moment ripened the already dull thirst for both redemption and physical substance, I removed what I perceived to be a slightly less than its net worth. I had satisfied my spiritual thirst and upon completion of the service, immediately proceeded to satisfy its physical counterpart by visiting the vending machine conveniently placed in the hallway next to God's house.

Allan Ginsberg's flirtatious mixing of toga, yoga, and

Buddhism and the Beatles subsequent pilgrimage to India, vexed the religious paradigm with such a verve as to vanquish all vestiges from the vestry where any investment in the vestments were changed forever. At least from the standpoint of the vertical yet spiritually inclined hippie, traditional religion had helped sharpen the senses, but failed to take them to the next level where spiritual acuity was essential in understanding any purpose in being.

In order to resist the temptations presented by any quantum leap forward, many of us chose to move freely from side to side in the hope of capturing the essence of being. The whole idea was to explore self with the realization that somehow the supreme deity was the bonding factor that brought it all together and therefore, made it all possible.

By looking at philosophy, many hippies combined the thoughts of Spinoza and Nietzsche; the concepts of free will and intellect being driven by the energy of self to create in harmony, the superman. The catch, this would only occur when all was unified by purpose, by striving to reach a defined goal. The problem with most hippies, and us was that there were no goals. Yes, we were free to move along a lateral plain, but our parameters were firmly entrenched by the social mood of the moment.

We were not detached observers of the world, but existed within the delicate framework. No matter how much we strived to escape or alienate ourselves, the world had become a very small place.

If we existed, and most hippies I'm sure, based on the constant hunger panging, scratching and bed sores, were convinced that life was more than fantasy. Existence, life and the future must be determined by both chance and action. This existentialistic viewpoint didn't tell us how to choose, it simply implied that there is a right way and a wrong way. Wouldn't it be great if all our choices were right? However the surreal implication supplanted our reality, because we all knew that the complexities involved in any decision- making could in effect, throw our existence out of balance. So you see, the less said the better. In truth, we were quite happy, living the way we did.

Being in a sense egocentric and stimulating the survivability of ego, we soon decided as a group, to move more into the metaphysical world, with the idea of waking and developing the id. The ideology being not one of idiocy or that of being idiomatic, but ideally cultivating the idyllic pleasures of the psychic plane; here tele transporting of the senses would make up the premise behind this workshop. We had discovered astral projection.

The state of being outside which was a struggle unless looking for a free meal or tying to score, was expanded to include actually leaving one's physical body. This could be achieved if you were psychically endowed, which was a definite chic magnet. A hippie, who was also physically endowed, obviously had the best of both worlds. Thank God for those Swedish penis pumps!

Now, if you were lazy, you could always kick start the process by drinking good old "Dartmoor Tea," a delicate blend of fungus and other herbal delicacies or take a short cut by popping a tab of strawberry mescaline.

Either way, my research as a wannabe hippie scribe or green horn shaman, unearthed four potential pitfalls that all novice practitioners of the astral state must be aware of.

1. All beginners must display the required "red on white" L-plate. This is easily accomplished by fastening the plate securely to the silver cord, which connects the physical body to its astral counterpart. However, many trainees fail to observe the age-old practice of obeying both the posted speed limit and giving way to merging astral traffic. The result can be astral chaos or worse. There have been documented reports of disoriented apprentices making quick turns

as they swerve, snapping the silver cord. This in effect, catapults the confused visionary into a parallel universe. If they are lucky, and find their astral counterpart, the merging of two similar yet different astral bodies can cause Schizophrenia, or in the worst-case scenario, having the ethereal recipient die in their sleep.

2. Many astral newcomers fail to hone their navigating skills. Rather than paying attention to what lies ahead, they became transfixed with the ground below. The result can be a calamitous head on collision, involving two heads actually colliding. For the most part, the recipients simply wake up the next morning reaching for bottles of aspirin.
3. STAY AWAY FROM AIRPORTS! There's always the concern that the astral body will be sucked up and through the turbo fan of a large jumbo jet. This will generally paint a very nasty picture for Doppler radar as the astral body, - parts are strewn over much of the UK and a wide area of the North Sea.
4. Never astral project during a major thunderstorm. There have been numerous reports of lightening strikes to the silver cord causing severe cardiac arrhythmia to the ethereal body. This can cause the cord to snap forcing the receiver into hyperspace where time and space converge. In practice, a very primitive form of time travel, yet not one without consequences. I think the recent discovery of mysterious humanoid footprints, preserved forever in Pennsylvania next to those of the Paleozoic reptiles helps to substantiate this claim.

Feed Your Head

The answers to the questions remain sequestered,
answered not, by putting in,
but by reaching in,
and pulling out.

Inspired by:

White Rabbit
Jefferson Airplane

Monastic monks, ascetic clerics, panhandling prophets, religious zealots living on the edge, and even some, for whatever reason, dangling so perilously by their fingernails from it. Fanatical freaks have done it since the dawning of time. Fasting, meditating, hanging upside down, flogged, frail and broken, the supreme and holiest of sacrifice. Disciplined deprivation, the physical oasis, and the waters that nourish the manna of consciousness, cultivated and modified the body's chemistry so to promote heightened awareness. If it didn't kill the determined, this psychophysical stress manifested through faith was believed to create a bond with the Great Spirit or creator.

Hippies had reached this state by a life style choice. Fasting just happened to be the major component of it. The rest was a rapid onset desire to jump start and complete the process without the usual 40/40. A month plus 10 where back packing Death Valley or closer to home, the area adjacent to Dartmoor Prison would hopefully bring about some sort of revelation.

The probing or merging of self with the divine soon

eliminated the pain from the physical. The cleansing of the soul that preceded the search for solitude and oneness with all that is, only dented the mind by nourishing the head. The vastness of the universe and the questions that abounded rebounded to ping the psyche. The universe became the "innerverse" where the mind and the connections made, rivaled that in numbers to the twinkling stars.

Hippies could either tap each other, tap the core within or even the core, the earth harbored 'neath itself. It didn't matter. All that was needed remained a clearly defined map and since the RAC had trouble servicing those in transit, the map became the unsolicited jaunt. This round-trip junket was serendipitously provided, thanks to a tripped out formula developed by Albert Hoffman, an overly zealous white-cloaked Swiss chemist. Distribution rights to LSD were quickly gobbled up by a bi-curious bunch of control freak operatives within the clandestine clutches of the US government.

MK ultra represented a policy shrouded in a secrecy blemished by a desire to propagate the *Manchurian Candidate* through mind control. It however fostered mind obliteration through careful design as a new weapon to instead, contaminate both water reservoirs and subway ventilation systems. Its test subjects included the avant-garde thinkers of the time, who viewed it from the perspective of enlightenment where the mind would indeed open rather than close.

It was Ken Kesey who unwrapped and exposed Pandora's snuff box or more accurately phased, Pandora's pantry. Here was hidden not only her party favors and forbidden fruit, but her secret stash as well. However, it was Dr. Leary who spun the psychedelic web, stranding together as an arachnophobic "Spin Doctor," the phrase "turn on," "tune in" and "drop out." These words advocated the use and ultimately the abuse of mine altering drugs.

> "We are now in the psycho-chemical age. In the future its not going to be what books you read, but what chemicals do you use, to open your mind to accelerate learning."
>
> Dr. Timothy Leary

You know, Leary was in a sense right. Ask any hippie what the last novel read during the height of a trip was and I'll guarantee the answer will be, "I can't remember or you've got to be kidding."

Any desire to read was quickly substituted by a desire to let the senses take over. Tripping became the logical follow-up, the next step in the evolutionary spiral that involved the quest for spiritual knowledge and truth. It became far easier to pick up a comic book, rather than a novel. At least the story was set in motion, where the senses particularly the visual aspect, could direct and even determine the outcome. All this was without involvement, by use, a secret code to decipher the written material. It allowed you to create by design, offering any number of story lines and endings depending on the number of people reading or I should say, attempting to read with emphasis on following the pictographs, versus the printed word. Hey you could even read or more accurately, flip the pages a second time, getting a completely different story with an equally strange and bizarre ending. In actual fact, the same comic could be panned innumerably during the context of the trip, offering an equal number of scenarios with a similar number of endings, comprising the entirety of the experience.

If one were to examine fully the drug experience, there were four reasons why hippies befell to the allure of hallucinogenics, or a mortar and pestle mentality of perceived medicinal pleasures.

1. They provided a glamorous mystical experience, including visions, ushering forth a fuller awareness, well beyond the five senses. A way to reach out and touch the face of God. However, beware, many

hippies have reported that their hands have actually passed through the apparition's face. Of the two remaining heads, many have imploded, exploded or just melted like a Wall's ice cream on a hot summer's day.

2. These drugs often brought people together to interact and share the experience. Be careful of bikers bearing gifts. Be suspicious of anyone in dark glasses with a nervous twitch, selling Durbin poison in a bag marked Oregano. Never let anyone in wearing shades, accompanied by a white cane and a German Shepard, - especially if they ask to see a map of Cornwall.
3. While they made you feel good; many however, suffered from recurring nightmares involving large saber-toothed black rats, swan diving from the white cliffs of Dover. This in all likelihood was caused by the chemical agent in question being laced with too much strychnine.
4. The drug experience often allowed the user to convene with nature. The most asked question: Can animals really carry on a conversation? Besides Mr. Ed consoling Wilber's obsession with "penis envy" and Francis the Mule kicking Ronald Reagan in the head, the list's rather short, so don't be fooled. The whole idea of gathering around the camp fire and pretending to be Dr. Doolittle and indulging badgers with your knowledge of a hedge hog's sex life are overrated. It only happened to people like Rex Harrison who by the way, was motivated by something far more powerful than any drug. MONEY!

Carlos Castaneda said, "Live every moment as if it was your last dance on earth!"

Easy for him to say! It's not hard to party hardy when you're "el blottoed" on peyote. However, the notion of the last dance is disturbing since I'm no Fred Astaire. It's even worse when stoned, though the inhibitions wane. I still have two left feet, a hallucinogenic affect I'm sure, or maybe just a simple error in judgment. It's not hard to imagine actually putting on two left shoes when one is wasted.

Castaneda's journey through the world of the Yagui Indians shamanistic existence was booked through tour guide Don Juan. It was a visionary excursion involving an encyclopedic mind bender, where powerful hallucinogenics dominated the first three books. Elevated consciousness became a means to an end. The experience was a bizarre interlude of alleged inter-dimensional phase shifting or sliding where mysticism and sorcery dominated the plane. An education in mass hallucination, predicated by an astral experience, where the door to the inner universe, slightly ajar, jarred the imagination—just enough to conclude that some things are better left to the teachers, though Amazonian bound, rather than a few disciples, captured like mice running blind through the labyrinth of time.

> "The ego doesn't melt like an iceberg in tropical waters, but expands to the point of suffocation."
>
> Aldous Huxley

In truth, tripping was a double-edged sword. Huxley stated in *Heaven and Hell*, that, only those free from negative emotions, have a door opened to visionary experience. I can safely attest that many flaunting negativity in terms of fear and anger, have either slipped under the crack or managed to peak through the keyhole. Here, the nickelodeon display, featuring the pink elephant in a tutu and tennis shoes and carrying a parasol, often became one's headmaster in drag, doing a burlesque where total removal revealed the grim reaper, complete with scythe.

I've seen it all. I've been to Oz, followed the yellow path through the poppy fields, forever red. I've been to hell, shook hands with the devil at the foot of my bed. Promises none, Faust, I am not, so I survived to pull the covers up over my head; to feed on the nativity of my naively striven, naked quest. The only pact I ever made was to come down with the promise I'd never reach blindly for that doorknob again.

Of course I eventually realized there were ways to gain entry, without actually turning the knob and walking through. Like listening to other hippies recount their experiences. A reckoning of minds over what really mattered. A long haired recital where many recalled, with vivid recollection, a repertoire of reckless renditions. A Renoir turned upside down, a reflection of the mood where like the Red Sea dividing, separated the real from the surreal. This, without warning could spill back allowing the user to drown in emotions dictated by the tide. A Looney Tune in reverse, where a bumbling Elmer Fudd, after dropping his gun, shoots himself in the head.

A simple noise could envelop the senses, an ever expanding opening capable of swallowing everything. A sudden cessation and then, the sensation of free falling through a tunnel resembling a Kaleidoscope turning in sync to the sound of Hendrix's white stratocaster serenading the beat in harmony to the changing colors. The feedback echoing a whisper that tickled the hairs inside the grottos of both ears.

"If I don't see you again I'll see you when we cross paths in the next world. I'll be waiting at the gate, so don't be late."

Inspired by:

Voodoo Child
Jimi Hendrix

Christ! I knew I shouldn't have closed my eyes.

Each experience was different. You might find yourself standing in the middle of a meadow, after a light shower. All at once two mirrors appear. One moves to the front, while the second places itself deftly behind you. A series of rainbows manifest and grace the glass, repeating the effect into infinity. But wait! You're suddenly standing next to the rainbow, repeating the sequence again and again. The onlooker becomes the reflection. The paradox of the parallax, paralyzed in time, caught between dimensions without recourse for action.

"Suddenly the sky turned blood-red.
I stopped, and leaned against the railing, deathly tired –
Looking out across the flaming clouds that hung like blood and a sword."

"The Scream"
Edward Munch

Ah, the quintessential acid trip, existentialism lingering within the confines of expressionism. To the layman, a bizarre marriage to say the least. I remember my initial reaction upon viewing Munch's painting, "The Scream." It followed, double time, lapping at the heels of a double feature, which heralded the timeless cult classics, *Attack of the Killer Tomatoes*, and *The Man from Planet X*. Now talk about strange bedfellows, or maybe more appropriately, soiled bed sheets. Mind you, this was not the most invigorating way to start the day!—sliding off white sheets slimed red with ketchup, unless of course, you're an extraterrestrial resembling a large "Hot dog." The painting reminded me of an alien, looking out over our world through paranoid chestnut shaped eyes.

I just had to confirm the visuals. So while "tripping" through Scandinavia, I managed to find by chance Oslo. This wasn't easy since I possessed the proclivity to map read while suspended upside down, usually from a lofty bridge, in this case, spanning two quite impressive yet vertically challenged fjords. After experiencing both a nasty concussion, and the customary two month coma that followed this type of closed head injury, I was convinced that the sunset I witnessed was more an after affect produced by a near death experience, rather than the tab of

California sunshine I had "dropped," not down my gullet, but to the gully below.

So you see, there was always an element of danger attached to the hallucinogenic and the pathways it bore.

The realization that the dark side was indeed only a trick of light and shadow away. It often held the hallmark of a journey to Mordor, during a total eclipse. With arms outstretched like tentacles, you probe forward into the catatonic curdling abyss of the blackened catacombs.

Visual distortion and paranoia create a motif resembling a crude but effective vignette; the meshing of style, falling somewhere between the hues of gray, taupe, black and more black. Just imagine Picasso and Salvatore Dali blind from birth and drinking insatiably together over the course of a long weekend. But, there's only one problem. In addition to the obvious hangovers, only a single canvas and one lonely brush decorate the austere room.

Even the layman practitioner, such as myself, was exposed to a seemingly idyllic mosaic of patchwork fantasies laden with a reality or dreamscape promoting an animated theatre where anything and everything could occur.

Dungeons and Dragons

Hooded, I can see his face,
as he rides reticent,
charging the darkness.
Wind flowing, hair and mane.
His face is my face.
My pain is his pain.

Inspired by:

Rainbow Demon
Uriah Heep

"Hold on JF, what's the rush?

He turned and grabbing for his crotch exclaimed, "I've got to piss!"

He stood there, hands on hips, a prodigious specimen of a lad, one able to ingest mega quantities of drugs and wash them down with the gusto presented by an endless parade of full "to the brim" pint glasses. An assembly line of thirst quenching goblets that caused many an Innkeeper to surrender in frustration, the chore of filling and then under handing and guiding the glasses down the length of the bar. No easy task, since every pub that blanketed the area between Davenport and Plymstock knew Big John's appetite for brew. It was even suggested that he take up permanent residence as a beer tasting brew master at the local Courage bottling plant.

The realization that I too, had to bleed the lizard, prompted a quick release, accompanied by a prolonged sigh as I proceeded to put out a non-existent fire that raged against the garden wall, just short of our front gate. As I re-buttoned my Levi's, I noticed John was nowhere to be seen. Being the stereotypical lightweight, I had consumed nowhere near the quantity of mind-altering substances or the tonic that soon followed. Needless to say, I found the distance to the front door equivalent to a safari lost somewhere in the African savannah. By the time I discovered the ascending staircase, I was somewhat out of breath. "Christ I hope I'm in the right house!" I whispered just under my now normal rate of respiration.

I looked up. There were definitely more than thirty-nine steps, remembering the book. I giggled, I preferred the movie.

Wait a minute. It looked more like the steps leading up an Aztec sacrificial pyramid. Lucky for me, I wasn't a virgin! I tapped my closed fist against my lips. The sensation was numbing. I suddenly knew what I had to do.

After relieving myself again, this time on the next door neighbor's shrub, I decided to leave the buttons unfastened, just in case. I assumed the same position, staring in desperation at the seemingly endless array of wooden steps, which now reached the ceiling.

"Oh, fuck it!" I muttered, charging up the stairs, which posed the same challenge as an escalator moving in the opposite direction. I seemed to be descending rather than ascending as though walking down rather than up. I decided maybe the best way to accomplish this endeavor, was to turn and walk up the stairs backwards. To my surprise, this slight of hand maneuver worked.

"Success!" I clenched my fists as I turned, only to discover a hallway, instead of a wall. It was dimly lit, with torches that hung at a slight angle from both walls. It appeared medieval.

God, I thought I was in trouble for a second! The notion of Aztec henchmen waiting and being mistaken for a transsexual virgin was obviously still quite apparent.

As I accepted my good fortune, a warrior on a horse appeared at the far end of the passageway. I rubbed my eyes, looked, pinched myself and then slapped my face as hard as I could. As I picked myself off the cold damp floor, I closed my eyes, slowly opening them and exclaimed, "Ah, what the hell is this?" He was still there. It wasn't Odin, even though I felt I had just been struck by Thor's hammer, obviously it wasn't the black knight, since whomever it was, was clad in an all white sheet and there was no sign of a hood or burning cross, so a lost clansman was definitely not a possibility, nor a knight's Templar since the sheet bore no evidence of a red cross.

Just then the knight galloped in full flight toward me. His lance, outstretched like an erect wooden member, swayed slightly from left to right, but stiffened quickly as he poised to strike. Instead of turning and presenting my ass as an ample target, I stared with unabridged amazement, as he and his steed grew ever closer. I noticed dangling from the point of his lance, a small triangular flag.

I swore as I closed my eyes and screamed, the flag bearing the word, AJAX nipped at my nose as the sound of hoof meeting wood refrained.

The door suddenly opened and only a head revealed itself. It was Fluff.

"Are you okay?" His concerned voice sounding somewhat mellowed by the distinct odor of hash.

I darted in, closed the door, opened my mouth to talk, but forming only the letter "O" said nothing.

Fluff looked down and noticing the open buttons on my pants, laughed and said, "Down Union Street for a quick blow job, huh?"

"Where's JF? My voice now tempered yet still stymied by the frustration of the experience.

"Christ, he came in, said nothing, yawned and went straight to bed."

I shook my head in disbelief, walked over to the couch, grabbed a pack of # 6 off the coffee table and lit one. I uttered not a word to anyone. By the time I finished the pack, all were asleep except the sun, which was rising just beyond the bay window.

By the last of his fifteen books, Castaneda concluded that drugs could be eliminated altogether. The vestiges of the overall experience he reasoned could be attained through alternative measures, such as yoga and meditation. Christ! I wish I had known this from the start. I would have read the last book first!

Even though we thought we honed the experience, that being spiritual nirvana, by taking the lift, instead of the stairs, the thirteenth floor, was indeed only apparent to our mind's eye. We instead found a tangent where escapism was a world flavored with the magic of laughter and buffoonery. This was a phase of friendly jousting, horseplay and hilarity, which soon gave way to the realization that the mind, including the eye, was indeed a terrible thing to waste. Besides, cannabis in its various forms was more readily available and high for high, on all levels, a hell of a lot cheaper.

High Times and High Crimes

Give Ulster back to those that barter the land.
Shamrock or Orange, which has the upper hand?

Inspired by:

Give Ireland Back To The Irish
Paul McCartney

It was the best of times and the worst of times. When it was good, it was sooooo…ever so good. When it was bad, man, it could blow your mind! I always thought, particularly from my point of view, the onus of being born in Northern Ireland could present with certain difficulties. I could hide the fact, hoping to wrought, serendipitously, a silver lining validating my standing, proclaiming in truth, it was okay to be Irish. However, the sign of the times, fresh with neon exposure, highlighted the reality, sadly, of the historical timeline, which pitted Sinn Fein and the IRA against the Reverend Ian Paisley and the Unionists. Even though orange appealed to me, and being green with envy was never an issue, my passport, typeset with obvious prejudice, was potentially a burden, if and when questioned by the local authorities. I quickly concluded that the worse stereotype during the uneasy period that followed "Sunday, Bloody Sunday," was being a Catholic of hippie stock, born in Ireland, heaven forbid, Dublin, now residing in London and living on the dole. It became painfully clear from this day forward, in addition to an empty wallet, I would carry only my student identity card. Though technically expired, it showed my citizenship as being American, giving a UK address without reference to place of birth. I now felt reasonably secure, but chose however, to mingle and travel in groups whenever possible.

It's interesting to note how hippies living in different environments react, based on a set of circumstances that intrinsically affect their lot. In America it was the war and racism; here, it was war and the Irish. I guess, in truth, it was also a form of racism if the definition of "black Irish" was changed to draw a parallel to its Afro American counterpart.

In the US, it led to hippie protests and violence. In Britain, it led to Irish unrest and terrorism. After January 30, 1972, when a rally over illegal internment of alleged IRA members led to the shootings in Bogside, Londonderry, the question of who sparked the incident resulted in a "white paper" soon turned red with both the blood of the Irish and to the British. It offered no real leverage to the hippies who were too busy chastising the sandman for sewing their eyes shut, to march in unison, especially against an already very nervous and trigger happy police force.

Besides, the only real inconvenience for us was if the Plymouth scene was dry. It forced the Shagger express, a London excursion, a road trip, where British rail acting as our hosts, provided the round-trip tickets. The sticky point, due to the threat of terrorism, all the baggage lockers at Paddington were off limits. The quandary? We had no place to stash the stash. This meant the customary pub-crawl before departure, had become the proverbial pipe dream.

The BBC and the British press gave both a cold shoulder and a smattering to the real issues.

The Irish, particularly the IRA, skewed the issues to enhance their position, eliminating the protestant question concerning, as a majority, their right to self determination and desire to remain a part of the United Kingdom.

The random bombings in Birmingham and London brought terrorism to our doorstep. The Northern Ireland Emergency

Provisions Act coupled with the Prevention of Terrorism Act, gave both the Police and SAS sweeping powers. If history is an indicator and indeed repeats itself, the stories we read, whether from the Herald Tribune or other outside sources, such as Amnesty International, showed beyond a reasonable doubt, a brown shirt mentality. Unfair search and seizure, arrests, brutality, torture and in many cases, coerced confessions, led to false convictions and incarceration. The trial and fervor created by the Guildford Four brought back the memories of the Weathermen and their doom and gloom forecast, a storm front against the US Government, raining in terror by randomly bombing police stations.

The Rorschach Redemption

And if all our friends clamored aboard,
    to celebrate my misfortune.
All to a man would have paid the piper.

Inspired by:

Yellow Submarine
The Beatles

The fog, famished for affection, like an albino tabby begging to be fed, cradled my feet. The street lamps yearned to run, since their faded light had already taken flight. The specter, a ghostly presence, reflected the chill of the night as its blanket shrouded the black top below. It nurtured and protected the ground as each step of our caravan forced its lace to swirl and retreat.

It was cold, but instead of a great coat, I wish I had worn a toga. The entire scene hinted of a Cecil B. DeMille epic and since we were about to break a handful of commandments, it only seemed appropriate for the Holy Ghost to appear, complete with paint and brush. He could then at least, mark the doors of any copper and military man who may reside incognito, as the eerie cloak continued to assault the street.

Big John appeared to rise above the simmering pea soup, fluttering to tower like a colossus of roads, seemingly blocking both lanes. He stopped and as he did, the cavalcade reeled, congealed and as a serried mass, halted. To a man, the process was complete with one exception. My inertia, which carried my weight, rammed Pete who careened the Blade, who like an oversized domino, road Fluff, tipping his body into JF, who turned, catching him just before he disappeared forever into the mist of vapors that reached up to snare him.

There was an impromptu, unrehearsed log jam, created by the flinging of single words, all I knew aimed at me, would fall short of their mark. Hey! Idiot! Fuck! Bastard! Wanker!

"Shussssss, come on, piss off, quiet, this is where we'll climb over." Big John, moving stealthfully, almost tiptoeing as he finished, all while pointing like a used car salesman attempting to sell to the rest of us, our point of entry.

The fence was imposing and each spire, acting as a sentry, contained a deterrent in the form of a very sharp and rather large chrome-tipped spear. It looked like a phalanx standing at attention, awaiting orders to charge. I noticed where John was pointing that two of the guards had broken rank, since their spears, at least the most dangerous part, were none existent. This is where, ironically, a sign was mounted, in turn, to act as a ledge where our feet could balance before stepping through the opening.

No one seemed to pay attention to the faded print that hung tortured and exposed, listless and lackluster, just clinging to life as the swaying branches of a nearby tree fanned with a whisper of light.

WARNING!
Entry Strictly Forbidden
Property of the Ministry of Defense

By the time I read and digested it's meaning, the group from the other side flagged my attention. Pete teased and challenged my resolve.

"Come on, Yank, let's go."

I managed to squeeze both myself and the cocoon provided by my great coat through, arriving by way of the ground. Pete smiled and offered his hand, which shackled my wrist, bringing me to eye's length.

"Come on Yank, this is no place to get lost."

I followed and once again, joined, as the rear guard, the forward moving caravan. We marched, tethered by sight and smell. JF leading, following the cobblestone brick toward the quay where the hollowed shell of a gray lady, perched from below, rested eternally against the break wall. She was majestic and soulless, marking time, forever silent. Anchored by a lifeline, which kept her at bay with only the tide and occasional gull to crew her at rest. Awash, an antique of antiquity, awaiting a burial at sea, forage for target practice or worse yet, a chance to make steam as the new flagship for the Indian Navy.

Next to the gangplank Fluff stopped, turned and looking directly at me, pointed to a large can of yellow paint, which stood demoralized in isolated solitude atop the metal monster. He leaned forward using his arm to part the others so he could see and muttered something about "clumsy" and me in the same short sentence. Pete and the Blade nodded and giggled, but left me without escort to fend for myself.

I quickly concluded that I would be better off blindfolded and forced to walk the plank. I would surely miss the obstacle, but undoubtedly continue until captured by a free fall, providing a free ride straight to the bottom. I only hoped that Davy Jones's locker, conveniently located next to Mike Neismith's vacated stall, contained at least one dry towel.

As I crossed the makeshift wooden bridge, my glances darted between the planks, the group, the can and the narrow confines of the deck. My visual range of motion was quickly drawn to two partly etched narrow yellow lines, running parallel on opposite sides of the wooden causeway, obviously acting as a guide for those making the trek onto the submergible.

Once on board, I carefully navigated around the container that contained, if spilled, enough paint to cover much of one side—not a bad combination if by design, the vessel was to be converted into a banana boat and sold as a surface raider to a banana republic.

Fluff had stopped short of the conning tower, which

appeared to be in the process of dismantlement. It was roped off, steering the remainder of our band toward his position, straddling a raised cover, which appeared from my vantage point to be a hatch.

He rubbed his hands together and gleefully pranced, doing a poor rendition of a jig, exclaiming, "Oh boy, lets do it! Come on then, who's coming? Let's get inside this bucket, find the engines…"

"Yeah!" JF followed with bold enthusiasm, throwing his support so lassoing the rest of us, making any possible riposte only a glimpse of fleeting thought.

Our unbroken circle, like a wagon train under siege, protected Fluff from any outside distraction.

"Give me a hand, then?" Seemingly probing and then reaching to bring into view, the largest spanner I had ever seen. This would be the tool by which the latch cover would be tamed, bribed and then removed. It took all of us just to hold it, and as I looked over at Fluff, it gave a whole new meaning to the phrase "grease monkey," as I hoped we weren't about to end up as chumps to his chimp.

"Okay, on three, remember, righty tighty, lefty loosy, so Ian, to the left, right!"

That in itself seemed complicated, but as we brought the wrench to hold, the count down began.

One, *oh God no, please, not now,* I thought; two, *Christ, the itch, it's unbearable! I'll just reach around and,* three, as my right hand scratched my ass, in synch with the last number, I lost my footing, brushing against Peter, who in turn knocked Fluff to the ground.

If its true, the speed at which sound carries at sea level is roughly seven hundred miles per hour, I estimated that just about fifty-nine minutes and fifty-nine seconds before Seismologists picked up the ping in Inverness, the royal marine garrison, patrolling the estuary, would be here, en masse to help remove the wrench from my left foot before arresting us.

I was pleased that no one condemned me to death or even serrated my misguided mishap, at mishandling the situation with a further berating. The only problem, they didn't help me either as I limped toward the exit point. I figured God had aptly punished me until my good foot, which had no consideration for its gimpy counterpart, ran a foul taking with it, the can of paint. It was like the parting of the yellow sea, the tempera inflicting not only the rising sun with dipping flares, but also a fellowship to Kandinsky, as it proceeded to take shape and then reshape, dripping down the side of the sub.

As I turned to witness the metal canvass, I noticed Fluff, like a munchkin following my yellow brick road. "Come on, put your arm around my neck."

He guided me to the fence, only to finish by uttering commands from the other side. As I scurried, bracing myself with my good leg, my lack of balance shifted my center of gravity, forcing me around to catch once again, the masterpiece I had left. I was now impaled, crucified, thanks to my great coat, which left me at arm's length reaching out to any one who could help, including the MP's who had successfully captured the wharf.

"Don't move," the Blade's voice, soothing as it was, was not the chord I hope would be tossed in my direction. I felt like Carlos the Jackal as the massive search light scoured the path, sniffing its way toward me, holding it's ground just inches away from my yellow boots.

My life review was now underway, unfolding in tempo, pacing my beating heart. It however, refused to page back, scanning the here and now, focusing on my capture, trial and incarceration as a "hippie spy." I looked once again at the sleek, elongated banana shaped craft, honing in on the patch of yellow, which formed as lines, islets of paint, dripping between the dark, forming bars. I imagined Long Kesh, a cold dank cell and Bobby Sands. Shit!!! I wished someone would throw a lifeless lifeline into the light, to let the wind make a stake to remedy my mistake.

My arms were as a Mandrake, a deadly nightshade, silhouetted by the large Oak tree that dominated the scene to my rear. From behind the massive trunk that shielded my misery, the Blade, my bulwark, like cork, floating in whirling wisps of Avalon, laughed but continued to reassure me.

His demeanor rallied mine with the reliance of a Lion heart, a Templar to the night kneeling before, bowing to my plight, a crucifixion soon to be in plain sight. I was now in flight, imaging myself watching as my body responded to each and every command.

"What ever you do, don't freak out. Very slowly, bring your arms close into your body, that's it. Now, look down at your feet, so the top of your head, good. Now freeze."

It was so effortless, I, as a puppeteer with no strings attached, was able to bid farewell to the moment, capture myself, and release from struggle, the obedience to survive through submission of self; all this without the uncontrollable urge to panic.

The small craft, puttered and petered, allowing for my retrieval. JF and the Blade extirpated me, leaving my shell to extol in absentia, to be extradited in my stead. I was free, but hoped our paths would cross again in the dingy back room of the local Oxfam shop.

Hard line, main line,
  sewing death, the needle, quilting,
  to cover those screaming in agony.

Inspired by:

The Pusher
Steppenwolf

I guess, in a sense, paybacks are a bitch! Just maybe there's validity in suspicion when dealing with the accusations that the world-wide drug problem originated from behind the curtains of the Kremlin or somewhere deep under the Forbidden City.

It's truly amazing what the English will do for a cup of good ole fashioned tea! Looking back into the same archives housing the likes of the great "British War Heroes," references to an age of "I came, I saw, I conquered and oh yes, I took everything I could," echoed a pattern that by 1830 was a perfect blue print. Now I understood how Karl Marx became obsessed with a manifesto that proclaimed religion as the opiate of the masses. Maybe the word religion should have been substituted by the phrase, "The British Government."

The British Empire soon became the largest drug-trafficking criminal cartel in the world. They grew mind-boggling amounts of opium in India, used the East India Company to ship tons of extracts into China through Canton, which was then traded for manufactured goods, and yes, a windfall, that would make even Earl Grey blush, of brown and green teas.

Now, with both the police and their canine masters sniffing, it became apparent that it was not just IRA planted explosives they were rooting out. There was also a second front underway, another war being fought on the back streets, alleyways, pubs and homes dotting the gray scapes of many British cities. It was the war against the pusher and the user that fueled the credo that all drugs with the exception of alcohol, tobacco and anything offered by a licensed physician was indeed, capable of destroying civilized man. Of course, people like the hippies became the focal point and as usual suspects, allowed a variation of the search and seizure mandates to posture with hands against brick, as others with briefcases in tow, headed hurriedly to Boots and a smiling, wide-eyed chemist.

For us, the 28th of September 1928 was the day that will live forever in hippie infamy. This was the date when Cannabis Sativa, the leafy drug, not the demented Roman general, first became illegal in the UK. Of course, it didn't help that people like the Egyptians and Turks denounced "Hashism" as a plague that rivaled that of Moses and the Israelites. It was argued that excessive smoking caused upwards of sixty percent of the insanity in Egypt alone. It's a shame that the decision makers didn't take into consideration that the average Egyptian smoker, already suffering from both malnutrition and dehydration, had a myriad of ailments including rather stoned, yet, patient liver flukes. Many of these same crestfallen sods were descendants from the followers of RA, who maintained a working relationship with the sun god by copping a few zzz's face down in the sand. This show of solidarity gave new meaning to the term "high noon." It was though the Islamic lawmakers, while facing east, were deliberately pointing west, shielding all blame, thus allowing the profiteers to stamp their resin, "destination" Amsterdam, London or West Berlin.

As history makers, only if a true capitalist like William Randolph Hearst had known, just how much money could be made by selling kilos instead of newspapers, then maybe he wouldn't have introduced the word "marijuana" into the English vocabulary. This was done to dupe the public that dope, including all forms of hemp were indeed, the by products of the devil's weed.

So, it followed that the black and white world of *Reefer Madness*, the film of course, since hippies knew that smoking a joint made everything brighter including the vivid dreams that followed; tarnished pot, turning the experience into a salacious affair, bordering on criminal intent.

By the early sixty's, the US government and its bourbon sipping old boys network, forced, using the always-persuasive threat of economic sanctions, the UN to sign the "Single Convention on Drugs." Now, all the usual drop, snort, smoke or inject, feel better about yourself and the crummy world you live in pharmaceuticals were banned. This unfortunately included grass. These same, used to be, bath tub gin drinking adolescents, somehow forgot what happened the last time prohibition was exercised. So once again, the underground, including the London transit system, became the sanctuary where it became "hip" to partake and at the same time, thumb a nose or two at the establishment.

As a wild fire, it burned and as it consumed, many enjoyed the pleasures it wrought. It spread from beatnik to peacenik, to a teenage wasteland, where the basements of many a white middle class suburban neighborhood bore evidence as youth questioned the morality of an era. It became the sexy, rebellious and "rock" thing to do and in Europe, it became the "American" thing to do.

The 1965 Dangerous Drugs Act began to bring the UK law in line with parts of the UN Single Convention. Some police used this new power trip to stop and search anyone suspected of carrying drugs. Of course, all this did was piss off the victims who coincidently were either black or ripe with hair.

> "All laws which can be violated without doing anyone any injury are laughed at—he who tries to determine everything by law will foment crime rather than lessen it."
>
> Spinoza

The music mantles, mantraed spinning the habit to justify it's worth, but they too were harassed. It didn't matter if you were Beatle or Stone, the Old Bill didn't put a face on it until you were charged. The hippies got more out of Mick Jagger's and Marianne Faithful's half eaten Mars bar incident than they did out of the customary hefty fines and suspended sentence circus that usually followed this closely-knit concert.

By forcing, in particular, pot and hash inside or underground, the only people besides the rift-raft that profited, were the makers of dead bolts and window shades. But, thanks to the efforts of British musicians, artists, writers, journalists, doctors and (coughing slightly), a couple of MP's, some of the stiffer laws were modified. At least now, if you were busted, you didn't have to share a cell with Bubba who was serving five life sentences for murdering an entire village in Dorset and raping a prized herd of "Black Angus."

By the end of 1966, LSD was illegal in America. But it was the US's involvement in Vietnam and the Golden Triangle, harpooning with sharp precision that dulled the pains of war. This forced Nixon's hands, signing into power, a super agency to collectively deal with the aftermath. The Drug Enforcement Agency, or DEA, became the new cowboys, taming a frontier that included many of the same tactics that were already commonplace in Britain.

But for the hippies it was evident that the American government was taking a no nonsense approach to the drug crisis well before the DEA began breaking in both doors and skulls. The images of Elvis Presley, shaking hands with President Nixon upon receiving a special badge, advocating his position as a Federal agent at large, prompted a little sneering, especially after the "King" was found dead with trousers dangling below his knees, espousing an expose of hysteria and controversy, especially when the medicine cabinet bore a cornucopia, a cornerstone that became his head stone, of substance abuse.

"Freedom of the press belongs to those who own one!"
Thomas King Forcade

It was an age where the heads took on the feds, but fair is fair, and all may not be lost, even in the grappling that was underway. The same lawmakers that tempted fate, by attempting to stifle and smother, also lived by decree, a proclamation, a protocol that we hoped, though drafted to protect the freedoms of all, wouldn't be the prototype for something more sinister. So, the media, historically a mouthpiece for those in power, was also by way of our freedoms, a way to voice opinions reflecting tolerance and hopefully, change. *High Times* magazine spoke out, indicted, debated and questioned the issues involving particularly, grass and the laws that left fallow, the tracts that formed between them and us. It was no surprise that the best pot was grown, as super genetically altered hybrids, flourishing in protected environments, in the Southern states, all under the watchful eye of the US government!

So, they had their stash, excuse me, I mean laboratory grown, just for testing and nothing more Cannabis Sativa, and we had our stash. Ours was mainly resin, compressed, packaged, stamped and shipped from near or around the "Holy Land." Any grass was a luxury and if it wasn't contaminated with the toxic "weed killer" paraquat, sprayed by low flying helicopters with US markings, it was probably related in some peculiar way to the super weed being developed in those protected plantations. The magazine just helped keep us informed with lots and lots of very colorful pictures. But it was their monthly THC centerfold that highlighted our high life. To any pot smokin' enthusiasts, this often proved more titillating than the plastic overcoat, depicted erotically by wet unclad vixens, retouched carefully through a paint by numbers sequence followed by most of the high class skin mags of the day. To say the least, a Panama Red spread, framed in Acapulco gold was enough to ignite the senses to feast on an ephemeral aroma capable of baking the mind in a display where fantasy crashed a fleshy oasis of maids seducing the mist, vibrating with a sultry twist. Of consequence, depicting for all to see, fresh blotches, predictably fashioned to the crotches of our already stained jeans.

CHAPTER FOUR
THE NEW AGE NUANCE

"Sex, Karma and Rock n' Roll"

To see the World in a grain of sand.

William Blake

Astrologers, Charlatans and Harlequins

I am the past,
I am the future.
I am the eyes cast in illusion,
    Bathed in the mists of persecution.

Inspired by:

Nostradamus
Al Stewart

The mumbo-jumbo that was traditional religion, by way of the lesson, or applicably speaking the allegorical fairy tale, gave rise to not only a desire to look elsewhere, but also the impetus for people like the Grimm brothers to write variations using this very theme. Hippies in particular wanted more than the political denotation exemplified by the different religions and the multitude of different sects that each spurned. These were based primarily on the connotations, conservative, liberal or radical being attached to them. The New Age movement brought together a belief system bathed in the holy waters of Christian apocalyptic doctrine and the divine through paganism. It tended to borrow from an archaic religious dogma called more cosmological than cosmic, being in truth, religious naturalism. I'm certain this caused many a follower to strip down to the "au naturale" state of being when convening not only with god, but finding salvation through the obvious connection made between the unification or "cumming together" of the physical on this very physical plane of existence.

Since New Age beliefs are a simple synthesis of many preexisting movements including nineteenth century influences channeled through the likes of spiritualism, theosophy, philosophy and new thought, it was easy to establish a new frontier with new parameters and hence, a whole new handbook of rules. It became a true spiritual subculture and like its physical counterpart, the more three-dimensional counterculture, shared the ideas of societal transformation. This brought them together, each offering the other a viable platform from which to operate. The New Agers now rippling with the effects caused by far eastern influences, had the hippies to use as new age mouthpieces. The hippies on the other hand, had the spiritual apparatus they so desperately needed to help elevate their awareness without sacrificing any more brain cells. Of course, the whole definition of the trip became a religious pilgrimage when combined usually taking the pilgrim to the cosmic extreme, where the hinterland of the sojourn brought forth the master or rogue soul. The result? "Well, he told me to," when the booking officer designated the new stomping ground, a rather Spartan eight by eight, a postscript to the arrest at the chemist's counter, holding the under "lock and key," I need to come down now, "helpers."

The blame, sorry I mean the stimulus for this, lets depart from the norm, and create the most bizarre, far out, spiritual awakening possible, lies within the works of a New Age nuance or "holy trinity" equivalent. This electric, eclectic and empirical euphoria harnessed the energies of Alice Bailey, Helena Blavatsky and Charles Leadbeater. As a group, don't ask me why, we focused our attention on the *Secret Doctrine* of Madame Blavatsky. This mountain of paper work proved to be a difficult read for anyone who boasted an IQ of over 150. Since collectively our IQ was just slightly less, it became a migraine wrapped in the unparallel twisting, rather than the synchronizing of the synapses. This promoted a skewed synopsis of sense; seeding a schematic schism where the schmo became the throw rug covering the abyss that existed based on our convoluted misunderstanding of the issues. Her mantra became "There is no religion higher than the truth." Well, the truth is, most of her dodgy dogma launched a sense of bewilderment that rocketed as empty capsules, ricocheting harmlessly from hemisphere to hemisphere like a pin ball machine running amuck. She was, however, both controversial and colorful, filling a room; it was said with not only her free-spirited personality, but also a physical presence that forced many to retreat to the safety of the passageway. The plain truth, she was big! It was said that when she "hauled ass" she had to make two trips. Madame Flabatsky's ops! Excuse me; Blavatsky's propensity toward self-destruction would have been better served if she had truly understood more earthly issues such as not smoking hash, just before a meal.

One has to suspect that its feasibly possible cattle mutilations began not in Colorado in 1967, but a hundred years earlier in Hereford, England, suspiciously coinciding with a Blavatsky visit. Synchronicity or not, rumor has the rather roly, poly, beefy and pudgy Madame receiving a twenty-five gallon drum of brown sauce just about the time the cow, or what was left of it was discovered.

By rethinking her position and using her influence with the masters she should have followed up the *Secret Doctrine* with two additional books. A New Age cookbook, "The Secret Doctored Book of Arkane Recipes," with true metaphysical menus that featured her specialty, Hyperborean Hash Brownies with just a hint of Lemurian essence of whey.

Her second effort, a more relaxed rendition of the Doctrine, focused on the "cleansing," ideally of the soul. A collaboration of ideas with let's say, a prepubescent Edgar Cayce, who under the influence of her Hyperborean hash brownies and for an added pleasure, a liter bottle of French wine of coca, could have scanned the horizon, glimpsing the non didactic passion of the 1960's. The result, a less intimidating enactment of the decade, the focal point instead of gritty Sanskrit would have been the karma sutra sprinkled with just enough violence to keep the reader intact. You see, we hippies, contrary to popular belief, loathed the whole idea of mind expansion and its attachment to karma, through the mental assimilation of torpid, yet visionary assertions that taxed and taunted the spirit. We were diehards, resistant to a database of nonsensical ramblings. In truth, the truth was, keep things simple!

Life had become a very complex assortment of do's and don'ts, rules and regulations, assertions and assumptions. The Paradigm was fixed, leaving little to the imagination. But it was the wanton desire to seek and find an alternative to a vexed mainstream that offered a Swiss cheese conglomeration of fact verses fiction. So in the minds of men, and a few women as well, another alternative, spanning the glitch, which was time, brought forth a tangent. Here remnants of past civilizations, rivaling the likes of Lemuria, using the energy of the universe, laid frame to an era when the spirit evolved true, to sway the intentions of men and a few women too. The seven rays gave birth to the seven distinct paths of spiritual evolution, which relied on the original root races, which soon left. They conquered the space time continuum to dimensionally shift to a parallel, yet spiritually cleansed place. The Sanskrit wheel, the wheel within a wheel, intersecting, touching at points where the charkas ordained, holy places like Mt. Shasta, Stonehenge, Giza, Mt. Kailas and the rock down under. The lay lines of truth were energy fields that amassed the awareness for the few, who atoned for what? For they understood, but the rest did not! The lines of truth, dictated within, fed the hearts and minds of men, and a few women too. They aligned their personal chatkas, from heart to root to sacral, to the third eye, which became darkened and distorted; hence the desire. So unbending, they were unable to yield to the quest, for the search to find spiritual awareness. The wheel was not complete because men and a few women as well, failed to attach and hold the truth behind the seven rays of the elder race. - My God! I'm sorry, I was channeling again. I can't help it! It's my irritating pestiferous spirit guide. Well not my guardian angel, the female aspect being pure and illustrious, but the devious inner workings of my extraterrestrial walk in. My not so welcome soul squatter, the walk right in, sit right down, make yourself right at home in my soul, mate, from stellar hell, Master de'Bris. A sad, sordid, pathetic patron of the end times, relying more on his own heart-rending pitiful plight than that of imparting any real truth to the meaning behind all that is. He's a Drossonian who was banished to the Planet Mange for loitering about the universe and littering the fane of heart. His garbage, a collection of gullible insights into the vein of creation, bleeding dry the consciousness by associating everything that is to the concept of chance. Poised to add as a spice to life, the possibility that the elder race of man are really gods who incognito, pronounced the world fit to display by hand and a little help from a test tube, the Genesis being the biosphere we call, home. Christ, now I'm beginning to sound like him! A castaway, a throwaway to the celestial trash heap, Mange, located I'm been told, in the outer waste land of Andromeda, a cast off from the federation. Now he has chosen me to take refuge, as refuse, here to stay because he refuses to leave, the dustbin that is my brain. So you see I have been given the truth, or a portion of the truth. Okay, the half-truth. Fifty percent is better than no truth at all, which is terrible when you consider that everything we know and understand is predicated on the so-called truth.

A Vision Quest

Visions of the here and now, take me beyond reason.
Bring clarity bathed in light, scan beyond the season.

Inspired by

Moonage Daydream
David Bowie

The whirlwind tour had been the pub-crawl that eventually became the slow crawl home. Once there I became more and more frustrated. Beating my alter ego was like the act of punching a clown or flogging a dolphin. Sorry, let me rephrase that, I don't want to upset the animal rights activists. Let's see, how about slapping the serpent or in this case, it might be more appropriate to refer to this feather-minded fetish as simply a wanton passion to slay the dragon. I guess that's what you get when you do the beer fandango.

One might have concluded that Hans, my German soldier was suffering from shell shock. I had just about banished him to erectile dysfunction-grad when I heard this soft, almost muted female voice calling out to me, "Come."

I spontaneously replied, "If I had a little help, you stupid cow!"

"You must come!"

As I struggled to get my hands free, I blinked rapidly, hoping to lift the black veil that shrouded the room. I scanned from side to side, noticing an almost translucent outline of a woman.

"Who are you?" I retorted.

"Cing."

"Only if you give me a hummer," I snorted.

"Always with the jokes. My name is Cing, and I'm your protector, your guardian angel, and the purveyor of the word. I will take you to where you can find the truth.

"Well, to tell you the truth, I'm a little busy right now," I answered almost cynically. I paused a moment and before I could continue, found myself adrift, floating above my body, following her, still struggling to put on my astral underwear. "Where are we going?" I asked.

She turned and smiled, raising her long index finger to her lips. "In time," she leeringly whispered, gazing, I hoped at the fade line that traversed my jockey's, as her brazen hair glinted, fluttering ever so slightly in the breeze.

I felt a warmth of being and smiled back.

"Where are you from?" I asked.

She stopped and pointed above her. The entire sky was a myriad of stars each seemingly winking back as we held our position, floating peacefully above a sleeping world. She paused, touched my shoulder and replied, almost lovingly, "From beyond the beyond."

I looked at her with restrained disbelief and responded firmly, "You've got to be kidding, right?"

"Watch where I'm pointing," she said with a hint of a forced smile. "You see that star?"

I nodded in compliance.

"That's Alpha Centouri and if you take a sharp right and continue past Zeta Reticuli to a distance of ninety-nine light years, you'll reach a quasar. Treat this as a four way 'stop' and make a sharp left and continue another ninety-nine light years. Here you'll find a galactic stop over, what you on earth refer to as a 'greasy spoon.'" Before I could find any words, she continued. "Its open twenty-four hours a day, three-hundred, sixty-five days a year, but you have to time your arrival because its orbits a white dwarf and based on Bode's law and Keppler's third law, its closed half the day and not quite half the year."

This was now getting a little deep, even for me, so I interrupted sarcastically, "So I suppose I have to order something right?"

"Yes, how did you know? My suggestion is the 'Orion's belt.' It really packs a belt, ah, I mean a wallop," She replied, giggling incessantly.

I closed my eyes and thought, "Christ, belt," my mind darting back to France and the epitome of terrestrial greasy spoon where I managed to make contact with an alien invader of the E-coli sect.

I started to feel a bit queasy and with an almost condescending come back, snapped, "Okay, I order the bloody Orion's whatchamacallit! And then what?"

"You politely excuse yourself, proceed to the repository for human waste, enter, find the third stall from the left, and shut the door. Close your eyes and count to ten. You see, its not really a toilet but a worm hole or entrance into another dimension. The other side of this interstellar septic field is my home. But enough of this, I'm here to enlighten you, teach you and hopefully convince you of the truth!"

Her voice was now poignant, but still comforting.

At that moment, I felt I had a million questions, matching the number of stars that surrounded me like a cosmic astral net. I struggled to find the words, so I continued to listen.

"You see, your world is a dumping zone for all the galactic morons. Replete, to be replenished with the souls of the vanquished!

That profound anecdote prompted me to respond, "Listen lady, just what the hell does that mean?"

"After death, all those who exhibited moronic, dastardly and blatantly inconsistent behavior are reincarnated and placed upon the earth. The only problem, most of these poor souls don't get it right the second time around either."

"Then, is this the truth?" I inquisitively replied.

"No, you must come."

I thought to myself, I wish I had; my balls were really beginning to throb now.

We continued and I noticed what appeared to be mountains hugging the horizon. "Hey," I shouted, "where are we?"

"The Andes," she replied. "This is where you will find the truth. The arcane knowledge, hidden for thousands of years, lost in the epoch…."

"Yeah! Yeah! Yeah1," I interrupted, almost scolding her. "Listen, take me, show me, explain it to me and then whisk me back to my own bed. Okay?

"You see that white Llama! Underneath its back left hoof you'll find it."

As I looked upon the beast of burden, I instinctively turned and noticed she was gone. Damn! Not because I was abandoned thousands of miles from home, but because she was fine and I had this overpowering urge to do her. As my sexual thermometer dipped, I thought "Great! What the hell am I going to do? Ride this bloody thing back to England?"

It suddenly moved and as my feet touched ground, a matchbox appeared. It had been secluded underneath where the animal once stood. I reached down and opened it. I found a neatly scrolled piece of paper. As I unwrapped it, there appeared only to be one word. "Nascar."

"Yeah and I'm Richard Petty." I rubbed my eyes and refocused. "Nazca."

I thought where the hell is Nazca? And, as I scratched my head, I turned the piece of paper over. There was an arrow pointing down with the instructions to construct from the many stones that were strewn everywhere the word, "seeker." Upon completing the task, I sat down and waited, and waited, and waited some more. I was just going to start, and hopefully complete this time, what I had originally started before being so rudely removed from my bed. A man appeared. He was tall, blonde, very Nordic in appearance, wearing only a long white robe. "No way, this couldn't be the same dude that appeared on that horse in the hallway."

He looked disgruntled and in a mocking voice, began to ridicule me.

"We would have been here sooner, but you blocked our landing strip with all those big stones! Now follow me. Hurry! We have very little time."

As I entered the spacecraft, I heard the all too familiar sound of giggling. "All right then, boy!" Christ, Cornish was the universal language of the heavens. I turned and there was Steve, standing side by side with Fluff.

"What the hell are you guys doing here?" I exclaimed, almost overcome with emotion.

"I don't know," Fluff responded, "It's your fucking dream!"

Steve, bordering on incoherence as usual, laughed, stringing together the best he could, an explanation.

"It was great, just great, simply marvelous, it was. You see, we were abducted against our wills, we were," and as he paused, grabbed his posterior, "but it doesn't hurt any more, no, not at all really."

"What?" I blurted out in a very perplexed, yet still somewhat euphoric voice.

"Yeah man, we were probed, you know, anally probed, and then forced, well I wasn't, to have sex with these Venutian women and what tarts they were. I mean they left nothin' to the imagination. I've never been gobbled like that before mate."

Fluff finished what Steve had started. "Ian, it was simply great. Each alien had three tits, each with 2 nips. It was like, wow man, simply heaven!"

"Fluff, in a sense you were. I think I found the answer!"

"What do you mean?" Fluff stated in an almost anticlimactic monotonic voice.

Before I could answer, everything suddenly stopped, frozen in time. There was a sense of foreboding as I pulled away without control, being drawn back through a tunnel of swirling light.

"Ian! Ian! Hey man! Are you okay?"

I looked up, rubbed my eyes, as Clive smiled back. "Rough night, eh?"

I closed my eyes, squinted and opened them again, just as he handed me a mug of hot tea.

I've never been one to star gaze, unless of course it involved drooling at the sight of a starlet in skimpy attire. Okay, most of these starlets were aiming for the stars, hoping to be "B" movie fox femme fatales, flaunting what, by the grace of God, or by a good surgeon, they were given. These photo shots, or money shots, spread eagle, appeared on the back pages, or for that matter, every page before the back page. Vamps that vamped, scenes between the scenes when large green elongated vegetables and table legs were the only props required. Even though dumbfounded, and like a survivor, post fit, the drool was the lube that initiated the dream, fantasizing about a future where a camera or director's chair would be the only props I would need.

Excuse me; in all honesty, most New Age hippies loved the idea of actually stargazing. Most of which was achieved flat on their backs, looking through stars to see other stars. This in truth was not a Newtonian experiment involving mapping distance between the constellations to determine galactic gravitational pull, but the result of the individual not being able to stand without assistance. The precursor being the affinity between the now supine participant and the joint that still burned between the catatonic clutches of a chiseled smile.

Astrology, or the discourse between man and the heavens or in our case, the discord between hippies and the uncertainty that loomed involving the reality of the next meal, played a role in the everyday lives of many. The daily horoscope programmed the routine of the bored housewife, the disillusioned secretary, the challenged teacher, and the badgered waitress. I'm sorry, I was beginning to stereotype the many people who would actually scramble to find solace or redemption before finishing their first cigarette and their last cup of morning java. It's no coincidence that most of these practitioners of non-pragmatic planetary propaganda provided by a framework of theoretical non-observational assumptions, to in effect, program a daily routine, ripe with a preordained approach, were women!

Well, what about chance? Well, for us, there was absolutely no chance that this dogmatic diction could effectuate change. This was due to two reasons:

1. Most newspapers hanging around our digs were the results of discarded, grease soaked wrappers from the local fish and chippy.
2. If by chance, a current paper was available, by the time we answered reveille, the day for the most part had already passed us by.

However, if introduced as informal chit-chat, it was usually worked into the parley by a stunning chic wearing a long Indian sarong or spring dress with roses in her hair, a daisy necklace and the smell of colitas rising up through her. You get the picture. The only thing on our minds was not what the heavens had conveniently mapped, but what our second brains had already decided. When it came to the possibility of sex, nothing was etched in stone. Everything was subject to change including not only the fate of the individual in question, but the fate of nations as well. I mean, she could have announced the imminent arrival of a large cache, like Captain Kidd's treasure trove, complete with an armored car full of gold bullion and we would have remained poised, not for instant wealth, but for the other booty, if you know what I mean.

Talking about destiny, fate and the future…who cares! In the big picture, everything had already been decided. We were all doomed. It was for many hippies, the end times, at least according to every soothsayer we had been introduced to. There was no reason to move on. So why not avoid everything including work and take each day one at a time. For billions of years the laws of nature specifically gravity, have governed the behavior of the heavens including that of our own planet. The earth possessed a tight spiral or elliptical orbit around the sun, being ever so careful not to run interference by ramming into its neighbors. Each celestial body tended to mind its own business, except maybe the occasional comet and those nasty little asteroids. Put it this way, there was more of a chance that our future could be determined by one of our own solar system rogues rather than by the planets, and how they decide to align, relative to our sun and us. Just ask T-Rex, the dinosaur, not Marc Bolan the magician, oops, I mean musician.

Scrying, I know I'd be cryin' looking at the future through a mirror presented by most clairvoyants. It wasn't a pleasant thought, whether looking at yourself or pondering the years that lay ahead, especially when relating it to what others had seen and recorded.

Nostradamus had a unique ritual that incorporated the placement of a lit candle next to a bowl of water. He would stare at the water's surface and record what he saw as quatrains. These visions were highlighted by poetic verse, double-entendre and twists and turns; reminiscent of a python shedding it's skin. I'm not implying that he was a snake, or even a snake oil salesman, but my God, the quandaries that he created through his riddles allowed truth and supposition to squirm somewhere between fact and fiction. This experience, though trance like, obviously suppressed the conscious state, inducing a subconscious response. I've always wondered what would have happened if unforeseen forces such as poltergeists or a stranded spirit had decided to play God by introducing just enough havoc to disrupt the process. You know, like shaking the bowl, or forcing a fly to make an emergency landing right smack into the middle of a vision. This could account for some of those strange references to beasts from the sky and destruction on a massive scale. However, the most poignant misgiving I have is the fact that Nostradamus was French. I've never seen a Frenchman biting his tongue, though on several occasions I have witnessed many a frog tripping over theirs. I find it a distinct possibility that he may have, in addition to sipping from his bottomless carafe, inadvertently bummed out on a variation of ergot of rye. Lets not forget this man was a physician first and foremost. It's not a stretch to envision him understanding the dynamics of lysergic acid and its relationship to mind expansion. Don't' you think this might account for that rather free flow tabloid style of thought, utilizing just enough mumbo jumbo to tax the spirit.

From back to marble, the walls will be converted.
Seven and fifty peaceful years.
Joy to mankind, the aqueduct renewed.
Health, abundant fruits, joy and honey making time.

Quatrain 10:89

Just what the fuck does all that mean? All he had to do, assuming he could actually do it, was explain what he saw as simply and concisely as possible. No beating around the bush, involving a nursery of rhyme, or crime, where twenty different interpretations involve one single line. Hey, Nostra-damn-us to hell, just tell us, the wherefores of how, when, where and why, the fucking world is going to end! Not that it's going to make a whole heck of a lot of difference in how we live our lives. If the world is doomed, then why protest? Why be concerned about the environment, civil rights, and global peace? Is there a real possibility we can change the future?

I found it strange that the great predictors always cling to the vines with a safety net strung between. Think about it! These people play it very safe. Why? Because it was and still is, their bloody livelihood. If they prove wrong, then people like the hippies will stop reading their books or on a broader scale, simply stop paying attention. So it's simple. They build in a fail-safe system. If everyone concentrates, prays or meditates together, then maybe, based on the harmonious vibes bathing the collective web, the future and all its doom and gloom can be changed? Simple, yes! But, if you think about it, brilliant! This brings to mind certain issues involving time and the consequences involving time manipulation or time travel.

1. The Time Paradox—I could see myself traveling back in time to Northern Ireland before I was conceived; killing my father for sending me to boarding school only to find out that the rumors about the milk man were indeed true.
2. Unraveling History's Mysteries—If I could go back and had only one trip involving time displacement and not acid, I would place myself in Dallas, November 22, 1963, on the sixth floor of the book depository building. If my hunch were true, it would prove once and for all that Lee Harvey Oswald was indeed the lone gunman. It would also prove that his was a pathetic shot, since he was actually aiming at Governor Connelly and not in the wrong place and the wrong time, President Kennedy.
3. Shades of Armageddon—I don't doubt John the Revelator moved through time. But, did it ever occur to all those *Bible* thumping fanatics that he might have landed just short of his ultimate destination, placing him unfortunately right smack in the middle of a Black Sabbath concert. If you think about it, his experience alone would account for the four horsemen, the loud trumpets, the tribulation and the final vision of hell.

I think most people do have some sort of ability to utilize the extra senses. Whether this is validation that some type of fundamental connection between the elementary particle theory and the way some people sense or actually perceive events, either in the present or future is debatable. Vibes or feelings relating to the subconscious or it intersecting with others, or situations as they unfold, have fascinated hippies since the subculture decided to forego all other means of entertainment with the exception of recreational drug use and meditation of course.

I do confess, even I have achieved some sort of third eye opening when dealing with prophecy. It was the summer of '69 and I was walking innocently along the banks of the Cuyahoga River just outside of Cleveland, when without warning, boom! The river spontaneously combusted, the flames were intense, holding my attention long enough to lap and burn forever a horrifying glimpse of the future. It gnawed at my soul from which I visualized an eco-disaster, where our biosphere cursed by giaia, became a mutated mesh of crab grass and cockroaches, forcing even the rats to scurry in disarray, beholden only to the chemical abyss. Oh, I wept and wept, not because I succumbed to the emotion, but from all that damn ash and soot. Upon reflection, my personal quatrain became a one liner.

Christ, I wish I hadn't thrown the last remnants of that
smoldering joint into the river!!

Hanging around a bunch of freaks had its advantages. The more people you interacted with the better insight you possessed when it came to understanding the truly bizarre and strange. The mainstream, whether a lifestyle or a mode by which the subjects viewed life, didn't offer a broad enough panoramic vista, visevis, the important issues; especially the uncertainty clouding the future. Hence, the New Age fascination with the prophets; however, from *Daniel* to the *Book of Revelations* to *Nostradamus,* the writings are smothered with both ambiguity and cryptic messages, more often than not, conveniently applied not as a cryptogram but an actual explanation for events. Unfortunately, in many cases, after they had already occurred.

Even the Mayan calendar ending December 22, 2012, didn't foster undue panic among the hippie ranks, I guess the guise presented by drugs, helped mask the pain associated with this eventuality, which eerily coincided with hippie retirement. This simply meant that a majority of non-working, longhaired dropouts would be of legal age to receive social security, or an old age pension, when their world actually ended. This was another reason to forego the plowshare, anvil and hammer and the donning of a hard hat. Now each and every participant had an excuse to party hearty for at least the next forty years or so. Maybe the Mayans who mysteriously disappeared as a viable civilization simply got pissed off with their general state of affairs. You know, high crime, recession, pollution, too many people and not enough resources, always being at war and a government out of control. This may have been enough to force the young to flee in disgust toward a simpler less stressful existence deep within the friendly clutches of the jungle. With no one around to pick up the hammer and chisel, the calendar was never finished.

Edgar Cayce, in addition to being considered the father of Holistic medicine, was also a pretty damn good psychic. At least he refrained, for the most part in the copious over-use of double-entendre, blather and poetic jabberwocky. He did most of his predicting from a self-imposed deep sleep, where he would vocalize his visions in a slow monotonic voice. I've actually attained a similar state of mind. However, according to witnesses, my concoction of foresightedness often exhibited a cognitive recollection of events that for the most part had already taken place. This rigmarole I attested was not of happenings in real time or for that matter our time, but a brief glimpse of events in a parallel time.

The thing that impressed hippies about Cayce, in addition to his bleak rendition of earth changes, even though it placed much of their current habitat under water, was his uncanny and unconventional look at history. Like Blavatsky, he saw projections, which included the ancient but lost civilizations of Atlantis and Lemuria. Unlike Blavatsky, instead of over gorging on pastries, rather than idioms, he preferred to overdose on catching forty winks, which proved over the long haul, to be far less of a health hazard.

He paved a connection between Atlantis and Egypt, pushing back the construction of the Great Pyramid to almost 10,500 BC. Here on the Giza plateau he envisioned the Great Hall of Records, buried somewhere near this Sphinx. This storehouse of knowledge if we can find it, will provide answers to all our questions concerning creation, life, and the cosmos, God and why we are here. Well, that's only five questions, but I'm sure, based on this assumption, it will ultimately answer all our questions. So someone with access to a paper mill and a gross of pencils better start jotting them down. I don't know about you, but heaven forbid if we accidentally exclude any, like why do plagues mysteriously appear (usually during any apex of fun, where debauchery and carnage rule the moment)? Or, why do flukes, tapeworms and other disgusting parasites infest hippies' lives after simple pilgrimages to the sacred lands in search of the truth? I guess we'll just have to hope that when we discover by fluke, this library of knowledge, all are not barred simply because they don't have the right library card.

Where did these great civilizations disappear? Was it the result of cataclysmic consequence, or simply an explanation that can be pieced from clues plucked from close scrutiny when dissecting ancient manuscripts?

I wonder if Atlas had anything to do with the disappearance of Atlantis? Having to hold up the entire planet on his shoulders no doubt prompted in addition to severe lower back pain, irresistible hunger as well. I can see this ghoulish titan, twitching as he placed the globe atop the back of a large elephant. "Hmmm, Should I?" Thinking aloud, but being careful not to displace the waters at Delphi. The premeditated act soon to follow offered no viable deterrent, thus allowing his irritated neck to sway slightly as he attempted to rid eons of cramping. It's not hard to visualize the quick movement of the orb toward his now unbarred gaping oral cavity. Crunch! The removal in one large bite, the area that once proudly flew the colors of Atlantis. I'm sure he then proceeded to wash down the continent with the equivalent of all the known world's reserves of wine, which assuredly forced slumber. Slightly less than twenty-four hours later, Mt. Olympus time, he squatted, grimaced, dumping a load or should I say, giving birth to a nation, remarkably similar in size and shape to the country we now know as France.

I'm sure Zeus was pretty lenient, taking into consideration his centuries of loyal service by banishing the lug to the extreme fringes of the universe, where his new job pitted his strength against the ever expanding cosmos. You know something, this would lend credence to those eight pairs of Hindu elephants being chosen and trained to take his place.

The Outer Limits: Stone and the Unknown

The Outer Limits

Music is the vibration that moves to extol.
Music is the universe in tune with the soul.

Inspired by:

Space Truckin'
Deep Purple

If the universe was created by a burst of energy and the law of conservation of energy is true, then the lifeblood or marrow, which is the universe, is essentially energy. If all that flourishes within, from the sub-atomic particle to the nuclear blast furnaces that are the stars, then surely every thing that falls between is also of substance, being that of pure energy. Then the lay lines or earth chaktras may be the earth's nervous system, where pulses of electromagnetic energy keep the planet alive by regulating the system.

The Chinese referred to the natural energy of the universe as Chi. This energy is really spiritual or supernatural and permeates all that is. Using this energy to heal, elevate the state of consciousness, or attract from beyond are quintessential for the belief of not just hippies, but other practitioners of the New Age Movement. The ultimate experience, regardless of drug ingestion, to promote the senses, was for a hippie to reach sexual nirvana through copulation by placing the symbolic sacrifice on the alter designated by the lay line. So with the backdrop being

Stonehenge, rather the Giza plateau (the sand was literally a pain in the ass), getting laid on a lay line was the ultimate trip.

It's interesting that other paranormal experiences are often associated with these earth bound centers of energy. Like a beacon, it was not uncommon to see strange lights abound, scampering between celestial bodies, seemingly under intelligent control, wink back.

Some ufologists have suggested that this phenomenon, which gained international exposure in 1947 with Ken Arnold's famous, flying disc encounters, coincided with the detonation of atomic weapons and the beginning of the Cold War.

Looking at it from another angle, just maybe they were attracted and further fascinated by the advent of the beat movement. You never know; this platform and the hippie juggernaut that followed could have offered a refreshing change to the natural laws that govern the universe. Bingo, Bongo! An age where the tempo changed, highlighted by a sound that plastered space, creating an echo, which drew these extraterrestrials to the source. An era where fun, music and escapism stimulated the minds and senses of an advanced civilization, which over time, had either never experienced its recoil, or if it had, had forgotten.

Stone and the Unknown

Beyond the Pillars of Hercules, before our time ensued,
stood in calm a place undaunted by the seas.
The power of the ages, challenged by nature's wrath,
spilled vengeance chopping them to their knees.

Inspired by:

Those Were the Days
Cream

Before Clive expanded my visionary horizons, the book that stirred my slow awakening was Erich Von Daniken's *Chariots of the Gods*! His theories, later coupled and reinforced with the likes of Robert Charroux, proposed that our dark past was really an attempt by historians and archaeologists to cover up and bury the past or prop-up the status quo, by using, or in this case, not using anything out of the ordinary to shed light with the idea of illuminating the truth. Primo history borrowed from theosophy, the idea that a series of civilizations, existed before the cradle had a chance to rock. These blue prints for man had a charismatic power, influenced by the Midas touch, a four fingered imprint that boasted of extraterrestrial intervention. The evidence purported and stung the imagination in photographs and drawings where spacecraft and inhabitants issued a mandate, allowing a newer age for infusion. Now, one large step for mankind became a quantum leap of both faith and the mysteries housed within the texts that drew quarters on the shelves next to the likes of Blavatsky and Bailey.

The idea that Atlantis and Lemuria flourished thousands of

years ago was more than Plato weathering a near death experience after sampling from Socrates cup, or Blavatsky suffering from delirium, praying to the porcelain god while retching in agony from a severe bout of botulism.

Hippies in general, viewed the traditional narrow minded and mind you, rather boring history lesson involving the now abandoned cradle, as being more of an aftermath to what really happened.

The great pyramid at Giza seemed to be the focal point of not only energy and enlightenment to the average hippie, but also evidence that it was conceived, constructed and conceded by a greater power. The first thing I noticed when introduced to the concept of "Pyramid Power," was not their staying power, but that their mystique had become an over commercialized by product, created by a Nouveau capitalistic venture put forth by either ex-hippie converts or better yet, New Age entrepreneurs. These connivers had saturated every possible avenue including the backsides of cereal boxes in a desperate scam to flog their wares, which in truth were just a simple variation of the box kite.

It was Clive who galvanized my quickly evolving sense of the strange and bizarre. Cayce was right. There existed a great library where the arcane truth, including the ancient manuscript of the 7 Rays and the elder races were securely kept. However, it was not buried under or near the sphinx, but existed right here in Clive's bedroom! I'm certain, if all his books, magazines, articles, scrolls, papyrus rolls, stone tablets, miscellaneous tablets, excluding paracetamol and parchments were categorized and alphabetized, it would dwarf even the once great library at Alexandria. What a haul! In order to read just the books beginning with A and ending with C, I would have to change my original thought concerning reincarnation, that coming back as a garden slug and opt instead to re-manifest as a book worm!

While submerging myself in paperwork concerning the pyramids, I couldn't understand why there was a copious over-use of name associated with one, albeit, titanic, ops! Better play it safe. I don't want the damn thing sinking into the sand. Ah, whopping, I'm reasonably sure the Italians won't get the pun, immense structure. The list included the Great Pyramid, The Great Pyramid at Giza, The Pyramid of Cheops or Khufu's Pyramid. Hey, if they couldn't even decide whom the colossal monument belonged to, it's a lot easier to fathom why all those so-called archeological pundits couldn't figure out how and why it was built in the first place.

If there is a link to Atlantis or some extraterrestrial encounter, then maybe the notion of an energy capacitor or reservoir, capable of opening the space time continuum ala, Christ, I better watch it. I don't want to offend any Moslems either. Now where was I, oh yes, a type of star gate—could the sarcophagus really be a tele transporter or even a time machine?

New Agers, especially the hippies, loved to theorize about questions like this, making it decent discourse between those desperately attempting to avoid everyday issues, like whether it was actually Monday and not Sunday since Saturday's status remained a mystery. Of course the notion of time and where does it go, remained a distant topic for discussion as soon as all the participants forgot what the original topic for debate was. This coincidently surfaced just about the same time the second tea break occurred. I often thought, I wish I could use the sarcophagus to move back through the sands of time. I'm sure the gang and I would find, in addition to the ungodly temperatures, a slew of engineers scratching their heads, not because they were lost or confused about the entire undertaking, but because all those bloody sand gnats and fleas were driving them insane!

The problem to us and any other longhaired freaks, wasn't moving the large blocks of limestone from point 'A' to point 'B', but doing the job as easily as possible. Any hippie believed that the total energy expended in any activity including all those that were considered sedentary by nature, had to be less when converted to calories than the total caloric intake of the previous week. Since our food pyramid consisted of brown rice, lentils and dustbin fodder, it was easy to conclude that the "weakly" intake, being slightly less than twelve hundred calories, would allow for us to simply point and offer direction versus actually participating in any physical activity. So let's assume the same situation befell the Egyptians including the slave labor work force. If it were up to us then how would the Great Mysterious Pyramid at Giza have been constructed? Easy, for crying out loud, the plateau is located right smack in the middle of the largest sand box in the world! The main constituent of even primitive cement, sand of course! So you build the bloody forms, mold the blocks and after, let's say a few years including reasonable breaks for brown rice and lentils, viola, a Great Pyramid!

Now, if the Egyptians were anything like us, the reason for the pyramid is quite clear. It's simply a focal point for energy where it can be focused on the individual. If directed at the participant using the right dose for the prescribed amount of time, then maybe the level of consciousness can be raised, achieving a state of euphoria, very similar in principle, to getting 'high.' This idea was probably lost after, let's say, those silly Atlantians brought with them, not only the psychedelic drugs from the Amazon, but the coca leaves from Columbia and Cannabis from the Yucatan. Here's a thought, I wonder how much the experience would be enhanced if you smoked a bowl and then entered the sarcophagus? In retrospect, if the early Egyptians had done this, they certainly would have never found the energy or time to construct anything resembling a pyramid again, probably opting instead to roam the desert, searching for the Atlantians, carrying only tents, which were a hell-of-a-lot easier to assemble, even when stoned.

The Druids, who originally emerged from ancient Celtic tribes, cohabitated with nature and conjured through spirit, a life force that transpired from the tides of the sea, the light of the sun, the wind in the Oak and the cry of the deer. In many ways, the hippie, besides resembling the stereotypical Druid priest, with long flowing locks and loose attire, adhered to this same basic philosophy. It's unfortunate that in Britain most of the deer and a great many of the Oak were huddled together in relative obscurity, either within the imposing walls of large private estates or small, rather well guarded and for the most part, non user friendly, especially to the hippies, animal parks. However, there existed a place for both aspired Druid and inspired hippie where each could share the experience of tapping the mother lode of folklore and the sacred template of the past, Stonehenge. The horseshoe configuration opened up in the direction of the midsummer sunrise, the traditional summer solstice in June. This became the magnet that drew the throngs and the Stonehenge people's free festival became the piper that played, keeping all in tune with the vibration that flowed under, over and between the giant trilithons. This sparked the coming together of souls where crystal signaled the connections between all that congregated between the pillars of forever.

Stoned Henge

The pillars of strength did reap,
passion to explore, an age when man suffered,
just to live.

Inspired by:

Solsbury Hill
Peter Gabriel

The aroma was pungent, stingingly magic, as the smoke drifted in harmony with the breeze. As though driven by the hand of the necromancer, it danced to the beat of the distant drum. It involved everything and everyone, all oblivious to its presence. The spicy seasoned allure, an inner atmosphere of pleasure had drugged the mindset of the horde, which rippled to its intoxicating sway as fires burned, a trick of light, as time seemingly stood still. The dark silhouette of the massive stones, beckoned the crowd, a celebration of life, as vibrations from the past teased the frenzy. They stood poised, erect and carried the power of an age where man and nature together, worshipped the holy ground where they stood. I was in awe, star struck, as the night sky paid homage, the heavens, a concert of flickering lighters, begging for more. The sight was unbelievable as hippies like gypsies, their station, Stone-Henge, captivated the mood, allowing all to synchronize thought and the connection.

Jim had disappeared, I knew where, and the idea of women, at least for the moment, seemed anticlimactic. As I sat transfixed, a round stone my seat, the cold and damp seeped to peep as though moving up my jeans to gain a better vantage point. I didn't need to roll a joint, so I put away both the stash and papers that Jim had so thoughtfully left in my care.

The hoot that was the moment, as the music and laughter thrilled also stood above me, though hanging upside down from its perch.

"Who, whoo, what, where the hell am I?"

I concluded was a hippie, rather than the owl as he slipped or keeled over, keeping with the current trend I had witnessed since sitting.

Maybe the power contained within the circle of stone, reached out to gently force those that were too high, to marry the ground until the honeymoon was over.

Jim returned, alas with lass or more correctly two.

"Hey kid, looky here, the blonde's mine!"

"Yeah, what ever! I struggled to comprehend, knowing if I didn't purge my indifference, this chance encounter would probably be lost until at least the following weekend.

"This here is Monica and her mate is Di. That crazy fucker is Ian."

"Hey girls," I replied with the enthusiasm of someone who had just banged an entire harem and now was looking for a one-man tent to sleep it off.

Of course it didn't help that Jim had started this trip, impromptu, as the sun dipped, making this cross country gallop in hyper drive, forgetting that we had both forsaken the necessities of sleep and the need to eat by partying the night before. It was his uncanny ability to bury the night, allowing two separate days to merge that amazed me. The only problem, my personal biorhythms were set to a different clock, which was slowly running out of time.

I watched intently as he maneuvered between the two, assuming the biblical position, arms outstretched as though crucified. But only his hands weren't nailed, but I knew deep down inside that one or both of these unsuspecting wenches soon would be.

For the moment I didn't care. The energy of the hour had eclipsed any desire I possessed to whip into passion, the meeting of skin on skin. There was something so special about this encounter as I lay back, my hair created a nest protecting my head. I was tired, but it was the tingling from the ground that stimulated my eyes to close. I was carried upon the wings, not from the owl, which signaled my retreat, but the canopy, which cradled my feet. I was going home where everything was complete.

Hippies didn't seem to be concerned about who and why, concerning the building and significance of Stonehenge. It swayed us not whether the stones were dragged hundreds of miles from Wales or levitated and moved using the power of the lay lines. The closest thing I ever experienced Stateside in terms of mystery associated with how, rather than any ancient pithy epiphany was the Coral Castle in Florida. Legend purported that one man built this lair of secrecy as a memorial to a woman who jilted him in love. Here even rational observation would attest that due to the immense size of the stones, many blocks weighing over twenty-five tons that some mysterious power akin to the forces used by the ancients to build the great pyramid and Stonehenge, were employed in the construction. It didn't matter whether he imported Cornish pixies or seduced fairies from Key West to build it, like other sacred or ancient enigmas, it was the power or energy that emanated from within that captivated the New-Age converts.

There was a commonality or common denominator that infested many of these ancient sites. They seemed to be hot beds for UFO activity. The idea that the Atlantians and Lemurians remained or are watching us with interest seemed a stretch since I'm sure that those who survived probably reached a pure state and were able to, at least according to people like Blavatsky, phase shift and move beyond onto a more fertile spiritual plane. Even though a vibration away, would they want to return and observe us? It would probably sicken them to see that by allowing technology to outstrip our emotional intellectual abilities, we have as a race, become desensitized and remain spiritually anemic. Therefore, unable to uplift in terms of enlightenment, we have become psychically dysfunctional, unable to harness the state of consciousness whereby to improve our standing as a people. Consequently, our primitive urges, controlled by greed and lust float our continued quest to ferment hate and a willingness to wage war.

Well, that was easy. I've successfully taken the mindset back to 1947 and the advent of the Atomic age and what was historically speaking, the dawn of saucer mania! Hippies like myself could either dig deeper, using the New-Age preoccupation with detail when dealing with the unexplained or sit down with Clive, indulge a chillum and wait until he offered to take those present once again, into his confidence by escorting all through the vastness of the dome of the tome where hard copy, soft copy, paper back and books with no backs, formed the canopy which became my storehouse of knowledge.

My first exposure to the UFO phenomena occurred well before the midnight serenade where Cing wanked—excuse me, whisked me off to a fancy-free fling involving a magic carpet ride or close encounter of the astral kind. Between the slipper fights and later toke sessions, I actually spent a few moments while shackled to "higher education," reading in the school library. I became infatuated with "project blue book" and the U.S. government's marvelous attempt to shadow and eventually hide, by disinformation, their study involving UFO's

Swamp gas, refracted or reflected light, birds, meteorites, top secret black projects, it didn't really matter. If you were close to and accepted as a result, the so-called expert's explanation, the mind precluded all other possibilities, leaving little to the imagination. It's fortunate as those who dared to challenge, included both the New Age explorers and hippies alike. The mind, a microcosm of the universe, is boundless in its ability to venture forth, expanding, ever scanning, and forever questioning the scope and validity of the spirit through imagination.

If our puny section of the cosmos, as religious zealous attest, is young and immature, being only 6,000 years old or as science dictates, six billion years old, then to preserve the integrity for both purists and highbrow, one has to only merge the two, therefore leveling the playing field. So, with our solar system and planets celebrating well over 5.9 billion candles, then surely life somewhere in the evermore that agars deep the agenda where the agent by suggestion, aggregated life, an ageless and hence, more advanced intelligence, surely exists.

If by worm holes, star gate, pyramids or even inter-dimensional transference, by chance or perhaps design, someone from somewhere, has visited this beautiful,—well it was, until touched by the hands of men; but if viewed from afar, still manages to maintain its innocence, - planet.

One can examine all the archaeological propaganda seeing what they want to see or seek the truth from the testament, spoken by those who believe. The Dogan, an ancient, isolated tribe, found untainted by added dogma, have for centuries worshipped the Sirius binary system where from the belt of Orion, it is said our ancestors arrived to spiritually awaken and as some believe even re-create the manner of men.

If love makes the world go round, then sex fuels the ever-expanding universe. In the *Bible,* Genesis speaks of the Nephilium, the watchers or those who came down, were the extraterrestrials who actually "got it on" with the first of the naïve, those swayed by false promises, glitzy cosmic attire and flashy spacecraft. It also didn't hurt that these carpetbaggers came here to capitalize in the first documented gold rush, by flaunting for all to see, especially the women, the wares of their trade.

So the first universal law was passed and then passed onto man, to be examined and ratified, the decreed as statue before it could be stamped and initialed as such, "A stiff member hath no conscience." Hence, from the loins, our early visitors who stood twelve feet tall and being anatomically correct came the first interstellar orgies. It featured studs who when not aroused were still able to model for and promote the first commercialized tripods. Many of these early encounters were documented and sold as porn on the back streets and "red candle" districts of Sodom and Gomorrah.

Zechariah Sitchen wrote of the long lost planet, Nibiru, which he postulated orbited our sun in the opposite direction mind you, every 3,600 years or so. The Sumerian culture made reference to its inhabitants, the Anunnaki, genetically manipulating the human race to both help in the mining of gold and also to better serve their personal needs and desires. The Hammurabi code provided an insight into the mind of the ruler who bestowed it upon the empire. Well hung, like the gardens of Babylon, Hammurabi often enjoyed a good piece of ass, - Syrian booty. So, an eye-for-an-eye, a tooth-for-a-tooth and ah… head for about three shekels, eventually forced him, if only to save money, to form his own large, and I mean large harem, which I'm convinced also acted as a small gene pool for his Anunnaki guests.

I'm certain that the "ever horny" Anunnaki entrepreneurs, those left behind to run the resorts and casinos in Atlantis and Lemuria were responsible for the first true abductions.

The 1961 Betty and Barney Hill incident, though probably the most famous, is just one of many classical abduction cases scattered throughout history. I wonder what "Joan of Arc" would have confessed if placed under hypnosis by the English. Instead of being burned at the stake for heresy, she might have been banged in the derriere for being a nymphomaniac.

Whether Raelean or Pleiadian, Zeta, or Beta, Alpha and Omega, the connotation affixing the label as the watchers is probably more accurate than describing them as cheap celestial playboys or gigolos. In all likelihood, those who visited and are by many accounts still visiting, are here to watch, study, examine classify, reclassify and document our ever increasing appetite to wage war against each other, slicing at the same time, portions of our planet to feed the greed of a race intent on both genocide and the systematic murder of the biosphere. Let's hope long-term intervention is part of their prime directive. If not, and we indeed survive, it wouldn't surprise me at all to remain quarantined until collectively we pose no threat to either ourselves or our cosmic neighbors. So old soldiers stop your cryin' and fade away. Drift as the stellar wind, dust on wind, wind to wing, fly captured, forever free.

Hippies viewed space travel as an extreme endeavor. Many believed that the same state in theory, relatively speaking, could be achieved without warping the space time continuum or suffering from time delineation and the rigors of extended periods of suspended animation.

Carl Jung first introduced from his theories involving analytical psychology, the concept of the collective unconscious and the archetypical images that rose through dreams and hallucinations. UFO's were simply manifestations, projected from the power contained within the mind, specifically the collective unconscious.

Terence McKenna, followed in the footsteps of Aldous Huxley, using his brother's Dennis' intuitive theories involving molecular bonding and electron spin resonance. He was convinced that dimethyl—tryptamine (DMT), a powerful hallucinogenic when combined with the power of certain vocal manipulations could summon and create an interface with the memory bank of galactic history. In essence, a simple way for a hippie to leap frog through space and time, meet and interact with various alien life forms, smoke a joint, share a laugh, enquire about the truth and return relatively intact and unscathed to the earth bound mattress, on the earthen floor behind the beads forming the curtain, separating his reality from the rest of the world; an interesting way to explore space without being launched atop a Saturn Five.

Myth or Magic; Witches and Their Niches

Myth and Magic

To see a light through the darkness,
is to see a shadow, cloaked in black.

Inspired by:

After Forever
Black Sabbath

In a sense the "New Age," or era of enlightenment, was a revolution. It spiraled like a waterspout, shedding mounds of information in its wash with droplets once clouded or ignored, as others flowed together after they fell. This era offered a rainbow of choice, a wide spectrum covering with a hue, the investigator or reader, saddling the imagination with a slew of ideas, both reasonable and radical in thought. However, it often brought a storm front, darkened with a depth, a visionary's nightmare, where the uncharted heralded so much bleak with a weight, the albatross being, the dark side. It rallied the witches, the magicians, the researchers and sometimes, the hippies who like a blind dart player could play pin the tail on the Donkey by hopefully facing the correct wall before tossing the dart. Since the affiliation spoke of escapism draped in the cloak of mysticism, it was easy to dabble without any thought of retaliation or ostracism unless of course, one crossed the line tapping the spirit load where unforeseen forces could interplay causing more than simple embarrassment. This was the world of witches and demons, white magic and black masses, the arc of a secular covenant, smeared with the blood of an ancient time where religion zapped the fears of an age, warning all not to trip over the line.

Witches and Their Niches

The wind carries her spirit,
caressing the mood,
as clouds nibble the ebbing nook,
crunching a frightened moon.

Inspired by:

Witchy Woman
The Eagles

If there's one true book that defined both the allure and the power of the unknown and the mysteries associated with it, the *Cabala* stands on a shelf all by itself. At least it did in Clive's parlor. Here it stood so reticent and haughtily aloof, yet reserved at arm's length, waiting patiently to be grabbed by the hand of the inquisitive. The naïve yet lettered scholar, an empty vessel, and subservient only to the intellect. In truth, and probably for the best, it gathered more dust than it did the probing curiosity of both resident and houseguest alike.

Though a new-age magnet, the followers of light including hippies and the like, respected its lore, but amassed instead, just enough insight from other sources. Magazines like *Man, Myth and Magic* and *Fate and Fortune* offered a poor man's rendition and interpretations of the world of occultism, the supernatural and the unexplained.

The *Cabala* influenced the Knight of the Templars, freemasonry, magicians and secret societies. In many ways it became their *Bible,* whereas a microcosm of the universe, it linked man to God. It borrowed from both ancient Egyptian mysteries and the Persian Magi. It was a table without chairs, of destiny where the practitioners were left to stand, pondering, until their legs gave way due to unseen forces.

A "Tree of Life" where knowledge could only be achieved by inching along one branch at a time, all the while hoping it wouldn't snap, hurling the visionary into the abyss of lost souls. Cosmic knowledge, pathways and precursors to different dimensions where the doors were always locked and the keys were never under the mat.

They say many possess hearts of clay, well, the hippies even though exempt from possessing hearts of gold, had hearts that beat to a different drum.

One area of the *Cabala* that fascinated us was the *Book of Creation*. Here tradition boasted that a man made clay figure or Golan, could be brought to life by the recitation of a formula fashioned from the creative powers of numerals and letters. This creature would forever act as a faithful servant to its creator. Oh, the possibilities. Its no accident that many hippies chose the Southwest of England to live since the Cornish "China clay pits" proved to be a favorite stamping ground. Hey, it offered a viable alternative to trouping off to Morocco in the feeble attempt not to score resin, but to barter in bedlam with the local Bedouin over the selling price of a fourteen your old slave girl.

Witches enjoyed a resurrected reprieve, rising from the ashes like a phoenix leaping forth from a cauldron; perking and spewing life back into the ageless practice of coddling with nature. The repealing of the 1951 Witchcraft Act, gave British witches, whether traditional or following the more modern Wiccan philosophy of the Gardnerian or Alexandrian teachings, a chance to exist without fear of reprisal.

Their general feeling against hierarchies allowed the covens to flourish and coexist, but estranged from one another, to remain fervently independent, led by their own high priest and priestess.

Being a religion where the horned god of the forests and

mountains and goddess or earth mother, coexisted, as equals. It was no secret that over time witchcraft evolved, to champion the female aspect.

I remember an early encounter with a Warlock who talked with a lisp and after a long day at the alter, preferred to relax at home in front of the fire, dressed in only bra and panties.

He proclaimed himself a sage, capable if the vibrations were conducive to the foretelling of the future; a clairvoyant who preferred to be called Claire rather than by his Christian name, Ralph. In order to reach an enlightenment state he insisted that his guest bring, in addition to the customary bowl and stash, a can of alphabet vegetable soup, and a bigger bowl with spoon and ladle. After simmering the soup, he would politely take the last toke, returning the smaller bowl, while reaching for the large one. Filling it to the brim, he would sip from alternative spoonfuls, deciphering from every second, the meaning behind its garbled contents. If he was in a rush, for it was rumored he kept as a pet, a goat, which was unfortunately not house broken, he would induce a quickening by use of the ladle. It was thought his banter incorporated various aspects of speaking in "tongues," but after serious debate, it was concluded that he was simply dyslexic.

History had been unkind, especially when dealing with female witches, engendering them with a distain that fueled a fire that burned across much of Europe. It almost single handedly wiped out an entire gender. The aftermath still kindled the kindred and its fever pitch scorched with an ardor, forcing many to keep with the age-old practice of cold isolationism.

I always wondered what would have happened if the National Front, sizzling with its own brand of searing hate for anything that hinted of being different, gained acceptance to eventually hold the administrative reins. I'm sure all those would have been drawn and quartered, diced and minced, pulverized and mixed, and sold as cattle fodder.

Witches and hairies, dykes and fairies
The caldron knew,
Eye of brute, dancing to Pan's flute
Into a frenzy, ready to shoot
For a breakfast of champions it continued to brew
In a world so cold, light as magic, became darkened
For the naked at lunch.

It's amazing what we can accomplish after a couple of double scotches.

It's a little wonder that those who perceived a world blanketed in prejudice draped in hate and so covered by the sins of man they chose to drench their pleasures and feed on the souls of the sacrificed. It was an area that for the most part, warned many a hippie that trespassing could incarcerate the soul, removing the sanctuary of the heart—land, to be forever beholden to the rites of the fallen. If the line was crossed, the err of the experiences, the life blood that kept the hippies free and easy, could suffocate the curious, turning the lights off forever.

Loch Ness was not the morning mist, shrouding the lair where Nessie would occasionally bare a hint of existence; but the castle that walled the other beast. This was the divining rod that drew the dabblers to the waters, which quenched the thirst of the fire that burned within. Aleister Crowley's legacy still tills the soils and his spirit filled the air with a presence that dwarfed the Loch. New-Agers all, didn't seem to care. This and other temptations, kept the dark side and its flair, dimly lit, just enough to offer a scare.

Witch Way to the Car?

She rules the eventide, separated by light,
the fire burns the darkness, to singe the lust,
as she tramps underfoot, cries rape the roused dust.

Inspired by:

The March of the Black Queen
Queen

The car, borrowed from Roy, followed the command of the road. The cat's eyes that weaved with it signaled the jalopy, hoping to force Jim's hand, which teased his feet. As it zigzagged between menacing thicket, the hedgerows bowed in awe as his feet fought back, making his hand work harder to still navigate with ease, each and every curve.

I turned to watch the last lights flicker as though extinguished, one by one, only to wink; as the ink of the matte rose to meet the black night. It sandwiched all, and though the moon was full, the clouds seemed to push it away from the loathing black hole that once captured the imagination of the now consumed village.

Stonehenge was gone as well, but the tingling still made me think and pay homage to an experience that electrified the passion, I now realized was more than a simple folklore.

Jim leaned over and chiseled away at the silence by first humming and then strumming with the other hand, the keys, which he bounced effortlessly.

I turned my eyes, being careful not to dislodge my head, for fear that if the last pint had indeed been his limit, his foot might deceive even his concentration, forcing the car down the escarpment that suddenly appeared to my left.

"I know that bloody lane is around here somewhere. Christ, I wish I hadn't lost the directions!!"

I knew better, and still looking out my window, angled my eyes down, giving the impression that we were contradicting Newtonian law. As I pulled myself back with the G forces needed, I turned to him and teased back.

"You didn't lose it, it was on that piece of paper you gave those chics."

I smiled to my self as my voice began to question the wisdom of his act. "Come on Jim, do you really think two chics who live in Carlisle are really going to make the effort to call us?"

"Hey, you never know, oh, hold on, there it is, see the church. I'm sure we turn there, yeah, right there!"

As the car slowed, he tapped both his hands on the steering wheel as though copying a drum roll, announcing our arrival.

The car was now motionless, but the dull pounding of the lifters, hitting the engine cover, superceded his drum solo, eclipsing even the tingling that spiraled my head, giving way to an uncontrollable urge to grit my teeth.

I forced my next response, sounding a bit antagonistic, but still inquisitive enough not to isolate him. "I hope this side trip is worth it?"

"Oh, it'll be worth it all right. Come on, cheer up, and think about it." By this time he was leaning over me giving the impression to anyone who might be cavorting between the headstones that he was just about to go down on me.

"I'm telling you, you can't beat a good ole fashioned, out in the woods, back to nature," he paused and simpered a grin that almost sliced his face, "orgy!"

He punched my softly and continued, "I'm going to park the car down the lane a bit, and then we'll hoof it the rest of the way, okay?"

The dead space that was, now rose to the occasion, giving

wing to my loon's that accepted without reservation, the invitation to join the party that had just erupted in my pants. This serpentine intrusion was the crotchety act that doddered my entire body. A change I felt tapping the energy I had borrowed from the capacitors that shaped Salisbury Plain. I was now in the mood to get laid.

He pulled the car into an opening that housed a gate, which by the look of it, had been scraped numerous times by cars no doubt, doing the same thing we were doing.

Before I could wake my legs, he was already out of the car and politely opening my door as though I was for the moment, a foreign dignitary.

"Now be quiet and follow me and be…" Before he could finish, I had already made the acquaintance, being introduced as I slipped to the now cold pile of sludge that pot marked the lane. I felt the wet mark its territory, not just on my rear, but half way up my back as well. One would have thought that a large herd of dairy cattle would have dispersed their wares, equally, while working their way down the road. But as luck would have it or I should say, bad luck being the prime focus of my existence, these fifty or so, decided to leave for posterity's sake, enough in one spot to mark forever my posterior and the rest of me too, creating a Golan, or better yet, England's only Mudman.

Jim laughed and offered encouragement by saying, "No need to worry mate, you're not going to be wearing your clothes much longer anyway. Come on, you can rinse them in the stream, or better yet, of what I'm sure is going to be many a babe, one will feel sorry enough and beat your clothes against the rocks while you sleep."

I had to laugh, catching a whiff as I scurried to follow. All of a sudden, I didn't care.

Like a pathfinder, Jim split the darkness and as he jockeyed with the night, managed to forge ahead with me in tow. I couldn't see a damn thing, but Jim's nocturnal instinct, like a compass, kept pace with the last cloud, which seemingly fell prey to the jagged edge, provided by an irregular dome, fastened to the larger wooden trunks that stood at attention as we passed.

Jim inexplicitly stopped and turned, offering only an eerie representation of a hooded reaper. He quickly moved his right index finger to his lips, "Sssh! Can you hear it?" his muffled voice was about as dim as the scene itself.

I focused my hearing, trying to eliminate all remnants of existence, including the rapid pasting my heart was inflicting against my chest wall; and there it was, voices.

"Come on then," he whispered again. "Follow me." Jim continued as a seeing eye dog, almost panting as his gait quickened. I followed, thinking it might have proved better in the dark if he had fallen instead of me. At least I could follow the scent.

Beyond the large border of Rhododendron bushes, which were more like trees, a large fire shimmered. Its flames danced toward the sky, taking with it, embers that escaped to remain suspended just above the angry clutches of its white-hot tentacles. Around it appeared people, mostly in undress, rhythmically moving, clockwise, with their arms raised to silhouette the backdrop.

At first they ignored us, allowing the ash, like a canine, to sniff, touching both my eyes and tickling my noses as it settled.

Jim, said nothing but pointed and as I excavated the scene, allowing my squinting eyes to dig through the smoke, I noticed, outlined in white, the shape of a pentangle, holding at bay, an alter where two lit candles seemed overwhelmed by the juggernaut that burned unopposed to their right.

"Holy Anton La Vey Batman. This ain't no simple meshing in the flesh, but a bloody congregation of witches celebrating mass." No sooner than I uttered the words, since I'm sure I wasn't whispering, the partly clad, but mostly bare partiers, advanced, menacing a cry that forced our retreat.

This time I was leading, hoping Jim's nostrils weren't

battened from the smoke so he could follow the scent I had burned in my stead. I didn't turn, and hoped my legs remembered the route, which my brain failed to detail. Like Cleopatra's needle, the steeple from the church, silent against the black, stood erect, a finish line where I hoped the car, by some sort of insight, had already started, just waiting for us before screeching away.

Jim, somehow passed me, then passed my legs, which were now in full gallop, but failed to cross the line, ending in submission by bowing to the ground at the head of the hearse like Cambridge. I reached for his hand, which mired mine with the same organic sludge that had since congealed against my pants. By the time the car sputtered up the lane, catching the turn that catapulted us back toward the main road, I chuckled as I realized that neither one of us had wiped the mess that now gloved our hands.

To paraphrase the *Bible* in a paragraph or less, when referring to the creation that is earth, is to exercise a parable based on six days, rather than the billions of years it took God's hands to mold the clay. The paradigm constantly reworks the parameters to include the ever changing scope by which we view and include as possible, the wide range of variations when looking at our home and what it represents.

Witches and others treated it as a living entity, manifested in the ways of the goddess and her relationship to mother nature. It was however, James Lovelock who modeled space ship earth, being every so careful not to sniff from the glue, - Gaia, the hypothesis. This is where temperature, oxidation, acidity and other parameters are maintained and regulated by a homeostasis, practiced by active feedback, which operates automatically and unconsciously by the biota. This was comforting to many hippies who were convinced that whether unconsciously or consciously, the Chatkas and lay lines were somehow actively involved in pushing the right buttons, so to either turn the earth's thermostat up or down according to these changes, whether acid rain or green house gases, the world could and would somehow compensate. However, the concern, that by fuming and continuing to fume, an endless bounty of hashish and grass the waste products, though small, just might be enough to tip the scale. We decided to deflect this issue by condemning the automobile for belching CO_2 and other pollutants and even the dairy cow for lifting its tail to expel both a slippery mess and methane. It was the higher ordained servants; many of the ex-hippies who decided to tackle the problem, literally in many cases, by coming to the forefront as activists. The Green Peace Advocates became a reckoning, especially to the whalers, nuclear submariners and polluters who took to battle stations whenever their flag dotted the horizon.

The Rhythm of Love

I'm dreaming to be awake, free to hold,
so sincere, yet bold.
A woman, I'm told, so much better than my hand.

Inspired by:

Dreaming From the Waist
The Who

We all over indulged in the practice of dreaming, since much of our spare time was expended either idly wasted, or comfortably toasted. This usually occurred stoned and buried under a goose down comforter. The only problem, there was only one eiderdown to be shared between a half a dozen or so weary eyed or for the losers, teary eyed freaks. Mind expansion allowed the abuser to fantasize about everything, including the masculine preoccupation with the practice, or I should say, to practice as often as possible, the hormonal driven desire to find refuge and solace between the legs of either a similarly driven female counterpart, or more appropriately, a chic who had unfortunately decided to conveniently pass out under our roof.

Free love was, for the most part, free or at least negotiable. Since money was rare, the obvious Casanovian precursor approach included the all too tempting power of the HERB! Let's face it, desperate times often called for desperate measures. It's no coincidence that sexual famine followed all to predictably actual famine. It's almost impossible to wine and dine with the ultimate goal of satisfying your sexual appetite when Mother Hubbard's cupboard was forever bare.

So, pick up lines were refined, rehearsed and perfected. Whereas the traditional hippie approach seemed so mundane, boring and so very predictable, our approach was different. We varied it, and honed it, so it came across as more of an impetuous plea for sexual gratification, usually taking place on one knee with hands outstretched toward the very surprised and hopefully now commiserating and ready to be taken, partner.

The Pick-Up

Traditional hippie:

Hippie:	"Peace baby—hey darlin' what's your sign?"
Chic:	"Virgo, what's yours?"
Hippie:	"Like wow, baby, it truly matters not, because momma, all I know, my Taurus is rising and that's no bull! So what do ya say, about moving upstairs and burnin' one?"
Chic:	"Sure, dude, let's do it."

Our approach:

One of us:	"Like wow! You're hot! Hey, if you come upstairs with me, I'll roll a number and we can get high?"
Chic/Victim:	(The mood dominated by both hesitation and reservation). "Oh mmmmm ah, well okay.
(Once upstairs)	
One of us:	(Assuming the position and presenting the bag, shaking it at arms length) "Please baby, like if you let me shag you, I'll keep this joint and give you the rest of the bag!"

The hippie credo with its Bohemian ambiance could and did foster a free and easy, so matter-of-factly, nonchalant, given for granted that just because there were no rules, sex dominated the idyllic landscape. Like I said, free love was relative to the mood, negotiated by the parties in question. Women didn't have to sacrifice anything for their man since by definition, there was nothing to sacrifice except the lifestyle. Men were not driven to succeed since the only career practices were stationed, relative to the stereotype.

Moving up the hippie corporate ladder was not an issue since everyone balanced precariously on the one and only rung. Yes, love was free; sex was not! There's always a price to pay, especially if you were a hippie dude. In actual fact, for many hippie guys, there was the unwritten, but ever present rule of thumb, well, hand really, if you include the other four digits, because that's exactly what most of us ending up using, after we struck out.

1.Its difficult getting laid when you discover after dropping mescaline, that the passenger riding in her canoe, is a colossus when compared to the disappearing act perpetuated by the dead space that once proudly posed as your penis.

2.Its difficult getting laid when you discover what you thought was Spanish Fly was really a Tsetse Fly and spend the better part of the next three days trying to revive her.

3. Its difficult getting laid when you realize after binge drinking Tequila, Senor "Big Jim" and the twins have decided to take a siesta, forcing you to do the same.

4. Its difficult getting laid when you leave the bedroom to roll a joint and end up watching a test pattern on the tele for the next two and a half hours thinking it's a test match between England and the West Indies..

5. Its difficult getting laid when you realize what you thought looked like a leggy brunette, turned out to be an ex-royal marine commando and you regain consciousness behind the pub, upside down in a dust bin.

The primary precursor to this age, dominated by the love generation, was the introduction of the pill. This and women's lib promoted the sexual revolution, which unlike the French Revolution didn't really kill anyone, except maybe the odd participant who died from exhaustion or bleeding to death after his penis fell off. Most mores were quickly vanquished or at least, revamped. So too, were many inhibitions based on traditions and upbringing. Suddenly the barriers were gone, initiating the reconfiguration of the sexual paradigm. Now anything and everything was possible as the one night "fling" enjoyed immense popularity, except maybe with the Irish, who were still busy doing their own traditional version. Encounters were short, sweet and for the most part, discreet. The exceptions, the orgies, outside festivals and anytime the mood struck in the middle of a public park.

Since taking the vow of poverty, sexual prowess remained a distinct and separate issue still governed by the individuals in terms of being both blessed and disciplined. We didn't have to worry about it being tainted by materialism in terms of wallet girth, flashy cars and swank attire. Instead the ability to deceive, lull, coax, coerce and even lie, too often preceded the actual act. The greater the number of notches in the bed post, reinforced the belief that if your guitar was bigger and you played better than the next bloke, the chances of coitus uninterruptus was just a short toke away. Now you know why most male hippies never left home without either their Fenders or their stash.

Led by Wings, all the members with the exception of Blade and myself could at least pick up an axe and strum it. I do however, remember being sadly intoxicated, playing my own fifteen-minute rendition of "Louie-Louie" on the Xylophone. But, alas, music was not my forte.

If and when women presented, there was a mad dash to establish a territorial advantage and begin the courting process. Amps hummed and acoustic guitars twanged as the various suitors attempted to thwart all rivals. Personal alliances and even friendships were for the time being, put on hold. I ignored this very primordial display of virility and decided to jockey for position by using another visceral, yet primeval option. One, by which the dominant male, me, usurped the competition by pushing everyone to the side. By parting the way, the road was clear and the turntable became my guitar. The vinyl was placed, the sound check was a simple moving of the knob where the room became center stage, - Heathrow during the launching of Concorde. Suddenly all eyes shifted to me as my "air guitar," like a Dutch windmill in warp drive, lacerated the space between myself and the rest of the room. Images of Pete Townshend spring boarding into full flight as I imitated a ravenous Condor scanning an intrepid sea.

This deafening shrill consummated the thrill; with feedback upon landing. My imaginary guitar as a rapier separated those lost from those pretending to be found.

I however, avoided all ambiguity by deftly using my index finger from my right hand to point directly to the part of my anatomy that needed immediate attention. Needless to say, this impromptu rendering of "Live at Leeds," usually resulted in at least one chic offering to do her best impression of an "air" job or in the event the windows were left agape, my lower torso being blown by the wind.

There was the "X" chromosome or double X or my personal favorites, the triple X, or more appropriately, pure unadulterated anything goes, porn. Our concupiscent ways were based on the Caligulan rule of carnal knowledge. Simply put, the more you knew about deviant sexual behavior, the better the chance not only to score, but more importantly, bring the victim, ah, I mean the chic back for a well deserved encore. Any sexual advantage, whether garnered from the Karma Sutra or any plane brown papered package from Copenhagen, played an important role in indoctrinating each and every members' member. This carnival of sexual carnage represented the best in local curvaceous delicacies—especially when the bong was full. Some of us were even gluttons for sado-masochistic punishment. Those perverse acts were usually employed the morning after, when incessant prodding with a virgin broom handle was the weapon of choice in rousing the newly ordained dead from the hallway.

I'm certain that Women's Lib, as preached by the likes of Gloria Steinham, and more so Germaine Greer caused a rapid onset mutation of certain genes wrapped loosely around the XX chromosome. It appeared to be an example of how the power of suggestion could manipulate behavior through warping of the DNA Strands. Such female traits, as the irresistible urge to binge spend without external stimuli, with the exception of either paper or plastic currency of course, have been apparent since the dawning of time..

It was while researching this evolutionary epoch for evidence suggesting a possible genetic link between Hippies and Neanderthals; I was inexplicably drawn to southern France. While masquerading as a longhaired spunky spelunker at Lascaux, I found very faint etchings in some smaller less obvious cave wall drawings, affirming a relationship between female behaviorism and spontaneous needless spending. There it was, prehistoric graffiti, showing an early Cro-Magnon female tiptoeing past her dozing mate, struggling with a rather large collection of beaver, sable and mink pelts. Evidence suggested she bartered the deal, probably trading her partner's morning kill, for in the next drawing she is depicted being dragged by her now very irate soul mate holding in one hand her matted hair and from the other, primed and ready to use, one prodigiously ripe, and I'm sure soon to be tattooed with blood, club.

Further historical evidence wasn't hard to find, some literally frozen in time. At Pompeii, women as stone figurines, clumped together like a deranged Rugby Scrum, were found fighting over a stall of discounted jewelry. During the middle ages, as London suffered through a fever pitch, exacerbated by Bubonic plague many women, though ravaged by pox, boils and oozing pustules, collapsed and died in the vain attempt to carry home the final bargains from a close-out sale at a local flea market.

For the most part, hippies didn't have to put up with the distractions presented by equal rights, equal pay and equality through standing - it didn't really affect the hippies anyway—how could it! Both the chics and dudes shared equally in the state of being, reflected by the hippie mentality. It's easy to maintain a state of equality, when there's nothing to share. Most hippies failed to earn a wage, so distribution of wealth in the form of equal pay was also a non-issue. If you think about it, there was a reason why no hippie babes could be seen burning their bras. They didn't wear any—because they couldn't afford to!

Potentially, the only real problem occurred if and when one of us decided to pair off with some bird. Then the reality check! It was only a matter of time until the all too familiar words rang with the intensity to crack not only the Liberty Bell, but the fine line that existed between the sexes.

"Honey, can we score a microbus to follow the free festivals, where we can sell tie dye, incense and jewelry?"

"Hell no!"

There's a reason they call free festivals, free. I just wish, if they decide to make a sequel to the *Stepford Wives*, it's done with hippie chics in mind.

Double, Double Toil and Trouble

A medicated lotion,
    the notion, that I am alone,
    to suffer with the foolhardy,
    a reckless streak
My rash decision to bear.

Inspired by:

I Don't Need No Doctor
Humble Pie
(N. Ashford, V. Simpson, J. Armstead)

The weather was ungodly. The cold, the rain, the flashes of lightening, separated by the periodic blast of thunder. I looked out the front window, mesmerized for the moment by a section of newspaper that fluttered like a kite, transfixed as though impaled by a burst of angry air. Exeter two, Plymouth Argyle one, the paper waving as it disappeared from view.

Reality had set in. I scratched my right temple, convinced it was time indeed, to expose the rest of my head and torso to the titillating sebaceous pleasures provided by Fairy liquid. I put down the piece of cardboard etched with the lone word, London. I closed my eyes, took a deep breath hoping to clear the cobwebs. Besides losing the motivation to follow Rob to the capital, I felt like a million pound in counterfeit bills. Something, obviously, was not quite right.

I looked across the room, for a moment feeling less concerned for myself. There they were. Three reticent, Kabuki like mannequins, superimposed by rigor mortis. They were huddled in blankets around a paraffin heater, covered from head to toe with a white salve. Pete, JF and the Blade, with long flowing locks, looked like Indian warriors in war paint. Pete, as Cochise or more aptly, Chief weeping sore, sat between two Apache braves, all praying to the great spirit for relief.

For the first time in weeks Pete's harem was visibly absent. He had recruited uniformed schoolgirls from the local academy located less than a stoned throw away. It was not just our Lolita helpers, but also all vestiges of any female companionship that was painfully missing. Not a Florence Nightingale among them. I guess without the uncontaminated hand of a man to roll a joint they were content to ride out at a safe distance, any remaining remnants of this Biblical like pestilence.

I decided to scoot my chair over, making sure there was a safe zone between the Marcel Marceu groupies and myself. The heat just teased my feet, however, an uncomfortable silence managed to chill the rest of the room.

"Guys, so how's it going?"

I tossed the words gently, hoping for some sort of response.

Between the out of tune scratching, there was only Pete moaning as his hand reached behind his left ear.

"Hey, I'd love to lend a hand," but before I could finish off the sentence....

"Fuck off! It's called bleedin' karma mate and things have a way of evening out!" Pete's caustic, almost sardonic voice, like an arrow tipped with his usual dose of negativity, ripped through my self imposed no-man's land, landing a blow, forcing me back in my chair. As, I recoiled, I noticed his eyes, like Rasputin, creating a force field hoping to hold me at bay so to preserve what little energy he had.

What the hell is that supposed to mean? My words like salvoes were more strafing than mordacious, thinking this bastard might just go out of his way to contaminate my bed linen. He continued, a little calmer, but still on the offensive.

"Listen, just because you escaped this plague doesn't mean

you'll come out unscathed. The way you make light of it, poke fun and for the most part, act unsympathetic is beyond me."

"Bollocks, you know something Pete? You're full of shit!"

Big John and the Blade both looked up in unison. John looked unconcerned; the Blade gently shook his head as though telling me to back off.

I turned to Pete, thought for a moment, sniffed, rubbed my nose and decided to offer the olive branch.

"Okay, I'll tell you what, I'll make some soup and bring it out to the three of you. I just need to do something first."

The three nodded and Pete went back, this time to his right ear and mumbled something that I chose to ignore.

I walked back to the front window, turned a blind eye to nature's ireful display, picked up the placard and black marker and intentionally walked behind Pete toward the door.

I engaged the stairs, feeling a rumbling inside that agitated my gut with each descending step. I paused in the foyer, turned the cardboard and wrote, "Warning: Quarantine, Scabies." I walked outside, closed the door, forcing the cardboard against an exposed finishing nail so it hung at a slight angle. I now felt Montezuma's knuckles tapping against my rear door, separating the outside from a moat that contained what I now knew would be expelled forthwith. I turned and feeling like a battered salmon ready to fight a series of weirs, reached for the door in anticipation of the stairs. My worst nightmare was in hand as the doorknob refused to grant me entry. "Oh, no!" I could feel the little beads of sweat shin digging their way down my forehead. I began to tap dance like Beau Jangles, but it soon escalated into a solo featuring James Brown, begging poppa for his brand new bag, which incidentally if I possessed would suffice as a receptacle. I glanced to the right, left and back to my right again. There it was, the shrub, the one I had ordained with the yellow rain a fortnight earlier. As I leapfrogged the barrier between walkways, I caught a glimpse of someone in the upstairs front window waving as he closed the drapes, a Joker to my Batman. Looking rather like Rudoph Nureyev performing *Swan Lake,* I finally reached the bush, dropping my pants as the hot steamy Monkey's Paw presented for the finale. For the encore I delivered breach, the entire Monkey!

I closed my eyes and sighed, opening them as a piece of newspaper covered my face. It still read Exeter two, Plymouth Argyle one.

Music in the Word

The golden age where everything done was under the gun.
For tomorrow, the dreamer, may never come.

Inspired by:

The Golden Age of Rock 'n' Roll
Mott The Hoople

Music was a serious preoccupation and passion with the youth of the time. The period that spanned between 1967 and 1977 coincided with the peace movement. Music not only reflected the mood, but also changed as the mood changed. For me, it helped smooth the wrinkles and on more than one occasion, saved my life—not from forfeiting it all together, but from losing it. I didn't want to become a casualty by relinquishing all ties and succumbing to the ever-present madness.

Music was the glue; music helped provide a clue, music laminated the soul, music played a role. Music was life during a time of unrelenting strife. My God! I sound like a folk singer who smoked one too many banana skins! But what the hell, its easy to drift back, as the book firmly attests, to imprint and then print what the experience was truly like. So, where was I? Oh, yeah. Here we go, like a FLASH BACK!

It helped delineate position at a time when positioning was essential in establishing an identity. It secured the boundaries. It made sense during a time when common sense was in doubt. It explained the scene when making the scene was a tribute to the identity in question. It identified with the scene; it quashed all doubt to what scene was in question.

The hippies were a scene where chaos chose a partner and being that partner, you better know how to lead as you danced across the plain, the grass burning at your feet. In plain view was the plane, a plane of existence, where existence was measured in the pain and anguish that rose incessantly from the nagging injustice that sweltered the stage. Total chaos in a world where chaos was measured in thirty-minute increments that flashed twice a day before our very eyes, close to the true meaning behind the stories that they wrought.

Ah... but the universe, according to Nietzsche, without music, would be madness. Yet, religion as peacemaker or more often than not, as the incendiary, became the opiate by which Karl Marx envisioned the masses and all the brethren, would be ultimately subdued and hence controlled.

Now, wait a minute! I think I'm finally on to something here. What would happen if one were to combine the two concepts? Let's see. By using opiates to rid the psyche of negatively and music to open the doors of perception, a whole new universe awaited the practitioner. THAT'S IT!

My God, that's what we did! Hippies alike fashioned a level of consciousness where music advocated a sense of purpose through the lavishing upon the soul of peace and acceptance through submission. Submissions to the chord that carried the word, where the sound of pounding guitars guided the message across the plane, which downplayed the elements of realism so painful, but for the moment, so much easier to bear. It also captured this essence of truth, by allowing not only the words to repeat as often as we liked, (since many of our LP's possessed the propensity to stick), but the thrashing guitar riffs, thumping bass line and bludgeoning drums, to keep it alive. Carried forever on the wings of flight, through space to be captured eight light years away, by a more advanced civilization that for whatever reason, succumbed, eventually exhibiting mass hysteria and madness, forcing their extinction.

Hippieism was the natural corollary produced by this

madness, epitomized by a rampant technology that society was unable to keep pace with. Music was the pace car, the vehicle, self-protecting, yet constantly moving, that carried us, insulated from the vibes that haunted the rest of the world. It was a mode by which we chose to cope, escape, rebel and ultimately adapt, to an ever-changing world.

Music infiltrated all aspects of a hippie's life. It became a viable alternative to both politics and religion. It was a consolidation without possibility for ramification that reinforced our seminal virtues proclaiming life as a magical mystery tour. It gave the listener the option to either tune in or tune out. It became a ritual, a reflex and without hesitation, the knob could be manipulated to abdicate all sound, eliminating, let's say, the Queen's annual Christmas address, replacing it with Cream's Pressrat and Warthog. When the BBC ten o'clock news announced the latest crisis in the Middle East, it was time to focus on Focus. If the toilet paper inexplicably disappeared, one had to simply enlist the Daily Telegraph. Now if it headlined British Leylands latest strike, ripe with the all too familiar fallout created by the government's latest economic casualty list, the bearer of misfortunate could avoid any knee jerk reaction by listening to The Who's "Heaven and Hell." All this while lighting up and strolling nonchalantly to the bog!

At first it was the poetry, cradled in the lap of the reader. This spurned the poets to render the truth from a passion strummed in tune from a six-string acoustic. To reach the masses, the ever-expanding throng, growing from a puddle to a pond, they chose the electric. The acid test, the be in, the congregation that tripped inflicting a presence from Newport to Monterey. The amplified sound of the collective spirit, harmonized the tempo of the troop that lay in turbulence at their feet. The new prophets pounded out the beat to a new collection of converts, whose holy water spilled forth, quenching the thirst of the multitude cuddled together to receive this not so cryptic message. This measured a response instead of a sword or gun, the clenched anger of the fist. Joined by more rapping against the space between the ocean of discontent and the sky that littered above the heads of the discord. So, be the reckoning that harbored the masses in tune to the time instead of being rife with a determination to unleash a deadly sting. It had this affect, a profound affect, which helped pave the way. It was all a matter of choice and each choice was up to the listener. It would, in truth, enhance the will, through its' energy or obliterate the senses, leaving the listener wanting more, further stretching the imagination, to remain trapped, only craving more.

You know, sometimes, especially when there's a burning passion, its hard, I mean real hard to deviate from the norm. Well, my norm, when dealing with an issue that I'm convinced if it hadn't evolved into the plethora of types, life would have become unbearable. So long live rock! And, the children it bore.

The period that we hunkered down to weather the storms of societal upheaval was indeed, the Clapham junction of rock history. Here each platform stationed a train—a train of thought, manifested in ideas that differentiated slightly by choice, to a sound, modeled after the blues, jazz, country or rock 'n' roll. It became the focal point where each track became a fusion, to architect an archetype, the nexus being rock.

This period was truly the Golden Age of rock 'n' roll!

With the hippies, it became fashionable to associate by stereotype to the grass roots, being the San Francisco genesis. The focal point, the band Kesey encouraged to play at the first acid test, The Grateful Dead.

Coming down,
  the trip was more,
  then just a collection of sounds.
Now, the cold realization,
  that reality held true,
  the mistrust, bleeding,
—forever bleeding, through.

Inspired by:

Eight Miles High
The Byrds

It was a merging of philosophy with music, a coming together of poetry and prose with a melodious display pumped through speaker and amp. An evolutionary path, premeditated and in a sense, pre-medicated to be predicated by a time, where a quickening forced a reaction, dampened in both anger and rage. It was no coincidence that the Vietnam War, environmental suicide, civil rights and a new decadence seemed to steamroll change. As the US involvement in Vietnam deepened, so to the anger voiced not only in the lyrics, but the total affect produced by a much louder and more provocative sound. Special effects like fuzz, wah-wah, feedback and distortion helped carry it beyond the fringe. Better sound systems, synthesizers, over-dubbing and the use of multi-tracking allowed bands to stay clear of the AM driven top forty formatting.

Bands languished, as the new saviors played to the audience. The extended "jam sessions" became the signature of many alive gig. Hippies loved it! This was the period where music became intertwined with the forces of dance and the sheer power of the light shows.

To further enhance the program, LSD was added as a mixer, thanks in part to Ken Kesey's first trip festivals. Beginning in early 1966, acid tests became the first festivals, spread over three days. Bands like the Jefferson Airplane, Big Brother and the Holding Company and Quicksilver Messenger Service held serve.

It's interesting to note, many bands adhered to the idea that it was indeed safer to play into the hands of the establishment by easing or even extinguishing any potential spark, particularly involving drug ingestion. It was common to hear the proclamation, "No need to worry" uttered by bands that over indulged in creating the likelihood for a "mind fuck." The bizarre over use of strobe lights and later, lasers and pyrotechnics, coupled with the over synthesized surreal sound of distorted guitar and bass often contributed to the warping of the senses. This heralded a time when the mass consumption of acid was not needed because the band would create naturally, the entire experience. What bollocks! All this did was encourage drug use, particularly hallucinogenics, by inviting the participant to drop, creating twice the experience. I saw this first hand at an acid fest concert where more people huddled the foyer walls than actually witnessed the concert, which stretched like a hawk, winging its way across a large screen, riding the crest of a solar wind, gliding with the black velvet breath of Brahma, taxiing as it carried all…

Yeah, all except those poor sods bumming out in time to the beat, electrified by fright and paranoia, with only the wall to weep. These were not happy campers, but you know something? Many returned the next weekend to wax and wane to the next band with many ending up assuming the same position, against the same puke-stained wall. However, we loved it! Simply because our parents hated it! Let's face it, hippies were usually very slow to react and if they did, it was because they were either reaching for or passing the communal joint.

The average white middle class American kid protested as a last resort, fearing parental retaliation in the form of ….let's say, "you can't congregate with your friends and get high." But if you pushed and prescribed to the age-old adage of safety in numbers, it was a lot easier to turn a police car over when there were also a few thousand of your closest mates doing the same thing. All in all, it was much safer to join together, scream a lot, vent and eventually pass through or simply pass out, when listening to someone else playing to your emotions.

Allan Ginsberg inspired change using his seminal trip to London in 1965. From the capacious confines of the Royal Albert Hall his readings echoed from catacombs, catapulting as a caterwaul and acting as a catalyst, reaching an audience in lofty pursuit, flying high at the UFO club. This catharsis castigated any remnants reflecting "business as usual," giving way to an underground scene, which would, like water seeking its own level, surface, washing away the tell-tale odors of the past regime. Bands like Pink Floyd, Cream and the Jimi Hendrix Experience, pulverized reticule, slamming the airways that censored their music. You see, the publicity that was deliberately diverted, created an allure that lent credence to their manifesto, which further afforded them popularity. If the establishment attempted to bury them, then the spirit of the youth, especially the early hippies would resurrect them, and deify them.

Here they joined the already ordained, exulted through their craft, the likes of Dylan, Holly and the Crickets, Elvis and Berry, who influenced the changing of the guard, which escorted to center stage, "The Beatles!" They epitomized the quintessential musical mavericks, the hallmark of truth, the purveyor of change, carrying with them the ability to influence on one level or another…the mindset of a generation. Whether dress, language, attitude toward politics, or religion and drugs, they symbolized a renaissance that spiced with their charisma, brought forth change on a very massive scale. The "fad 4," probably influenced an entire generation, particularly the hippies, more so than any one group, individual or event.

Even though it was Dylan who pioneered the placement and the application of the cryptic message, it was the Beatles who introduced the enigma machine making it a mystical art form. They pioneered a lifestyle, a flamboyant ensemble of sight and sound. The marriage between the music and the message created a mélange, echoing freedom, peace and love.

If I preach politics,
I cannot preach religion.
For if I preach God,
He tells me, never to lie.

Inspired by:

Politician
Cream

In Britain, it was the staying power of the "blues." This gave lifeblood to the music that emerged during our time. It served as a template that produced the rock paradigm, which gradually swept the rest of the world. From the three Kings to the holy trinity of the guitar legends and the princes of the new frontier, it pounded out a new accord, one chord at a time.

I was introduced to the blues, one stanza at a time. It was the honing device that brought the gang together, not just our group, but more cliques that assembled based on different levels of disillusionment. But for me, being an immigrant, weaned on the San Francisco sound, rock, particularly hard rock, was my salvation.

The blues, by way of the emotional recoil, was like looking up and seeing bottom. Crisis, ordeal and suffering, a way to explore the human element in terms of its affiliation to the affliction and pain it wrought. I often wondered why the Buddhists, whose cycle of life, death and rebirth entangled in an existence woven in pain, didn't chant to the sounds of Robert Johnson and Willie Dixon, instead of the moribund and monotone distraction initiated by smacking that silly miniaturized gong with that little wooden stick. My tolerance, on a good day, very rarely exceeded forty-five seconds. The whole idea of being a hippie was to hopefully condition or at least minimize, the effects of negativity in the environment. Good old southern Mississippi delta blues mixed and recorded in a dingy Chicago tenement basement was, to say the least, not my cup of tea. For crying out loud, don't tell Clive, but I didn't even like tea! Listening to Muddy Waters commiserate aloud, about misery loving company, forced me to conclude that the Bluesmen's proclivity to an eternal pessimistic penurious state of constant peonage would further damage and further bloat my own level of anxiety and depression.

Now, the perfect antidote for me was to combine the drudgery of life, especially adolescence with high-energy music. This combination seemed not only to counteract or neutralize the potential for a catatonic episode, but provided a solution to remedy any chance to relapse into a state of chronic depression. I found this release by listening to the music of the WHO!

If I swallow the world,
don't let me choke on all its madness.

Inspired by:

Behind Blue Eyes
The Who

It was hard, gut wrenching and awe inspiring. It was high octane that provoked a feeling of anger, yet provided enough discipline to keep the listener bolted to the floor. It reflected the streets, the grouping together of lost souls at the crossroads where personal crisis thwarted any attempt to detour, right or left. It circumvented love and dealt with the issues. It encompassed an age where impasse often flirted with disaster. Youth, a microcosm of life, became an identity crisis, true to form gnawing at the lifeblood that fermented rage. The uncharted territories, the proverbial teenage wasteland, without boundaries, yet from within, the oasis that bathed the spirit—free to fly, to capture the truth. This was the Who.

They captured the mood of a generation. They were the product of the time! While they were neither heavy metal nor acid rock, they managed to personify an era. They dripped with the emotions reflecting a theme draped and smothered with the never-ending struggle to force change. The sound was layered where each layer acted as a conveyor belt, taking you to the next level and then the next. Daltry's twirling microphone, like a fan, forced the energy toward the crowd. Townshend's feedback and anatomical windmill complemented Moon's flailing, which always, no matter the mood, directed the energy toward Daltry. Entwhistle as the conduit reminded us that no matter how far the band took the audience, when the song was over, they were always anchored and able to return.

Feeling a sense of relief, but at the same time, a new confidence that someone else both understood and would be there to console, I hoped and prayed that the Who would be there for the next generation.

I remember my first Who concert. I soon realized what inspired Townshend to come up with the concept behind Tommy. I was certainly not the only concert goer experiencing blindness from the lasers, total deafness from the decibel, and being struck dumb by the sheer magnitude of the event. All my senses were put in touch with the music and the meaning behind the words—I had been set free.

Through the sordid mishap brandishing to bear,
the dead did sleep, never to keep,
the promises they made to silence the guns of war.

Inspired by:

Ohio
Crosby, Stills, Nash & Young

Much of the music was loud and angry. It reflected the mood of a generation. The music was the emotional outpouring, yet it also contained the word. The lyrics reflected the raw energy that carried it from the schoolyard to cars cruising from the highway to the by-way. From the streets to the fields, to the raucousing mania of the rabid masses, to an isolated rice paddy playing host to a line where the grunt on point held a radio in addition to a gun. The sound seemed to jingle and jangle through the jungle, whether a green canopy or a concrete embankment.

If the truth kills,
then let those who speak,
silence their words.

Inspired by:

Won't Get Fooled Again
The Who

From an age featuring long haired suits toting guitars to a short lived diversion where modernists taunted leather clad rockers, psychedelic blues, jazz infusion and heavy metal lay siege to our senses, drawing across and feeding the starving souls of a deprived menagerie, featuring the children of the blues. This was where the faithful followed and would follow their heroes to hell and back. In a sense many did, as bands like Black Sabbath played, ushering in an even more aggressive sound, reflecting a "working class" pittance that never seemed to skip a generation.

Upon reflection, maybe the CIA would have been better served if they had used, a variation of this pied piper syndrome. A simple concoction really; by combining an aggressive sound, subliminal messages and LSD, MK ultra may have indeed, separated the wheat from the chaff. Code naming it, Project Combat Rock featuring Death Meddle, whose motto would have been spelled out by the lyrics such as:

If there's a despot or dictator we don't like.
We'll just invade your country using our might.
After raping and pillaging and ridding the rogue
We'll set up a new government that ain't so bogue.

My God, rock was all encompassing. It was everywhere and everything. It could be gnosticistic, or narcissistic. It was mysticism and occultism. It was Hendrix on fire, playing like a god, his guitar exploding as his hands pleaded for it to burn. It was a revival smothered in a fog like haze, imitating magic, where theatrics projected onto an audience, escapism through lavish stage acts. It was science fiction rocketing the onlooker to a different time and a different place where all troubles, where all problems were transformed and for the moment, forgotten. It was where bands like the Beatles, the Who, the Rolling Stones, Pink Floyd, Deep Purples, Yes, Alice Cooper, Jethro Tull, the Doors, Lynyrd Skynyrd, Joe Walsh and the Eagles that gave even the hippies something to cheer about. They were our heroes, our mentors and ultimately our saviors.

But it was Led Zeppelin that rode shotgun on every road trip and impromptu excursion involving sojourn and quest. Zeppelin was hard; hard livin', hard lovin', hard luck and hard times. Their sonic vocabulary captured the last rites of the psychedelic era, pumped with the emotion brimming its wake. They possessed a capacity to uplift and carry the listener beyond the natural laws governing the senses.

The journey from now to an age where vassal and fief trampled underfoot sowed an allegiance to both ploughshare and lord. We let the land stand fallow, but chose to question our avowed obedience to the state. The state of being, a state of mind, a state in flux, where questions abounded and change seemed paralyzed by a resounding ever present neuroses.

> "Somebody once described me as the original hippie, and that's because of the flowery lyrics, you know, and also because of the 'buzz' we gave out."

Robert Plant

A Close Encounter?

I look beyond now,
and see yesterday.

Inspired by:

Ten Years Gone
Led Zeppelin

As I sat transfixed on a single point, my mind minced the foreground retreat and the background music, slowly forcing my eyes to do the same. The whole experience fed the sage, spicing my appetite for more. This gnawing, panging the imagination, continued to feed, taking the palate with the soul beyond the realm of reason. Led Zeppelin possessed the ability to wrap Celtic myth and English folklore with a fine thread dipped in the mystic afterglow of the arcane, a combination of Tolkien and Crowley held firmly in the throes of the blues, a magic carpet ride, unfurling a vision where yesteryear could be viewed in a different light.

In truth, there was no light except the full moon, pasty and surreal, yet conveniently primed. The mood was somewhat dismal. We were huddled with one flashlight, a boom box, a half empty flask of cheap brandy and damp rolling papers with only the company of stale "ole Virginia" to act as a husk to line its walls.

But, upbeat we hoped from atop the Tor, the barren of Exmoor bathed by streams of meandering light and veins of brisk melted snow; always reached the sea. The microcosm of existence, our little world, alive for now, tempered by a patchwork conglomeration of fields and hedges, cascading as a potpourri of confusion, attacked the roads and houses, anchored and unable to flee. We had fled, risking sprained ankles and knees to scale the mount where the ancients once tread.

The clouds inquisitively crept a blanket above to filter the dew. It sprinkled a sensation to guide my arm, gliding it skyward, a cotton candy array, sweetened the quest. I reached for his face but only teasingly tugged his beard. Laughingly aside, a whisper to yawn, his smile spread the ruffled linens, a sentimental rescue soon to stretch the new day.

I wanted to share the experience and as I turned, not a peep, but the galloping evidence of light. It shot right and then left, playfully dipping, dispensing to swarm, stopped and accelerated, tempting the hedges as a dragon to bite.

"Hey! Did you see that?" Forgetting momentarily what prompted me to rear my head.

"See what?" Clive hypnotically replied.

"That!" Pointing, knowing full well Clive, with arm draped, couldn't see.

Rob was bolt upright, a Frankenstein to my whim, thinking I'm sure, the drug squad was near, knowing full well that those dear, would, if probed, have the last laugh.

Clive, now kneeling, was like a carved figurine, scanning from the bow, a ship lost at sea. He appeared focused but removed his glasses to wipe them clean.

"That's bizarre! Look how it navigates the sky. Christ, that's amazing! I've never seen anything do a ninety degree turn like that!"

If anyone had the answers besides the dark side, the inner circles, the top-secret agencies of both the British and American governments, it was Clive.

"Cleaver, what do you think it is?" I probingly snapped.

"I, I'm not really sure. Maybe an optical illusion of sorts, you know like...."

Before he could finish, I playfully filled in the blanks, "Like swamp gas, right?"

Rob ambushed the segue, "Yeah, swamp gas, here, out here, right smack in the middle of the bleedin' moor. That's a laugh! It's just a car with its headlights misaligned."

Clive turned to Rob and shook his head, rolling the words toward me, pivoting in sequence to view again the mysterious intruder. "It's a bloody UFO! I know for a fact, the area adjacent to Stonehenge and the lay lines is a corridor for UFO activity, the southwest in particular."

"What Bollocks!" Rob exclaimed, simultaneously lighting the worst specimen of a hand rolled ciggie I had ever seen.

"Now let him finish!" I retaliated, pointing to the noticeable light.

Clive calmly picked up where he had left off. "I've read about farmers complaining about UFO's or balls of light, buzzing their grain corps, some even landing, leaving strange patterns like large nests.

Rob coughed as he rose and looking down at Clive, flicked the smoldering ash just missing Clive's nest of hair. Like a blind beekeeper, Clive swished his hands back and fourth, coordinating the activity as he jettisoned himself to eye level. It was the beginning of the classic standoff, a prelude to combat. The medieval joust, the eighteenth century dual and the OK corral, all rolled into one. Clive, the barebones visionary, the open minded liberal rogue, the typical no holes barred seeker of the truth. *There's got to be more than what we've been told,* freak eyeballed his adversary. In turn, Rob, *I could care less about anything far out and cosmic, I don't want to be a fanatical fringe member, but I'll still look the part, leave me alone,* long hair, defiantly goggled his foe.

I looked toward the heavens, hoping a strange beam of light would break the stalemate by reaching down to levitate Rob high above the scene, dropping him rear first onto the spire, which begged from behind to act as the skewer.

The silence was broken as Clive made the first thrust. "Rob, I'm telling you, it's a fact mate, whether you want to believe it or not, strange things are happening, especially here on the moors. Extraterrestrial or not, those lights are indicative of something beyond the norm."

I aligned myself with Clive. "Come on Rob, don't be so narrow minded,. They could be watching us. Christ, we could be their stepchildren. You know, an experiment gone terribly wrong, In actual fact, the more I hang with you, the more I'm convinced."

Rob waved back at me, "Ah, whatever! All I know is its almost breakfast and I'm in no mood to be abducted, so let's find a caff and woof down a mixed grill or two."

It was perfect timing. The sun spanked the horizon and from the hill next to where the lights once hovered, a distant shrill pierced the solitude.

Clive turned again, his outstretched arm following the faint outline of a fast moving aircraft, "Wow! It looks like one of the RAF's vertical take off and landing fighters, the P1127."

"Well, there you have it." Rob grabbed me, pushing slightly, hoping to kick start our retreat. I stopped to tie my shoe while Clive, finger pointing, followed Rob, talking as he walked.

"Hey Rob, how do you know those aircraft weren't dispatched to chase the lights?"

Rob continued his retreat with Clive in hot pursuit. Their voices echoing as one played off the other. The tone fading, as only their heads appeared, bouncing every so slightly against a lively grass ridge, which fluttered, heaving with the wind.

I felt the church, its cold presence, alive yet spirited by years of memories; covered with both neglect and ivy, which consumed its steeple. I couldn't shake the religious implications tied to the lights. They could be cosmic explorers fastened less to the vastness of the universe, but here in numbers by bending time and space. A cosmic connection, Kip Thorne's wormholes, watching us, so rotten to the core. What is their secret? Maybe a universal lottery? Where we as misguided children, lay claim to the fascination brought forth by our insatiable urge to tempt providence by continually prodding element ninety-two? I thought to myself, *We have become death, the destroyer of worlds*. Perhaps the universal odds read that we as a civilization have a one in ten chance to survive the next one hundred years. I paused a for a moment, laughed and looked up at fragmented sky as though our visitors were listening and whispered, "I'll take that bet."

Something happened with the Mod, by which I can say I formed a basic but tenuous affiliation. I loved the allure of Carnaby Street, the swank clothes, the badges, but cringed at the sound of Vespas in full throttle and plastic masks that were molded from the subtle, yet still, application of both make-up and mascara. I was too young to understand the difference between reds and blues, but dug Magic bus and the idea of scanning the horizon, able to see for miles, taking me beyond the structures that limited the senses. I was able to make the trek. Many made the trip with me. It gave new meaning to the word tolerance since the gestation period drew even small remnants from the ranks of the rockers. I admit I respected the balking, their alienated toughness and the deafening sound of the café motorcycle streaking the Chelsea Bridge.

But, Mods and Rockers together! What next, black and white? Capitalists and Communist? If the Blade and I could co-exist, then the sky was the limit. There was now hope for all.

But from hope eternal springs not only peace and love, but with the music, other sensations and scenarios.

This included fringe groups and fads. Based on Darwinism, sometimes a totally different species would evolve and the notion of survival of the fittest measured not so much by conflict, but by the strength in numbers. Marketing, in terms of catering to the needs of hippies, was never a corporate mainstay due in part to a lack of resources not aligned with the board room, but the hippies themselves, where deep pockets or pockets of any sort where uncommon. Hippies enjoyed not only the stereotypical slotting presented by psychedelia, but the spider mechanism by which it suddenly sprung eight legs, taking it in eight different directions. I guess the advent of the three-day festival, including Monterrey, Woodstock and the Isle of Wight, allowed the spider to, instead of shearing off its appendages, to draw them in at the same time, spinning a web. This captured bands and performers as diverse as ShaNaNa, Ravi Shanker, Richie Havens, Joni Mitchell, Crosby, Stills and Nash, Mountain, Johnny Winter, Jimi Hendrix and the Who.

For the orphans and outcasts, separated from the hippie movement came strutting, clamoring, glamoring, gleaming and with the splendor and pageantry of a force enlightened and highlighted with make-up and glitters, our quasi step brothers and sisters. Glam was really a short-lived sham! "Look at us, we're different. We're switched on and electric. We love to be noticed. We'll light the path, so follow us!" Yeah right!

A true hippie would never abandon the culturally acceptable, well tolerated.... Maybe that's even stretching the truth. Put it this way, a real hippie would never abandon the stereotypical roots manifested in jeans, tie-dye and beads for platform shoes, rhinestones, cultivated hair, lipstick, eyeliner, eu de cologne and a manicure. And I'm talking about just the guys! Since androgyny abounded, it was not uncommon to start out dating a chic only to end up bonking her brother. However, I sadly confess, I secretly admired David Bowie and I want to believe, many other hippies did as well. Ziggy's music breathed life into a sound, which had become rather predictable. A sound, which soon heralded the King is dead, long live Queen.

> "None ought to be lord over another, but the earth be free for everyone to live on."
>
> Garrard Winstanley

As the squatting movement grew, so did the notions of the Free Festivals. People generally became fed up with the exploitations, commercialization and the sense of having to survive a three-day mess, complete with garbage heap and if it rained, a swamp or muddy enclave. Baloney! The part about exploitation and commercialization, yeah, but the rest, give me a break! The average hippie was used to that kind of situation. In actual fact, living in squalor was in many cases, a huge step up. It was simply the idea of bread. Anything more than nothing was just too much. Now if it was free, 'what me worry?' No such problem, hey, a little bit of rain, mud slides, a few rats, over flowing out-houses, raw sewage, septic run-off, septicemia and cholera, never hurt anyone, except maybe the 2.5 billion or so inhabitants of third world countries that weren't used to that sort of thing.

So why not lobby for the idea of a series of free festivals, where everything, including the music was free.

So the Windsor People's free festivals became the annual event over the August Bank Holiday for the cool and not so cool cats. Well there were a few needed to kill the rats that didn't drown or suffocate in the mud. Needless to say, it was the scene for the freaks and hairies to congregate. It became the place to be seen, sort of like Cannes, well, without the sun, or for that matter, the caviar, champagne, servants (we were all servants to each other) and of course, money. Since it was technically free, you didn't really need money, except if you had to get out of Dodge in a hurry. Of course, this only happened once, because once was all it took for the police to remind everyone that the queen's back yard was no place to hold an impromptu August Bank holiday weekend barbeque.

Freaks, Festivals and the Fuzz

Thirty days in the "nick"
    just for having "blow.'
Next time, to the pub,
    Let the "brew" flow.

Inspired by:

Thirty days in the Hole
Humble Pie

"Christ!" I thought to myself, "I have to stop smoking."

As my heart and lungs caught up with the rest of me, I turned, still panting and saw my fellow escapee just as exhausted. He adjusted his head band, closed his eyes briefly and while turning toward a tree, cleared his throat, forcing a large lugge, which attached itself to the bark like a remora to an unsuspecting reef shark.

The sound of "Thin Lizzy," had accompanied our "jail break" since breaking stride. It was a beautifully executed ploy since our capture no doubt, would have resulted in our own blind folding, last cigarette, last rites and final countdown to a twenty-one gun salute, aimed unfortunately at the colorful targets placed as a pathfinder over our soon to be bullet riddled hearts. In truth, we were lucky that the impeccable timing of my ingenious plan had split the ranks of the "Bill." It was called, "Hey Officers! Do you see that bloke waving his hands madly, well, just beyond that tent there's a young woman tripping out and totally nude, surrounded by a crazed pack of very hungry and oversexed skin heads."

Happy trails, or should I say dusty trails, the remnants of which were still settling, well after our two heroes galloped off in chivalrous pursuit of both grail and booty.

"I think we'll be okay now." I aimed my words carefully, but I was still scouring the congregation for any parting of the way, indicating a plague of blue.

"Follow me there." As I pointed to my flag, the confederate colors swaying so gallantly just short of the fence, gracing the litterscape where bodies remained outstretched, some twitching with the music, as another anthem played. It could have been Gettysburg, but alas, it was just another August Bank Holiday, playing out or more aptly, playing host to a very turned on, and ever so vibrant but uneasy melee, a powder keg of potential hysteria. The police were everywhere and I was certain that before the day was out, some "Copper" with a nervous condition would inadvertently light the fuse, setting the whole festival ablaze.

"Here sit," offering my guest the only space, a small mound made up of a carcass of wood where I hoped its porcupine appearance wouldn't deliver a splinter to his already very scared derriere.

"Man that was just too close." As he spoke his accent hinted of a London tie.

"Yeah, been there, done that whole scene, man." I answered with the confidence of a worldly hippie.

"Why did you put yourself on the line?" He smiled, offering a cigarette as a token of his appreciation.

I politely accepted, lighting a match before he could reach for his lighter.

"Ta." He took a deep drag and I waited for him to exhale, "I guess it was after I heard you plead with him. If you went down for such a trivial amount, it would definitely mean jail time."

"Yeah, third offense and all." He seemed more relaxed, and far less pensive, as he continued. "I was giving my mate enough black to roll a joint, when out of no where, I mean it was just that quick, you know, boom! Busted! By the way, my name's Sid." As he reached to shake my hand, Clive came running toward us. It was obvious from his gait and his apprehensive expression that either the two blue knights were still in hot pursuit or something even more foreboding was just about to unfurl before our eyes.

On cue, it was the latter, "Okay lads, up! Pack your gear, its time to leave; the enemy is at the gates! The whole damn Thames Valley Constabulary is here and they aren't foolin' around! Let's move!"

Pete rolled over and in a disheveled manner, muttered a blasphemous blast of hot air, enticing the stampede that soon followed as each grabbed what he could in the frenzy that now gripped the afternoon turmoil.

I plucked the flag and feeling empowered by the yellow badge of courage that was now staining my shorts, yelled, "Every man for himself," as I charged without concern, the unguarded fence.

Hair, my tangled web of misfortune.
Rinse to cleanse the stigma did hold,
the dirt, that nestled the stench of despair.

Inspired by:

Hair
The Musical

Just when and where did it start? Was it the result of an extemporaneous jam session, applied eventually to vinyl, let's say with Iron Butterfly's "Innagodda Davita," or the Who's rock opera, *Tommy*. Who cares! The point here being that it marked the time, when music sold out. This is where rock attempted to advance its cause by slipping in the back door, off Broadway on Broadway to off shoots resembling Broadway to anywhere they could sell a ticket, fill an auditorium and hopefully, broaden its appeal. It had attempted to capture a wider market at the expense of loosing its mass appeal ostensibly with the youth. You see, by becoming mainstream, it wasn't part of our wading pool any more. It had managed to filter through the water shed, becoming part of the corporate scene. Here it could be marketed to a mass audience with the sole intent of raking in the buckaroonies.

Ah, but the critics will say it was rock's last stand, bent on finally capturing a larger more civilized and therefore more culturally ordained flock. I'm not going to argue over why. All I know, it changed the boundaries, allowing a more toned down version. This was designed to exploit the issues that for the last five years had been the hallmark of protest that had included the well intended, but flat broke hippies. Now politics through religion or for that matter, religion through politics or politics through music or religion, Christ! It all catered to the College educated black tie and gown lace draped thirties crowd, desperately trying to tap in with the sole purpose of being cool by association.

Hair, Godspell, Jesus Christ Superstar and finally, *The Rocky Horror Picture Show* captured the scene. While *Hair, Godspell* and *Jesus Christ Superstar* were over commercialized hype, *Rocky Horror* was a production with balls, tea-bagging the viewer, I mean impaling the onlooker with a series of dark eerie sensations begetting true horror through music and theatrical imagery. The kind of haunting visuals that danced poetically through a maze of erotica and absurdity that beckoned even the hippie faithful to applaud. In truth, just enough sex and rock 'n roll to warrant the inclusion of mind expanding aphrodisiacs.

Now, to create the perfect hippie experience, the traditional Saturday afternoon at the flicks, where *Rocky Horror*, preceded the ideal encore, *2001, A Space Odyssey*. Now talk about mind expansion on a universal scale; more like a space oddity. The epic clash of celluloid titans, where science fiction met the warped world of dark comedy through the genre of horror and I'm not talking about being lost in Harlem after dropping acid. Here reality was eclipsed and skewed by degree subscribing to the mindset of the viewer. Boy do we live in a fucked up world! Just think, if the world was really like Frankenstein's place, who in their right mind would want to leave.

Sock hops, greasers and leather, Elvis was king.
Cults anew, rebels, no causes, Dean couldn't sing.
Holly and Domino layed down the dancin' beat.
Pool-halls and motor bikes out in the street.
The first wave rocked while it rolled
And there's more that can be told.

From Hamburg to Liverpool a new sound did emerge.
The Beatles and Mersyside left the cavern to surge.
The Stones sang rebellion, but Jagger refrained.
Social uprising, the Who in concept did explain
The second wave was a stairway to heaven
And it took Jimi Hendrix at barely twenty-seven.

The marquee and the village were never really dead.
With safety pins and clothes that could be read,
Sex Pistols and Stranglers screamed thru the night.
The Ramones as harlequins just didn't seem right.
The new wave of energy, punk is their tact.
Music will give birth to yet another act.

The New Wave
1977
My last poem before leaving England

Between 1967 and 1977, the age of protest, more happened in music than any other period. From the marriage, let me rephrase that, the mange-à-tois that occurred between the blues, rock 'n roll and any of many lucky invitees, including country, R & B and Jazz came acid rock, hard rock, blues rock, jazz fusion, heavy metal, glam rock, country rock, and the advent of both punk and (bite my tongue and cut off my balls) disco—geez, what next!

Maybe we'll revert back, you know, the power of the spoken word, where a new generation of poets will ignite a crowd by simply talking in time to a simple beat. Nah! On second thought, it's too easy; it'll never fly.

Living in the past,
    the key, the verses to open the way.
Memories to enlighten,
    springing a new day.

Inspired by:

Life's A Long Song
JethroTull

Heroes and Villains

Those who died,
    speaking the truth,
    walk silently together,
    —pointing the way.

Inspired by:

Abraham, Martin, and John
(Dick Holler)
Dion

"If you want a picture of the future, imagine a boot stamping on a human face—forever!"

George Orwell
1984.

Nobody liked Big Brother, especially when he was watching us. It could be as subtle as the '*Bobby*' walking his beat, coincidently, repeatedly, marching in front of eighty or as blatant as the BBC with their seeing eye trucks patrolling and probing the same street, hoping to detect the TV license cheaters who also by coincidence, were rumored to live somewhere in our attic.

The early seventies were surely an exciting period, but this penchant for excitation also unfortunately bordered on absurdity. In practice, the world was an extremely volatile place, where the doomsday clock, which was rapidly winding down, reflected the chance for total annihilation.

"Totalitarianism" was a word that for the most part, had been eliminated from the hippie vernacular. Even though forbidden, it was the catalyst that graded the road by which the hippie movement still trudged. Whether fascist or communist, who were dynamically opposed, the word somehow reflected a commonality by stressing control. The National Front dominated the far right and many of these supporters, though stereotypical, thanks to the skinheads, were former conservative voters who had drifted away, expunged by Edward Heath's leadership. They were galvanized by a strong affinity to an "All white Britain," and adopted many neo-nazi slogans.

On the other hand, or I should say, swinging from the pendulum, to the left was the Communist Party of Britain. It adhered to a platform denouncing racists and fascists hoping at the same time, to crack the foundation that was "Fortress Europe." It grained support by organizing and promoting a strong working class.

The hippies realized that no matter what happened, minor tweaking to a political system and preservation of the current status quo was imperative.

Our biggest fear factor continued to be the "Irish question." The spill over affect being the internalization of a suppressive police state where abuse of power could challenge that of a rather complacent parliament. In addition to the Orwellian boot, collapsing doors, the sequestering of other undesirable and fringe groups, including the hippies, could redefine the meaning of the term underground. This might come to pass by simply incorporating the word genocide and the phrase "mass graves!"

Any major shift, either right or left, depending on which way the head was turning, could spell

"THE END!"

No, not the book! However, for those being left behind, relax, take a break, we're almost finished. Hey, grab a mug of hot java or some of that tea, have sex, smoke 'em if you got 'em, take a shower, eat a scone. I personally don't give a high flying…

All right then, back are we, fine! Good, okay, where was I? The end, ah, the end for a sub-culture still searching for its niche. We knew that mandatory haircuts would mean the blade, somehow severing the head rather than the locks that hung from it.

The cliché' that clipped the cliques, though marketed to an extreme, still held together and promoted the age old adage of survivability through suspicion.

"Never trust anyone over the age of thirty." The only problem, some of our fallen heroes were over thirty when they died, or sadly, as each day the sun rose, were gradually inching closer and closer to this hallmark. Our *Logan's Run* mentality, based on the laws of relativity, would soon grip our existence by one day adding the last of the thirty candles to our own cake of misfortune. Rather than using another eternally driven cliché', like, "Let them eat cake," and "snub the masses," the thought of old hippies turning and facing the sunset, and "simply fading away," held a somewhat numbing, though comforting consolation prize.

So, if our heroes were dead, they were immortalized forever, by tune, by prose, by poetry, or by the imagination. Their pictures were frozen in mind, a time, which kept their deeds and accomplishments alive, as our tongues flogged our mouths, to speak the truth. Dylan Thomas, the Kennedy's, Martin Luther King and Steven Biko, their legacies, whether channeled from within, heartfelt to begin or from beyond, a wall to keep, allowed us to sleep. Freedom was a blessed virtue, by which many such as we, though so few when compared to the millions that Orwell knew.

It was a time when the fat of the land allowed the likes of Idi Amin and his gluttonous appetite to rape and pillage, entertain terrorists and their hostages, without them first RSVPing. The most famous being his bash at Entebbe, which was eventually gate-crashed by Israeli commandoes who had the nerve to breach protocol by wearing black masks rather than black ties. A half a world away, Pol Pot cleansed by first dirtying his hands and then washing them with the blood that irrigated the fields that once fed an entire generation.

One man's freedom fighter was to another, a terrorist. One man's hero could be to another, the bastard that removed forever, the name from the town from which he too had come to know as home.

For each wretched insidious purveyor of hate and injustice, there stood a counterpart to harvest the ways of truth and justice where everyone including, yes, even the hippies, could have a chance at life.

With the New Age, and its renaissance, especially concerning the cycle of life, death and rebirth, the rationale behind karma and what goes around, comes around, kept hippies thinking, *It really can't get any worse, can it?*

Ruth Montgomery set the record straight, at least for us. As a practitioner of automatic writing and by maneuvering through the fogs of the ether, she was able to lasso Author Ford. From his spirit poured forth a one-way invitation, a travel brochure if you will, outlining the other side.

Here the souls of the deleted migrated, separated and clustered according to the scope of their existence. So, the likes of the once living who chose to murder and plunder, gathered forces with those that did the same. The scum of the earth resided literally together, on, in, and with the scum of the earth. If murderers converged and conveyed, an eon or two should produce but one, since I'm sure "its kill or be killed." This lucky survivor will vie for soul and space. An eight by eight with both Hitler and Stalin—oh, not an eight by eight in meters or feet, but molecular field where hydrogen atoms could coexist and provide just enough space to allow for the existence of only one survivor—ah, even "Darwinism" has an spillover effect.

Initially, I had doubted my guardian angel and protector, Cing, especially concerning the universe and its solution when dealing with its dander. As it expands, it has a habit of shedding, showering the earth with the souls of all those who failed to hold on tight.

If we, as a form of punishment are reincarnated with the sole purpose of "getting it right," then maybe the Buddhists, the hunter-gathers of the Kalahari, the Aborigines, the mud men of New Guinea, the bushmen of the Amazon, and the hippies of Devon and Cornwall, are after all, really on to something. Surely, after we die this molting pot will migrate and cluster together just beyond the scanning and meddling third eye of Author Ford.

It's important to take life in stride. Keep it simple, watch your diet, read a lot, love a lot and stay away from the temptations that beget greed, hate and prejudice. It's better to walk around or under any corporate ladder rather than attempt to scale it, one rung at a time.

So, hippies were ostensibly safe and well insulated. There were exceptions of course. Success didn't come often, but when it did, it shifted the parameters, which in turn, changed the configuration of the model, albeit ever so slightly. Whether it was the few, who flew, grasping the truth, through music, the arts or even the forbidden fruits of politics and the decadence of the free enterprise, capitalistic system; the system we abhorred, but which allowed us to exist, also allowed a few to succeed.

Richard Branson, even with long hair and jeans, was on the periphery. We would have loved to claim him as one of our own, but in truth, he jettisoned the scene well before the allure of doing nothing, had a chance to ice his veins, freezing him forever to the scene.

He succeeded in "Virginizing" an idea, keeping it pure and exempt from the traditional ideology, promoting both greed and corruption. By championing Tubular Bells and helping a friend, the new onset being wealth and opportunity, seduced him by seizing the moment to propagate the experience.

If only our lifestyle could flourish by succeeding, to promote by enterprising the endeavors of an age; the best of both worlds, where harmony with both self and everything else, could exist. The chance to capitalize and live without having to sacrifice; was to struggle just to live. I guess if this were true, all, well, most hippies would be rich! But alas, all, well, most hippies will never be rich, except in the hearts of both each and each other.

I was a soul survivor, whose sole purpose was to endure, by keeping my head above the preverbal water line. However, being driven, as with any organism, the desire to survive, supplanted any fantasy concerning the lust for life and its appetite to devour. In order to create and maintain a delicate balance between the physical and inner self, the physical had to be fed not only knowledge and truth, but also the sustenance that allowed the machine to function. I possessed not the discipline to fake it, to travel as a fakir, the never-ending loop, begging for a handout, between St. John's Wood and Torquay.

I had capitulated, now the consumed would become the consumer. The roots that held firmly the man had never really been torn. Transplanted by choice, I knew I must cease my ride, a boat against the current, to return intact, well, reasonably intact to the mainstream. Besides, it had become painfully clear, in truth, I was flat broke, and enough was enough!

EPILOGUE

QUOTE:

Flaming youth has become a flaming question. And youth comes to us wanting to know what we may propose to do about a society that hurts so many of them.

Franklin D. Roosevelt

Epilogue

I look back at the memories, and heed,
the deeds, of lost youth, in search of the truth.

Inspired by:

Free Four
Obscured By the Clouds

It had been a great run, but alas it was time to leave. The writing was on the wall.—Amazing! Everywhere I looked graffiti exploited the once dull exterior of the tawny colored brick barriers hiding the railroad lines from the hustle and bustle that was London. Freedom of speech promoted an emotional outpouring that prompted my head to reel haphazardly against the forward motion of the train.

Brits out of Northern Ireland! Beware! IRA. No to Europe, boy, someone was pissed off. This was soon followed by more political slander and racial slurring, No Nukes, Pigs are wankers, National Front, Wogs go home! Communist Workers Party equal jobs! Poetic injustice I thought, cracking a crescent smile. But wait, there was more; God is dead, drop acid and find Nirvana, life's an illusion, pyramid power. I doubted seriously that this was the work of just one individual. The train was fast approaching Clapham junction and the tracks began to branch out like an oriental fan. On the last section of wall, the Who rule the World, and what appeared to be remnants torn from a Dylan song, adverse to scrutiny, white washed and in tune with the "sign of the times." The final tag, a scribbled blur announcing, the Royals suck!

Now that one jolted my imagination. Somehow, if taken at its word, visions of the Queen performing oral on...Christ, I think I'm going to heave! Maybe it was just motion sickness brought on by the constant strain from stretching my neck when twisting my head from side to side.

I closed my eyes for a moment, and with my left hand spread apart, rubbed both temples with thumbs and forefingers. As I opened them again, they captured briefly....Liverpool rules! Ok, where the bottom of the big block "K" dipped and then disappeared at ground level. It was as though the poor bastard who was holding the brush was momentarily startled by two rather large burly Arsenal fans, who then proceeded to beat the shit out of him. A somber thought, but so true of British football!

I packed my memories, never lost,
always found, when time beckoned the call.

Inspired by:

Night Flight
Led Zeppelin

Deep down inside I knew. The job sounded good and I certainly needed the money. But once I left England, it would be very difficult to break rank and return. Being tethered to the "American Dream" once a nightmare was now a vision that harnessed my desire to reap rather than sow.

The train began to slow. My neck was still paining, as I peered out the window again. There it was, "Welcome to Gatwick Airport."

The writings of those who remembered to bring,
a lust for life, will always sing—when the music plays.

Inspired by:

Paperback Writer
The Beatles

I had only a few minutes until my flight. I needed something to read. I glanced around the area adjacent to the concourse and through the maze of folk, noticed a freestanding stall, complete with canopy. I couldn't see any sign since a pillar blocked my view. I made a crude attempt to estimate, based on the number and direction of the two purportedly endless lanes of pedestrian traffic, how long it would take to traverse the horde, find a book, pay for it, fight my way back and then finally make my way to the point of embarkation. I concluded I would need at least fifteen minutes. According to the loud speaker, located above my now ringing ears, I had only twenty minutes. I hesitated, contemplated pulling the fire alarm next to me and then dashed toward the stall. Using both arms as battering rams and displacing everyone in my wake, like an icebreaker before spring thaw, I arrived, panting and somewhat light headed. I looked up and to my dismay, saw the sign, "Confectioners closed." *Damn all living things to hell*, I thought.

I shook my head and noticed just beyond where I had originally stood, a Kiosk, taunting my predicament by waving the name W.H. Smith in my face. Adapting the same mode, I stuttered stepped, and rambled across. I imagined myself towering over my adversaries and in full Gulliver like fashion, stomping on anyone and everything in my way, leaving only carnage and rubble in my aftermath.

Upon entering I made my way to the bookshelves, created my own version of the domino effect in the Barbara Cortland section, and noticed a small paperback hidden just out of view. I grabbed it and brushed the dust. Perfect! *The Late Great Planet Earth.*

I had a strange sense of warped irony, based on my impending departure from England. Needless to say, I now had enough change left over if they would exchange what I had, to make, if needed one call home.

My house is only another mile,
wrapped in a distant calling.

Inspired by:

I'm Your Captain
Grand Funk

"Bloody headphones!" A silent anger began to seethe inside, elevating simultaneously my desire to scream and blood pressure to the boiling point. Finally, secure to my tangled locks, I reached down beside my seat and switched the system on. "What the hell is this crap?" The overall hankering to spew forth obscenities in a Tourette like manner subsided expeditiously as I maneuvered the knob to the off position. "Disco!" What a bummer. Just a brief interlude could cause an irrepressible urge to spontaneously combust! I must resist. I must at all costs, stay alive!

Suddenly there was a gentle tap on my shoulder. I turned toward the aisle and followed a pair of shapely legs from the floor almost to the ceiling. I opened my mouth, but couldn't speak. The stewardess leaned over, lifted my left earphone and whispered gently into my ear, "Are you okay?"

"Ah,"...I paused, my lower jaw in my lap, still mesmerized by her overwhelming beauty, I mean concern: "Yeah, yes, I'm fine."

She smiled while pointing to my seat belt, politely saying, "Honey, make sure your lap belt is firmly in place, we're going to be taxiing momentarily."

I nodded, replaced my headphone and as I watched, trying not to be too obvious, she gyrated gracefully toward the galley. I took a deep breath, exhaled and switched the channel before increasing the volume.

"Now, that's better," being careful not to even mumble a word.

The sound of Rush saturated my inner sanctum, reverberating the space between my ears. Lithium for the soul! Geddy Lee's vocals faded as the plane began to taxi down the runway.

A manic-depressive, I walk in the rain.
The sun in my pocket, to cope, the pain.
Rainbows bleed, each step I take.
To think what wealth, I hope to make.

Inspired by:

Cinderella Man
Rush

The End

"All good things,
come to an end," my friend.

I hope we meet again,
so I can put a face to the discerning eye.

Inspired by:

The End
The Doors

Or

The beginning of the end, or the end of the beginning? A sequel!—Sorry, I'm fresh out of paper.

"Peace"

IN THE NAME OF CHURCH

By Edmund DuBois

In 1572, there is an uneasy peace in the bitter religious wars between Catholics and Protestants in France. Madeleine, daughter of a nobleman, and Colette, her bright but unlettered maid, find themselves fending off strange attempts by a Catholic bishop who is determined to take control of the maid because he professes to believe she is bewitched. A royal wedding in Paris provides the opportunity for Madeleine to seek excitement and shield Colette from the bishop. Madeleine and Colette have romantic affairs, but the Saint Bartholomew's Day massacre of Protestants turns the happy royal marriage into macabre tragedy and gives the bishop the chance to attempt his evil intentions- yet once again, Colette escapes. In a final confrontation, the bishop's true motive is unmasked, and believing himself possessed by the Devil, he goes insane. Madeleine, because of the terrible happenings "In the name of church," disavows affiliation with any church, and takes her worship directly to God.

Paperback, 531 pages
6″ x 9″
ISBN 1-4137-1763-2

About the author:

Edmund DuBois is a retired Army officer. He served in the Pacific during World War II and subsequently had assignments in the Pentagon and with NATO. He has co-authored one publication and is working on a sequel to the present novel. He resides in Sonoma, California.